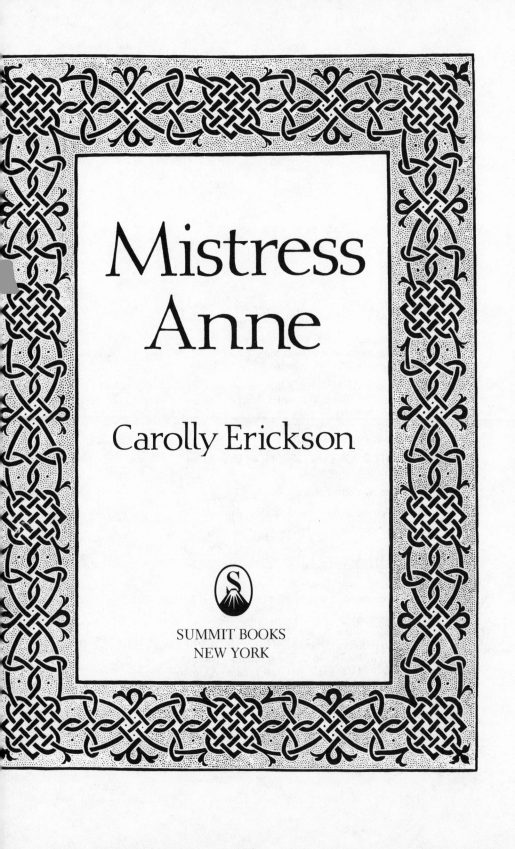

Mistress Anne

Carolly Erickson

SUMMIT BOOKS
NEW YORK

Published by SUMMIT BOOKS
A Division of Simon & Schuster, Inc.
Simon & Schuster Building
1230 Avenue of the Americas
New York, New York 10020

SUMMIT BOOKS and colophon are trademarks
of Simon & Schuster, Inc.

Designed by Edith Fowler

Manufactured in the United States of America

10 9 8 7 6 5 4 3 2 1
10 9 8 7 6 5 4 3 2   Pbk.

Library of Congress Cataloging in Publication Data

Erickson, Carolly, date
  Mistress Anne.

  Bibliography: p.
  Includes index.
  1. Anne Boleyn, Queen, consort of Henry VIII, King
of England, 1507-1536 2. Great Britain—History—
Henry VIII. 1509-1547. 3. Great Britain—Queens—
Biography. I. Title.
DA333.B6E75   1984   942.05′2   84-105

ISBN 0-671-41747-9
ISBN 0-671-60651-4 Pbk.

Contents

1

"This gentlewoman, Mistress Anne Boleyn, being very young, was sent into the realm of France, and there made one of the French queen's women."

In the golden light of a September afternoon, a long procession of horses, mules and wagons moved slowly along the Dover road. The riders, hundreds of them, were travelers from the royal court in London, and as they passed the country people ran up from the fields to watch them, standing in bedraggled groups and shouting and waving with enthusiasm.

The travelers held themselves stiffly in their unyielding brocades and thick felt cloaks, conscious of the splendid appearance they made and of the vast distances of class and income that separated them from the laborers and villagers they encountered. Pride kept them rigid and aloof, but despite their outward hauteur they grimaced inwardly with discomfort and hoped passionately that they would reach Dover before nightfall. Their longing grew greater as the sky darkened and rain began to beat down on their plumed caps and riding hoods. The rain was more than a present inconvenience: it meant storms in the Channel, and a dangerous crossing for Princess Mary and those who were to accompany her to France.

In this fall of 1514 the reign of King Henry VIII was five years old and the king himself, toweringly tall and energetic and youthful, enjoyed a hero's renown. He was only twenty-three, but already he had made himself a figure of legend. He was Great Harry, "our great king" to his people; to foreigners he was the awesome knight who had beaten the French at the Battle of the Spurs, driving them from the field with his thunderous horsemen. With his red-gold hair and beard, his laughing, hearty manner and his strong athlete's body Henry was dazzling enough, yet he made himself even more resplendent by costuming himself in flashing jeweled armor and golden robes and doublets of cloth of silver. Young and strong, victorious, flawlessly chivalrous, Henry seemed "a being descended from heaven," and the shouts and cheers of the country folk swelled to their peak as he passed by.

There were cheers of encouragement too for the exquisite young woman who rode by his side. She was his younger sister Mary, a delicate beauty of nineteen whose glowing complexion and charming features made her among the most admired women of her generation. Mary Tudor was the center of interest of the royal perambulation to Dover, for she was about to become a bride and this was the first stage of her wedding journey.

She was not only about to become a bride, she was about to become a queen. For her brother, having made his military reputation by defeating the French, was now about to make his diplomatic reputation by becoming their ally.

In the intricate sequence of treaties, battles and tergiversations that went to form continental politics King Henry was playing a quixotic role. He had been allied with his father-in-law Ferdinand of Aragon against the French king Louis XII; now he was abandoning Ferdinand for Louis. And Princess Mary, who had been engaged to Ferdinand's Flemish-bred grandson Charles, now found herself pledged to the "old, feeble and pocky" widower who ruled France.

Were it not for the fact that she loved another man Mary would have been willing enough to accommodate herself to her brother's plans. After all, King Louis was a man in his fifties, weak-limbed and drooling with age, and could not be expected to live long. He had promised to shower his young wife with jewels, and in token of his promise he had sent her a casket of gems, among them a unique diamond "as large and as broad as a full-sized finger" called the Mirror of Naples. Gifts of this sort, and the title of queen, might make a brief marriage to an old man at least bearable.

But if she was to sacrifice herself to an "aged and sickly" bridegroom, Mary reasoned, it ought to be with the hope that after he died she would be free to marry a second husband of her own choosing. No more marriages of state: her brother must guarantee this. And it was with thoughts of bargaining on her mind that Mary rode, thoughtful and preoccupied, along the Dover road.

At a little distance from the king and his sister went Queen Katherine, plump and round-faced, wincing each time the litter she rode in sagged unexpectedly at a dip in the road. She was heavily pregnant, only two months or so from her delivery, and though her condition was reassuring—she had yet to give birth to a thriving child, an heir to the throne—she was worried over the sharply altered course her ebullient husband's diplomacy was taking.

Katherine was not only queen, she was, in all but title, her father Ferdinand's ambassador to England. More than any of the official ambassadors he sent to the court of Henry VIII, Katherine knew the country and its ruler; she had lived in England for thirteen years, and if her spoken English was marred by a strong accent her reading of insular affairs was relatively unclouded by the cultural blindness of the foreigner. She was, however, biased in favor of Spain and the allies of Spain. She much preferred to have England allied with Ferdinand and his Hapsburg in-laws, and she was dismayed by her husband's rapprochement with the French. There were those who said that Henry's disenchantment with King Ferdinand went even further than a diplomatic breach, that he was thinking of finding a way out of his childless Spanish marriage and taking a French bride for himself. But his behavior toward Katherine lent no support to such gossip, and besides, she was now carrying a child, and this time the pregnancy might not end in stillbirth or in a fatally weak infant. This time it might be a healthy son.

Hovering near the king and queen was the royal almoner, Thomas Wolsey, the clever priest who had begun to make himself indispensable to Henry the year before during his military campaigning in France. A portly figure in his clerical garb, Wolsey carried himself like a great aristocrat and not like the son of a provincial butcher. His wary intelligence was unmistakable as he observed the royal party and their mounted attendants, watching out for obstacles in the road, for broken wagons and lame horses, and for the bands of robbers who lived from plundering travelers along this well-worn stretch of highway.

As the afternoon advanced the riders straggled on in an untidy line a mile and more long, now bunching together, now splaying out into smaller groups to talk, sing or pass wineskins from hand to hand. The journey had an official function, to be sure, yet it had the character of a family occasion. Many of the courtiers had brought their wives along, and a few, their children.

One of these children, a small, dark little girl of indeterminate age, rode inconspicuously among the princesses' maids of honor. She was much younger than the others, a thin child among nubile and handsome young women, and she must have felt out of place and awkward in their company.[1]

Her awkwardness came as much from her appearance as from her age, for Anne was afflicted with embarrassing disfigurements which made her hide her head and hands when anyone looked too closely at her. A large mole grew out of her neck, a mark too prominent to be hidden by her thick black hair. On one hand a sixth finger had begun to grow, and there was a double nail and an excess bulge of flesh. Such bodily marks, conspicuous enough in themselves, stood out even more conspicuously in an age when the extraordinary was always thought to be significant. Ignorant people might take the rudimentary extra finger to be a mark of the devil; to a more worldly observer, such as Anne's father, her blemishes were less diabolical than simply unlucky, for they were likely to lessen her value when she reached an age to marry.

As far as we know, Anne's sister Mary had no such disadvantages. Mary was older than Anne, sensual and precociously attractive. Her appointment as maid of honor to the princess was the second such post she had held—she had spent a year in Brussels in the household of Margaret of Savoy, regent of the Netherlands—and her enviable status as a veteran of life abroad must have made her seem infinitely poised and sophisticated to her younger sister.

Compared to Mary, Anne was plain and unpromising, the sort of child a less ambitious father would have sent to a convent to live her life as a nun. Convents were full of wellborn girls with crippled limbs or addled brains or ugly faces, and Anne, with her flaws and unfortunate coloring, was a candidate for a life of genteel obscurity as a religious. If only her hair had been golden like the princess Mary's, or rich auburn like the queen's, instead of black and impossibly thick; if only her skin had been fair and rosy instead of dark and sallow like a gypsy's; if only her eyes had been the sweet, light-filled blue of religious paintings instead of piercing jet black, there might have been hope for her. Yet as she was, Thomas Boleyn was determined to make a cultured French gentlewoman of her. And if she had to be eclipsed by her better-endowed sister, then so be it. He would make the most of the little that Anne had to offer nonetheless.

Probably Thomas Boleyn gave no thought whatever to either of his daughters as he rode along, sleek and prideful, beside the other gentlemen of the court. He was a handsome, shrewd man in his late thirties, with a hunger for wealth and advancement that his considerable success at court had done nothing to assuage. In the next few days he would take up his most important assignment to date, as ambassador to France, and his thoughts were fixed on the details of his embassy rather than on the welfare of his children.

In the previous reign Boleyn had risen to be esquire of the body to the king, and then had turned his linguistic skills to advantage in carrying out diplomatic missions to Scotland, to the imperial court of Maximilian I, to the Low Countries and now to France. Henry VIII relied on Boleyn's experience and suavity in foreign affairs, and rewarded him with minor grants of offices and incomes and land. His most valuable reward, though, had been a fortunate marriage.

When Thomas Boleyn married Elizabeth Howard he was an

energetic, strikingly good-looking nobody—or next-to-nobody. To be sure, his merchant grandfather had been lord mayor of London and his mother was the daughter of an earl. Still, in taking as his bride the eldest daughter of Thomas Howard Boleyn was entering the very highest circle of social rank, for the Howards had royal blood and under the Yorkist monarchy had enjoyed a ducal title.

At the time the marriage was made, the title had been withdrawn, forfeit to Henry Tudor's triumph over the Yorkist cause at Bosworth Field. But Thomas Howard had eventually rehabilitated himself and, ever the stalwart commander, had served Henry VIII in the battlefield with distinction and loyalty. In the previous year, 1513, the aged Howard had routed the Scots at Flodden Field. To reward him the king had restored to him the forfeited dukedom, so that now the fortunes of the entire Howard family—including the Boleyns—had taken a sharp upward turn. It was as the son-in-law of the duke of Norfolk that Thomas Boleyn was setting off, with his daughters, for France.

Swift reversals of fortune such as those of the Howards and their in-laws were commonplace in this age of parvenus. It was an unstable age, an age of upstart noblemen and gentlemen in muddy boots. It was, above all, an age of opportunity, for the old social order was shifting and the medieval hierarchy, with its triumvirate of kings, churchmen and peers of ancient lineage was giving way to a newer structure of power. The ancient titles were being conferred on relative newcomers to court, families only two or three generations removed from husbandry. Churchmen were still prominent, even pre-eminent, in the royal Council, as the thrusting career of Thomas Wolsey clearly showed, yet men like Boleyn and, even more, his bullying brother-in-law Thomas Howard the younger, heir to the dukedom and earl of Surrey, were challenging their right to dominate the king. And the monarchy itself was changing. Where the Plantagenets had ruled England for centuries, the Tudors had been on the throne a mere three decades, and unless Henry VIII managed to sire a son the dynasty would end with him.

For that reason the marriage of Henry's younger sister Mary was of the greatest importance. If Henry did die without a male

heir his sisters would inherit the throne, first his older sister
Margaret, queen of Scotland (and if he should survive, her infant son James), and then Mary, queen of France. A dispassion-
ate observer could have argued, in fact, that by her forthcoming
marriage Mary would become the most distinguished of all the
Tudors, for France was a far larger, far richer and far more
powerful country than England and as queen of France Mary
would surpass all her relatives, living and dead, in rank and
wealth.

It was thus a considerable honor and a great opportunity for
the dark little daughter of Thomas Boleyn to be allowed to join
the wedding party. Whether she looked on her coming journey
to France in that way is doubtful, however. While there is no
evidence about Anne's thoughts or behavior—probably no one
paid much attention to her, certainly no one noted down what
she did or said—she must have approached her embarkation
with a mixture of excitement and apprehension.

Her apprehension must have increased as the royal procession
neared its destination and the high towers and thick stone walls
of Dover Castle came into view, and beyond them, the gray sea.

It was an angry sea, its surface broken into dark ridges and
furrows by a treacherously high wind. The ships hired for the
journey dipped and rose wildly in the harbor, looking pitifully
small and flimsy in the heavy weather, and though there were
fourteen of them their number did nothing to decrease their
frailty.

In a day or two Anne must get aboard one of these plunging
vessels and sail in it all the way to France, a place that must have
seemed impossibly distant and alien to a child. Her sister would
be with her, but not her highborn mother; with the older girls in
the princess's suite she was being put into the care of the proper,
stern-featured Lady Guildford. To a little girl who had never
before left home the hazards of the journey must have loomed
as fearsome. Among the least cultivated skills of a gentleman's
daughter was her ability to swim.

For some days the wedding party and their escort stayed at
Dover Castle, taking refuge within the Norman battlements as
storm after storm beat upon the coast and whipped the water

into foaming peaks. Everything bound for the journey had to be stored in the castle—the hundreds of horses for the princess and her party, the dozens of sturdy oak chests filled with her dowry and her trousseau, the wagonloads of furnishings for her wedding and the clothing and possessions of her servants.

Each evening there would be hope for calm seas and blue skies the next morning; each morning there were cold winds and black clouds, and often a shoreline shrouded in fog. It began to appear as if the wintry weather would never lift, and as it was already the first week of October the king decided that he dared not wait any longer to commit his sister to the fortunes of the Narrow Seas.

The loading of the animals and goods began, the travelers said their farewells. Princess Mary, in a final talk with her brother, was promised her freedom in marriage when Louis XII should leave her a widow.

In the blustery dawn of October 2, Mary and her companions embarked. Only a few hours out from Dover the overcast sky darkened almost to twilight and the wind rose around the ships, making them veer wildly in the troughs of high waves. The noblewomen went below, where they lay, wretchedly seasick, in their uncomfortable berths. On deck the sailors fought to keep the ships on course, but the hissing wind and towering waves defeated them, and before long they too were seasick and all but immobile.

For several days the little flotilla foundered in the storm, rising and falling in the steep seas, the timbers and masts of the vessels creaking as wave after wave crashed against their bows. Many a ship had been lost in the Channel, and it was customary for sailors and passengers alike to pray to the Virgin Mary, Star of the Sea, Port of Salvation, to save them in their hour of danger.

Then at last, whether through the power of prayer or a strong tiller, four of the fourteen ships sighted Boulogne and three of the four managed to sail into the harbor. The fourth, the princess's own ship, ran aground at the harbor mouth and Mary herself had to be carried ashore in the arms of one of her gentlemen. Green with illness, she and her women were hurried to shelter and given dry clothes and a blazing fire at which to warm themselves. They were at first too sick to eat, and the cold and the continual fear had numbed them so that they could hardly speak. But after a few days of rest they began to recover, and soon were well enough to go on with the ceremonial events and official welcomes that had been prepared for them.

Princess Mary, her complexion restored to its usual enviable fairness, rode dutifully on to meet her husband-to-be at Abbeville, and their wedding was as grand and as splendid as brilliant hangings and gleaming plate and golden robes—all salvaged, miraculously, from the water-soaked sea chests—could make it.

Yet the dark child who watched the solemn ceremony with her sister cannot have been unscathed by her ordeal. She had known grave danger, for a time at least she had come very near death. For a long time to come her dreams would be full of screaming winds and green water—more often, perhaps, than of the home she had left behind.

2

*"The lovely freedom of France, more to be prized
than anything, makes our ladies more desirable,
lovable, and approachable, and better givers than
any others."*

N o monarchy in Europe was more magnificent in the
early sixteenth century than France. The realm was large, rich
and populous. A healthy peasantry cultivated fertile fields; indus-
trious townspeople supported a thriving trade; the nobles and
the knightly class, long an anachronism in war save as captains
and commanders, had found a new trade as courtiers, and lived
a gilded life in the shadow of the king. To be sure, there were
years of famine, when villagers starved and wolves hunted
through the towns, and feudal warfare still made chaos of country life, but to visiting foreigners France was a paradise of plenty
and contentment, graced in abundance by the beauties of Renaissance art.

Amid an exquisitely varied landscape of sun-filled meadows,
picturesque woods and winding rivers châteaux and palaces in
the new Italianate style were taking shape, their façades of gray
stone lightened by high arched windows and their outlines soft-
ened and made graceful by rows of elegant columns. The royal
palaces in the lush Loire Valley rose out of the river mists in
fairytale magnificence, the purity and charm of their proportions

offset by whimsical rooflines of miniature cupolas and turrets and towers.

Within doors all was splendor and color. A generation of military campaigning in Italy by the French kings had brought many shiploads of plundered artworks to the royal treasury, and the walls and ceilings of Blois, Amboise and Les Tournelles were adorned with luxurious spoils plundered from Florence and Pisa and Milan.

It was here, in this rich and beautiful place, that Anne Boleyn grew up, in surroundings bright with glowing tapestries and gleaming metalwork and painted wood. Carvings and statues of antique heroes stood in the halls, beneath huge paintings of battles or classical themes or voluptuous nudes. The wooden moldings and plasterwork of the walls themselves were carved into cornucopias of fruit and flowers, the gilded edges laced into intertwining geometric shapes of remarkable intricacy. Painters, sculptors and lesser craftsmen brought from Italy continued the work of ornamentation, and Anne must often have seen them at their work and must have grown nearly as accustomed to the sound of Italian as she was to French.

Against the backdrop of vivid hangings and artworks and colored marble moved the living adornments of the palace—the pages and esquires in cloth of silver and the household gentlemen in cloth of gold, the nobles and gentlewomen in their sumptuous court dress, black-robed ecclesiastics and guardsmen in the velvet livery of the king. Anne's sister was part of the ornamentation. Beautifully dressed, beautifully coiffed and jeweled, she sat with the other maids of honor, smiling and amiable, ever accommodating and ever ready to serve her mistress. No description of Mary Boleyn survives, but she must have been an inviting, eager girl, ripe and nubile; to judge from her later history, she may well have been intelligent and opportunistic besides.

Less visible at first, but gradually earning a minor place among the maids, was Anne, dark and thin and all but hidden among the older girls. Little girls were dressed like women, and Anne must have worn the many layers of petticoats and underclothes, the kirtle and gown and sleeves, the headgear, girdle and jewelry of a court lady—all of which may have helped to give her confidence and to take attention away from what was least attractive about her appearance. As the months passed she must have seemed less and less the inconspicuous little girl from Kent and more and more the cosmopolitan young French lady, in speech, manners and bearing more French than English. Her models were her sister and the other maids, and she watched them as they danced and conversed and flirted, mimicking their behavior, their turns of phrase, their ways of moving and speaking and smiling.

From those in the queen's formal household Anne learned how to curtsy and bow, when and how to enter and leave a room and how to observe the rules of precedence and court ritual. But her more deepgoing training came from the other young women, and she seems to have absorbed in full measure their ineffable qualities of femininity, their subtle ways of pleasing the eye and gratifying the senses.

An observer of the French court who lived a generation later than Anne and Mary Boleyn but who was able to rely on family tradition for much of what he wrote documented in copious detail the environment in which Anne came to maturity. Brantôme's *Vies des dames galantes* describes the nuanced arts of allurement she encountered, the way the women made themselves captivating by their "little magnetic glances," their "hundred thousand ways" of tilting the head, half-smiling, moving their eyes and lips expressively and hinting by their "ever rich and suggestive talk" at further delights to be revealed in private.[1] Those with beautiful necks wore their hair upswept to reveal them, those with beautiful hands whitened them with lotions and adorned them with sparkling rings. Cosmetics, perfumes, creams to heighten and creams to disguise, lavish hairdressings wonderfully arranged—all these, complemented by superb gowns and expensive finery, made the women marvelously beguiling. But it was the "charming, extravagant little gestures and intimacies" that made them irresistible, and all these, we must assume, Anne came in time to practice until her Englishness was lost under a glowing patina of Gallic witchery.

There were other arts to be learned as well, courtly arts of lively, witty conversation, of light banter and of sophisticated bawdiness. At this Italianate court young men and women were expected to imitate the patrician cultural pastimes prevalent in Italy, where their counterparts took pleasure in discussing music and painting and in debating the merits of ancient writers. Connoisseurship was easily acquired in surroundings so rich in artistic treasures, and Anne must have developed an eye for color and form and harmonious proportion along with her discriminating taste in gallant speech and erotic flirtation.

There was nothing fragile or fainthearted about this style of coquetry; it was bold, full-blooded, even greathearted. It sprang from the chivalrous tradition of the Middle Ages, which if it subordinated women also gave them much scope for courageous action and unblushing self-assertion. Drawing-room graciousness was one thing, the raucous comradeship the women shared in the privacy of the queen's apartments-another. When they were among themselves they shed their magnetic glances and charming gestures and boasted to one another about their conquests, roaring with laughter over the foolishness of their lovers and describing in graphic terms their amorous encounters with the gentlemen of the court.

There was a strong element of tension in these conversations, though, for a new mistress, Queen Claude, presided in the royal apartments, and she belonged to that minority of proper, conspicuously pious ladies who made the sign of the cross whenever they heard an obscene word and were coldly out of sympathy with flirtation of any sort.

Anne and Mary Boleyn had gone to France as attendants on Mary Tudor; within months of their arrival, Mary Tudor had been married, widowed, remarried and returned to England, and a new queen was installed in her place.

Mary Tudor's story was a romantic one, calculated to make a deep impression on a young girl such as Anne. After her marriage to old King Louis Mary had taken her place at his court as his dutiful bride, nursing him in his weakening state of health and, when he soon died, mourning him with dutiful sincerity. Her thoughts then turned, naturally enough, to the promise her brother King Henry had made to her a few months earlier, when he had told her she could have free choice of a second husband. The man of her choice, Charles Brandon, duke of Suffolk, was at the French court on a diplomatic mission, and the widowed Mary went to him, anxious to confirm his love for her and to secure her future as his wife.

But Brandon, a bluff and soldierly man deeply indebted to his great friend King Henry for his ducal title and everything else he possessed, was reluctant. The king had not yet given his formal consent, Brandon told Mary; let them wait until they had it before they went ahead, since any marriage between a princess, nay a widowed queen, and a recently ennobled commoner like himself was an extremely weighty matter.

To Mary, uncertain and among strangers, and already being pestered by King Louis's successor Francis I, Brandon's reasoning was suspicious. Troublemakers had been warning her about his trustworthiness. Had he in fact been sent to France by Henry to trick her, to carry her off to yet another loveless diplomatic marriage? Why else would he refuse to marry her then and there?

She panicked. If another marriage had been arranged for her, she told Brandon, she would refuse to go through with it, even to the point of death. She would rather be torn in pieces than repeat her experience in France, she insisted, and then, her will breaking, she burst into floods of tears. Wailing, accusing, now blaming Brandon for betraying their love, now vowing that he meant everything to her, Mary wore down his defenses. Let her obtain her brother's consent in writing, he said. That, at least, was essential, since before leaving England he had made a bargain of his own with Henry, promising not to give way to impulse and wed Mary in a hastily arranged informal ceremony.

But to Mary, who was by now in hysterics, Brandon's request seemed just another subterfuge. She was past arguing, past listening to reason. In desperation she told him that, if he did not marry her right away, he would never have the chance again. She was making herself available for the last time.

It took courage for so small a lady to confront the tall, broad-shouldered, athletic Brandon with her ultimatum. But as he confessed to Henry later, her tears, her distress and her defiance befuddled him and, not wanting to lose her, he gave in.

There were repercussions, of course. As soon as Mary and Brandon were back in England, King Henry exacted a large fine from them and warned Brandon that, if his councillors had had their way, he might well have been executed. But Mary, safe and happy with Brandon and pregnant with her first child, was content to ride out the storm of her brother's displeasure. And when her son was born, she gladly named him Henry after his royal uncle.

The swiftly moving events meant changes in the royal household. King Francis, hearty and lascivious, replaced the feeble Louis and his wan, retiring queen Claude established herself in Mary Tudor's place. Few of Mary's English attendants stayed on in France, but the two daughters of Thomas Boleyn retained their posts among the waiting maids—possibly because Queen Claude approved of them but more likely because their father had succeeded in ingratiating himself with the new king. Whatever the reason, their status had shifted. Whereas before they had been part of the suite of a foreign princess, they now became full-fledged members of the French court, on equal footing with the daughters of the noble houses of France and occupying a high and enviable position. As Marie and Anna de Boullans their transformation into Frenchwomen was becoming complete; they might expect, as the other waiting maids did, to marry French noblemen and spend their lives in their adopted country.

For the next five years—in Anne's case, six—they were steeped in the bawdy, flamboyantly erotic life of the French court, an atmosphere more like that of a brothel than a royal establishment. By the time Anne and Mary reached the end of their teens they had become, in manner, thought and outlook, French court ladies. Though they happened to have been born English their behavior was French—and not only their behavior, but their entire experience of human relations, and in particular, of the relations between women and men.

The dominant figure at the court was King Francis, tall, sardonic, in looks and temper a high-spirited, virile devil with a "grand air" and astonishing physical strength. Smiling, insouciant, glittering in his jewel-encrusted doublets and lace-trimmed shirts, Francis was a perpetual spectacle unto himself. Whether striding boisterously through the halls of his palaces, laughing and bantering with his courtiers, or riding one of his dozens of fine horses, accompanied by a retinue of fiery young noblemen, the king caught and held the attention of everyone around him. He was undeniably not only "the handsomest and greatest man of his court" but among the most cultured. He delighted in conversing about the fine paintings he brought back from his warmaking in Italy, he wrote accomplished verse, he held his own with intellectuals and men and women of letters.

But it was his sexual profligacy, his immense and infectious zest for venereal pastimes that gave his court its erotic flavor. King Francis was, as a contemporary wrote, "clothed in women." There were the three voluptuous brunettes who formed his "little band" of favorite bedfellows, there were his official mistresses, as haughty and proud of their rank as they were of their magnificent bodies, and there were, in addition, the dozens upon dozens of daughters, wives, and even mothers of courtiers with whom he formed more ephemeral liaisons. King Francis, it was said, "drank the waters of many fountains," and any girl or woman in his vicinity could expect to be called upon to join in the all-night revels he delighted in.

But Francis was much more than an eager, dedicated voluptuary; he was the self-appointed arbiter of the sexual life at his court. Having observed that at the exquisitely refined Italian courts every man had his mistress, Francis urged his nobles and officials to imitate this practice, and announced that any who did not were "foolish idiots." He kept himself informed about the identity of each man's mistress and took a solicitous—and no doubt salacious—interest in each of the women, promising to "look after them and say a good word for them." He even went so far as to interrupt tête-à-têtes between lovers, asking them what they were talking about and suggesting suitable language.

There was more than a little artificiality about this orchestrated lechery; just as King Francis imported Italian tapestries and paintings and marbles, so he was determined to import Italian morals as well. But what was at first imitative soon became natural, and he found that his courtiers showed a remarkable aptitude for unbridled amorousness. And ever eager for vicarious pleasure, he wanted to hear all about it.

The king was "most anxious always to know about the love affairs of his ladies and gentlemen," wrote Brantôme, who in writing his *Vies des dames galantes* drew on the long memories of his lusty grandmother and other members of Francis's court. Francis was especially intrigued to hear "of their actual joustings, even of any fine airs the ladies might assume when at those frolics, the positions they adopted, the expressions on their faces, the words they used." And the stories he heard made him roar with laughter, Brantôme wrote, though he made a great show of "recommending a still tongue and observance of honor" afterward.

King Francis presided over a little closed society pervaded by every shade of sensuality, from ribald teasing to bawdy conversation and the reading of erotic books to debauchery of heroic proportions. Dinner-table conversation was full of innuendoes and double entendres; books, plays and songs treated of the joys and pangs of fleshly love; tapestries depicted amorous pastimes while paintings gave explicit instruction in the art of love. Nor was it only the love play between a man and a woman. Sometimes "several lovely ladies" were shown bathing together, "touching each other, fondling each other, handling each other, rubbing each other, feeling each other, intertwined with each other" in such a sensual way that "even a recluse or a hermit" could not help but be aroused.

"We've been here too long," one of the prominent women of the court announced to her lover after "losing herself" in a painting of two women disporting themselves. "Let's hurry into the carriage and go home to my place, because I cannot bear this heat, I must go and quench it, I am too scorching hot."

Everywhere they looked the courtiers saw reminders of sexual passion—even in the platters they ate from and the goblets from which they drank their sugared wine. One goblet in particular was handed around at the French court as a sort of touchstone of sexual sophistication. The goblet's interior surface was engraved with copulating animals, and as the drinker drained it he or she saw, in its depths, a man and woman making love. It amused the prince who owned the goblet to have his servants present it to various women to drink from, so that he could watch their reactions. Some blushed, others whispered to one another in mild astonishment, still others tried to keep their eyes closed while they drank—while at the same time trying to ignore the loud laughter of the prince and the other men present.

Newcomers to court, or the youngest and most innocent women, Brantôme recorded, "maintained a cold smile just at the tips of their noses and lips and forced themselves to be hypocrites" about the goblet, realizing that they had either to drink from it—for the servants refused to serve them from any other —or perish of thirst. But those who had been part of the courtly circle for even a short time laid aside their scruples and drank from the titillating chalice greedily enough. And often it was those who protested most vehemently over the unseemliness of the goblet who were observed to take longer and deeper drinks from it than anyone else. "In a word," Brantôme wrote, "there were a hundred thousand jokes and witticisms tossed to and fro between the gentlemen and the ladies at table about this goblet," and no doubt it served to whet the appetites of all present for the love play that went on after the banqueting was over.

And what love play it was! Men consorted long and lustily with their mistresses, their virility enhanced rather than diminished by repeated erotic encounters. One renowned gentleman—a cleric, as it happened, the king's almoner Baraud—was known for his ability to perform no fewer than twelve times in a single night, and even this seemed to him inadequate. "I am so sorry, madame, for not doing better," he told his partner on one such occasion, explaining that he had taken some medicine which weakened him and kept him from doing his best.

Women expected Baraud, and others like him, to keep them satisfied, and goaded them to ever greater feats of passion. One lady, Brantôme recorded, agreed to a rendezvous on condition that her seducer live up to his boast that he could satisfy her six times in the course of the night, so greatly would her beauty stimulate him. But then, when he failed in the attempt, she berated him and threw him out.

"Don't you mean to do anything more than this?" she cried angrily. "Then out of my bed! I did not rent it to you, like the bed in some inn, to sprawl at your ease and take your rest. I mean what I say! Out with you!"

Sex at the French court had strong overtones of warfare. Brantôme called his anecdotes "descriptions of amorous combats," and the vocabulary of battle was commonly mingled with the language of love. When men seduce women, he remarked, they act just as they would in besieging a city. They first sound the attack, then call on the women to yield, then prepare the bridgeheads, build the earthworks, dig the trenches and prepare the batteries. They "attack the fortifications of modesty" and the ladies, after a suitable defense, "run up the white flag and receive their sweet enemies in their castles."

All-night encounters, many hours long, were referred to as "the great battle," while more hurried engagements were "mere skirmishes." Insatiable women, Brantôme wrote, "intoxicated by their pleasure," "kept their opponents with them on their own ground fighting till daylight came." And whenever intrepid lovers met, risking discovery by the woman's outraged husband, they always posted "good, vigilant sentries" outside the bedchamber door, to warn of an unexpected midnight assault.

War was an aphrodisiac. Just as Venus fell in love with Mars, though he was "all sweaty from the wars, whence he came, blackened by gunpowder and as filthy as could be, smelling more of the fighting man than a court darling," so the court ladies could not resist a soldier, and found any fighting man with a bloodstained shirt and a grimy face and hands irresistible.

But if there was an erotic charm to this intertwined imagery of war and love it held a darker truth: that overshadowing all the amorous combat, the banter and byplay and exchange of scalding words was the awesome fact that men had nearly absolute power over women.

It was, in reality, a power of life and death.

Men killed their wives for infidelity, and for even the faintest suspicion of infidelity. One husband stormed dramatically into his wife's bedchamber, bared sword in hand, and with savage strokes cut her to pieces. Another slipped into bed with his unsuspecting lady, laughed and joked with her awhile, then "gave her four or five thrusts with his dagger" and had his servants finish her off. Later he boasted of his deed to the whole court.

Some husbands turned a blind eye to their wives' doings, some were forgiving, and some, of course, had nothing to forgive. But honor had its imperatives, and in an age that equated manliness with murderous athleticism flirtatious wives were inevitably at risk. All cuckolded husbands were to be feared, but worst of all were "the dangerous, the odd, the bad, the malicious, the cruel, the bloodthirsty and the moody men, who come to blows about it, who torment, who kill, some for real cause, some for none, so much does the faintest public suspicion infuriate them."

At the court of King Francis many ladies were able to claim royal protection from their brutal men, for if the king was among their lovers he might well threaten the husband at swordpoint and command him to be lenient with his spouse if he valued his life. Yet outraged husbands had many ways of taking revenge. Subtle, slow-acting poisons could be introduced into food or wine, or smeared on gloves or jewelry. The unfortunate victim appeared to die of pneumonia or apoplexy or heart failure, or wasted away until she was "dry as a piece of wood," while the gloating poisoner played the role of attentive, grief-stricken spouse. Or a man could have his wife walled up in a convent for life, or could shut her away in her apartments, in a bare room, leaving orders with his servants to feed her on bread and water and punishing her himself by lashing her mercilessly with a whip.

Even faithful, blameless wives, Brantôme recounted, had reason to fear their husbands, for it not infrequently happened that virtuous women were poisoned, tortured or killed by husbands who "wanted fresh meat," or who saw a chance to marry a wealthy heiress if they became widowers. Impotent, jealous old men, or deranged younger ones, took leave of their senses and ridded themselves of unwanted women on any pretext—or none —and with virtual impunity.

So vicious did the intrigue at times become that men attacked their enemies at court by seducing their wives—who, poor women, might then be forced by their infuriated husbands to kill their seducers. It was never safe, Brantôme remarked, to trust an amorous woman, "since to escape her husband's cruel hand she will play whatever game he wants."

The cruel hand of husbandly anger was never far from women's thoughts. It frightened and awed them, it made rebellion or resistance hazardous in the extreme. More often than not it thoroughly soured the sweetness of their revenge.

Yet they took revenge. If their husbands had mistresses, they had lovers, though, as Brantôme pointed out, "in this they ran greater dangers and risked their fortune more than any soldier or sailor did from the greatest perils of battle or the sea." Still they braved it out, gratifying themselves, taking their pleasure boldly (if stealthily) behind closed doors and in dark corners, throwing themselves all the more passionately into liaisons fated to be brief and full of danger. And, when the game was up and they were caught, they stood their ground and showed defiance to the last.

"I know I am a dead woman, kill me, don't hesitate!" cried one court lady when her husband broke open her bedchamber door and burst in on her and her lover. "I am not afraid of death, but I die gladly, I can tell you, because I've had my own back on you and cuckolded you and put the horns on your head nicely!"

It was this bravado, this "fine feminine vigor" which Brantôme lauded and which the young girl calling herself Anna de Boullans must have watched with great interest. Anne must often have been witness to the kinds of incidents Brantôme later described; she must have grown accustomed to stories about embattled women confronting their husbands and about resourceful women, eager for romantic intrigue, who managed to outwit their spouses and so escape their punishment—at least for a time.

It was a heady education for a young girl, to observe the tumultuous, ribald gallantry between the sexes and the heavy price in fear and pain the women paid afterward. Anne must in fact have encountered the full range of erotic modes as she approached maturity, everything from friendship to lusty dalliance, from women paying men for their sexual favors to monastic celibacy and religious concepts of virginity and chaste womanhood. She saw good, trusting marriages and many ugly, hostile ones, jealousy, coquetry, bawdiness and prudery, flirtation, infatuation and that musty anachronism, now mostly embalmed in poems and songs, courtly love.

She saw only too clearly how King Francis treated his sickly, corpulent, perpetually pregnant queen Claude, whose piety and scrupulous chastity were worlds apart from his own high-spirited lechery. Claude was everything that virtuous mothers and confessors taught women to be: modest, devout, demure and self-effacing. She was regular at her prayers, bore her seven children in dutiful stoicism, and won praise for her "pudicity, sanctity and innocence." Yet she and those of her women who shared her way of life were pale, wilted lilies beside the dazzling hot-house roses of the court, and the king generally kept her apart from the others. It was rumored, at least among the diplomats and ambassadors—one of whom was Anne's father Thomas Boleyn—that Francis meant to have his rather displeasing queen quietly murdered.

"It was generally recognized in those days," remarked Brantôme of Francis I's time, "that it was a rare lady or girl indeed resident at court, or fresh arrival, who was not seduced." Mary Boleyn was no exception. Francis referred to her as a "hackney" or "English mare" which he and many others had enjoyed riding during her years in France. And two decades after her departure for England he recalled her as "a great prostitute, infamous above all."[2]

But what of the "great prostitute's" little sister Anne, the graceful, slender girl with the long, thick black hair and beautiful almond-shaped black eyes? Did she too become drawn into the vortex of sensuality or did she, from cunning or fear or simple innocence, remain within the chaste circle of Queen Claude's waiting women, observing all, gaining sophistication without giving up her good name? Anne had undergone a metamorphosis from thin, blemished child to fascinating, worldly young woman. Did she adjust her morals as well?

"Rarely or never did any maid or wife leave that court still chaste," Brantôme believed. But when they left, he added, they took with them the rich spoils of unchastity—heavy gowns of cloth of gold and cloth of silver, silken petticoats and robes fit for a queen.

When Anne left France in 1521 or early 1522, then in her mid- or at most her late teens, she may indeed have taken back to England trunks full of splendid gowns, along with the accomplishments of a cultured young lady who spoke fluent French.

But to judge from her later life, she certainly took back with her more than a little of the brave audacity of the dauntless French women as well. Like them she would live dangerously, aggressively, always pressing her advantage and rarely shrinking back in the face of danger or challenge. Beyond her coquetry and physical attractions she had more than a little of the great-heartedness Brantôme wrote of, that "fine feminine vigor which closely resembles that of the masculine heart."

3

*"And then was she sent for home again and,
being again with her father, he made such means
that she was admitted to be one of Queen Katherine's maids; among whom, for her excellent
gesture and behavior, [she] did excel all other."*

When Anne came home to England early in 1522, a young, vivacious Frenchwoman, she stepped confidently into the place her father made for her at the court of Henry VIII. Lithe and willowy in her stylish French gowns and kirtles, her long black hair flowing down her back, she had not only taste and the elegance it conferred but something more. She had magnetism, allure, together with a dark and elusive loveliness that made her memorable amid the pale blond beauties of the royal suite.

Anne had, in addition, an aura of singularity. Her unique and privileged position at the court of Francis I gave her a sense of self-importance, a conviction of her own worth and weight that, if it did not bring her to instant prominence, must at least have lent a hard edge of brilliance to her every act.

In France she had been the English ambassador's daughter; her attitudes and actions had a significance beyond the ordinary, for like her father she was a bellwether for the amity or enmity of the two kingdoms.

Her departure for England, in fact, had no small diplomatic import.

The two realms of England and France, traditional enemies throughout the Middle Ages, had in recent years been on terms of nervous accord. Their two splendid, high-hearted monarchs, Henry VIII and Francis I, as imperious and physically awesome as young gods, had alternately hailed one another as brothers and challenged one another as personal rivals. Both kings excelled in the manly arts of riding and jousting and fighting on foot in the tiltyard, and each was eager to parade these skills and prove his superiority in the presence of the other. In the summer of 1520 Henry and Francis met in a festive encounter called, for the magnificence of its spectacle and costuming, the Field of Cloth of Gold. On a windswept valley in Flanders, the monarchs strutted and postured and competed—though never directly against one another—while thousands of their attendants looked on.

As theater it was superb, and unprecedented. But its exaggerated chivalry was at the same time sublimated warfare, and within months of the grand meeting the brother monarchs were drifting toward fratricidal war.

The principal power on the continent, the Holy Roman Emperor Charles V, was at war with France, and King Henry, who was the young emperor's nephew by marriage, was being drawn into the conflict on the imperial side. Francis was dismayed to hear that the English were making preparations for war. King Henry, he wrote to his ambassadors in England, did not appear to want to "maintain his fraternal love and alliance" any longer. He was building warships and mustering his troops to march, so it was rumored, against the French. He was sending munitions to the emperor's forces at Antwerp, and allowing his English subjects to fight in the imperial armies. English and imperial diplomats, so Francis's informants told him, had just signed a secret treaty whose provisions could not but be harmful to French interests. And finally, Henry had just given an order which could only mean that war was imminent: he had summoned the English scholars studying in Paris to return home, and with them "the daughter of Mr. Boullan."[1]

Just as Anne's return to England was prompted by the shifting tides of diplomacy and war, so her first recorded appearance at the court of Henry VIII was occasioned by England's growing rapprochement with the empire. Envoys of Charles V were sent to England in March of 1522 to herald the imminent arrival of their master, and King Henry's mightiest subject and most hardworking servant, Cardinal Wolsey, gave them a costly banquet at his magnificent palace, York Place. To entertain the ambassadors after supper Wolsey had arranged for pageantry on a lavish scale.

The guests were led into a vast hall illuminated by hundreds of waxen torches. Around the walls the rich blues and reds and golds of Venetian tapestries gleamed dully in the firelight, while at the far end of the cavernous chamber there loomed a vision all in green. It was a fairy castle, its high battlements crowned with towers and its walls pierced with crenellations. Carpenters and painters had labored for two weeks to build the Château Vert, or Green Castle, first constructing the wooden frame and then painstakingly covering it, from top to bottom, with green paper and foil and liquid verdigris, a poisonous copper derivative mixed with vinegar and melted in earthen pots over a coal fire. The effect was unearthly; the Green Castle shimmered in the candlelit hall like a ghostly thing.

Standing on the battlements were apparitions clothed in white —eight lovely young women, Anne Boleyn among them, playing the roles of Beauty, Honor, Perseverance, Constancy, Kindness, Bounty, Mercy and Pity. Below these were eight others, dressed "like women of Inde." These were the defenders of the castle and its fair occupants, and represented Danger, Disdain, Jealousy, Unkindness, Scorn, and so on—the sentiments most hostile to love.

The pageant proper began when eight lords appeared, intent on assaulting the castle. Chief among them was the king, whose height and splendid physique marked him out from the others despite the mask he wore. (Only one other man at court, the king's cousin Edward Neville, was as tall and broad-shouldered as Henry himself; the resemblance between them was so striking, extending even to their gold-red beards, that Neville sometimes stood in for his royal cousin during the pageantry, wearing his robes and dancing in his place.) The eight lords—whose blue satin cloaks bore the names Amorous, Nobleness, Youth, Attendance, Loyalty, Pleasure, Gentleness and Liberty—ran up to the Green Castle and pelted the defenders with dates and oranges, and were showered with rosewater and comfits in return. Meanwhile the guests were jolted by a "great peal of guns" shot from the cannon on the walls of York Place, and after a last show of resistance Danger, Disdain and the others fled. "Then," wrote the chronicler Edward Hall, "the lords took the ladies of honor as prisoners by the hands, and brought them down, and danced together very pleasantly"—did Henry dance with Anne?— "which much pleased the strangers."[2]

Save that she was among the eight lovely ladies who were captured that night, nothing is known of Anne's participation in the pageant of the Green Castle. Was she at all awed by her surroundings, at all taken aback by the wonders of the great cardinal's mansion and the glittering personalities of the court? Or did she, as seems more likely, smile inwardly at the quaint innocence of the English pageant, with its ponderous allegory of love and its old-fashioned chivalry? English ideas of love were clearly nothing like those of the sophisticated, decadent French. Nor were English courtiers like French ones: they did not lounge familiarly near the king's person, exchanging roguish banter with him and joining him in debauchery or in romping through the streets, throwing eggs at passersby. No, the English observed decorum, and they must have seemed to Anne excessively stiff and formal, bound by etiquette (however often they abused it) and sexually ingenuous by comparison with the lascivious French.

Of Anne's companions in the pageant one, Gertrude Blount, countess of Devonshire, was a staid and pious matron, while another was the king's happily married sister Mary. Another girl, Jane Parker, would soon be married to Anne's brother George Boleyn, while the others were respectable young women of the court. All but one, that is—Anne's sister Mary Boleyn Carey.

Sadly, there is no authentic portrait of Anne Boleyn's older sister. Undoubtedly she was an attractive woman, perhaps a beautiful one. But whether she resembled Anne, either in temperament or in looks, whether there was jealousy or sisterly feeling between them, whether Mary matched (or surpassed?) Anne in cleverness, vivacity or allure must remain a mystery. The presumption is often made that, because Mary was so sharply and dramatically eclipsed by her younger sister, she must have been colorless and insipid—the docile, willing dupe of those who took advantage of her. Yet the truth may have been different. In fact Mary may have chosen her relatively obscure role with some degree of calculation, and remained within it less out of happenstance than out of a wise instinct not to tempt fate too far. Of the three Boleyn children, after all, only Mary lived into middle age, forgotten but content, and died a natural death.

In 1522, Mary was at the height of her prominence at the court of Henry VIII. A year earlier she had married William Carey, a minor courtier who to oblige his king was willing to marry the royal mistress.[3] Mary had been a member of the English court since the summer of 1520 at latest, when she attended Queen Katherine at the Field of Cloth of Gold, and she succeeded Bessie Blount, the first of Henry's more or less official mistresses, sometime in the early 1520s. Like Bessie, Mary eventually bore the king an illegitimate son, but though Bessie's child, known as Henry Fitzroy, was accorded a royal upbringing and was looked on as the presumptive heir to his father's throne, Mary's son was kept out of sight at the monastery of Syon and given no attention whatever.[4]

Yet Henry's connection with Mary, though an open secret, was very much a private matter. Whereas in France the royal mistresses were visibly, stridently at the center of things, completely overshadowing the wan, pathetic queen, in England it was just the opposite. Mary Boleyn was the background figure, Queen Katherine the dominant, gracious, chief lady of the court.

Katherine was certainly not handsome. She was middle-aged, short and stout, with hair that had been a rich auburn but was now fading to a dull red-brown streaked with gray. Her many pregnancies, all but one of them resulting in stillbirths or fatally weak infants, had thickened her figure, while her features, plain even in her freshest youth, had only their animation to commend them.

Yet Katherine's strength had never been beauty. Rather it had been force of mind, with an admirable firmness of will and high character. She was a formidable personality, intellectually vigorous, a good match for her curious, brilliant, and speculative husband whose own darting intellect was as impressive as his athletic prowess. After thirteen years of marriage she no longer had Henry's ardent love, but she had his affectionate respect—and his company. He was often said to be "taking his pleasure as usual with the queen," visiting her in her apartments, talking of books, ideas, affairs in the European states.

It was the king's affection for his queen, in fact, that provided the courtly theme for the entertainment at Wolsey's banquet. The assault on the Green Castle was meant to represent King Henry's suit for Queen Katherine's love; the "lady's hand gripping a man's heart" depicted on the castle's banners illustrated Katherine's firm grip on Henry's heartfelt devotion. Of course, these tender sentiments had far less to do with the state of the king's emotions than with the imperial alliance he was forging. Queen Katherine was the aunt of the Holy Roman Emperor Charles V. His mother Joanna was Katherine's sister; both were daughters of the famed "Catholic Kings," Ferdinand and Isabella of Spain. Through Katherine, Henry was Charles's uncle, which meant that he was uncle to the richest and potentially the most powerful man in Europe.

Charles V had become king of Spain at sixteen; by the time he was nineteen he was master of the greater part of the continent, and, as Holy Roman Emperor, nominal overlord of Christendom. The Netherlands, heart of his far-flung dominions, had for centuries been England's chief trading partner, and it was this firm link that made Charles, not Francis, Henry VIII's natural ally. Compared to this strong commercial bond, England's showy, skittish partnership with France was only a passing flirtation, and the presence of Katherine of Aragon at Henry's side reinforced diplomatic interests with dynastic ones.

Or rather, that should have been the case. In actuality, Henry's marriage to Charles's aunt had proven to be a dynastic catastrophe. Queen Katherine's many pregnancies had produced only one surviving child: a girl. Princess Mary was six years old in 1522, a delicate blond child with a precociously quick intelligence and a gift for languages and music. But a princess, alas, could not reign. Even if she did inherit the throne, she would be a mere figurehead; her husband would be the one to exercise the real powers of king, whether or not she granted him that title.[5]

King Henry desperately needed a son, and it seemed more and more improbable that his queen would ever provide him with one. She was reaching the end of her childbearing years, and even if she did manage to produce another male infant there was every likelihood that it would be like her others—either stillborn or too feeble to survive for long after birth. There was still hope, but it was lessening year by year. To observers it seemed more and more probable that in time there would be a succession crisis in England.

Thus when Anne Boleyn took her place as waiting maid to Katherine of Aragon early in 1522 she was entering a palace community agitated by impending war and uneasy over the state of the succession. But beyond this, she entered it, not merely as a well connected young woman, but as a Boleyn, a member of one of the most conspicuously ambitious and acquisitive parvenu families at the Tudor court.

In the early sixteenth century the old feudal order was rapidly giving way as the Tudor kings brought able but obscure commoners to prominence in government. The great noble families lost ground—and income—to "new men" who built up power and wealth through attracting royal patronage and making judicious marriages. From this societal maelstrom the Boleyns emerged successful. Anne's great-grandfather and grandfather had married heiresses, while her father Thomas Boleyn had become a leading courtier, making himself useful to Henry VII and his son Henry VIII in a variety of roles.

Thomas Boleyn, who was forty-five in the year Anne took up her duties as waiting maid to the English queen, had very nearly reached the summit of his ambitions. Handsome, worldly, with a strong constitution and an equally rugged sense of self-interest, Boleyn had spent nearly twenty years in the service of the Tudor crown. He had willingly undergone the hardships and punishing expense of acting as royal envoy to the European courts. Again and again he had traveled the muddy roads of Scotland, the Low Countries and France, sometimes coming dangerously near on-going battles and fending off exhaustion and disease—to which his weaker colleagues succumbed—in the course of serving as his sovereign's diplomatic advocate. Beyond this, he attended King Henry, decorously attired and suitably austere of mien, when the latter met King Francis at the Field of Cloth of Gold and escorted members of the royal family on other ceremonial occasions. Boleyn was among those who heard the trial of the ill-fated duke of Buckingham, who was executed for "imagining and compassing the deposition and death of the king" in 1521, and was also entrusted with the less exalted but equally impor-tant task of supervising several key household accounts. In re-turn he was granted a succession of court posts and offices through which he amassed a substantial fortune.

But the key to success at the Tudor court was patronage, and here Thomas Boleyn had a very considerable advantage. To attach oneself to a powerful patron, to make oneself worthy of his time and notice, was to benefit immeasurably from the favors he had to bestow. Thomas Howard, son of old Norfolk, in his ruthless determination to exalt the Howard dynasty by any and every means, built up an extensive network of political depen-dents, men connected to him through patronage and often through family ties as well. Among these men was Thomas Bol-eyn.

In its positive aspect, patronage benefited both parties. For the client, it opened the door to wealth and advancement, for the patron it enlarged the host of political allies upon whom he could rely. But there was a dark side to the system, in that it was based on secret agreements and covert deal-making, and in that it was built on no firmer ground than the quicksand of personal greed.

As a result, the court of Henry VIII seethed with intrigue. Snakelike the coils of conspiracy and disloyalty wrapped them-selves around every courtier, powerful or vulnerable, ultimately making him sacrifice everything—his reputation, his income, even his friends and relatives—for the sake of inching higher up the greased pole of preferment. It was a vertiginous and hazardous career, the career of courtier, made fatally precarious by the everpresent power of the king to sweep away titles, lands, even life at his whim. Yet some men had the shrewdness and flinty-heartedness to succeed at it—and survive. Boleyn was clearly among them.

There were bulls on the Boleyn coat of arms, and bull-like the head of the family lowered his horns and muscled his way past all obstacles, human and otherwise. His singleness of purpose lent him the stamina and strength of the fibers to shake off both the sleet of the highroads and the icy abuse and duplicity of envious rivals. He also shook off—rudely and unceremoniously —any of his colleagues who became a nuisance to him. A fellow envoy and traveling companion of Boleyn's, the elderly Richard Jerningham, complained that after they had journeyed together for many weeks Boleyn suddenly deserted him once they reached London, "and would not help him to a lodging."[6] Another ambassadorial colleague of Boleyn's, Richard Sampson, longed for "a more agreeable and liberal colleague" and wrote that Boleyn was miserly and ungracious about everything.[7] As surely as Boleyn garnered allies and dependents he made enemies—among them the most powerful man at court, Thomas Wolsey—and acquired a reputation for self-serving amorality. As a French diplomat wrote of him some years later, Thomas Boleyn "would sooner act from interest than from any other motive."[8]

Along his upward path he encountered continual frustration, the continued receding of his hopes. In 1515 he had had a fateful conversation with King Henry, in which, Boleyn alleged, he promised "to serve the king in the court all his life" if in return Henry would appoint him either treasurer or controller of the household. This was his aim, nothing more; "if he would grant him that," Boleyn swore, "he would never sue for any higher place." A bargain was struck, or so Boleyn said afterward. As soon as the present treasurer, Thomas Lovell, left office, he would be replaced by the current controller Edward Poynings.

This would leave the controllership vacant and Boleyn could count on filling it.

Yet when in 1519 Lovell did leave his office, and Poynings replaced him, Boleyn was not made controller after all, and he wrote to Wolsey from Poissy, where he was on a diplomatic mission, to complain. Despite what the king had reiterated "on his last departing," Boleyn said, that he could trust "undoubtedly" to have the office, he now found that the royal promise had not been kept. Instead he was being asked to shift his expectations, to "live in hope of the treasurership" itself, which might (or might not) come to him at some future date.

Boleyn's letter to Wolsey, though deferential to the point of servility, did not mask his exasperation and pique. What good had it done him, he asked, to put in so many years of tireless labor as a royal servant, especially in the thankless role of ambassador, "if the fruit of his service is the prolonging of the king's promise, and if his absence is to be accounted a hindrance?" If this was to be the reward of his efforts, "he had better have stayed at home," he wrote sourly. He was dejected, ill-served, and not only he himself but "his friends, to whom he had disclosed his hopes." He could only conclude, Boleyn ended with obsequious resentment, that Wolsey had "perceived some fault in him," and decided to promote a worthier man.[9]

More promises were forthcoming. When the new treasurer Poynings had served his term, the office would go to Boleyn. And in fact he did receive the controllership in 1520, and in April of 1522, about a month after Anne made her courtly debut in the pageant of the Green Castle and a wearying seven years after the initial promise was made, the king issued a patent making Thomas Boleyn treasurer of the household.

By this time Mary Boleyn was the king's mistress. Possibly she had already given birth to his child—or she may have been pregnant. Their liaison was no doubt crucial to Boleyn's further advancement, though just what his role was in bringing the two together remains hidden. At the very least he approved the king's intimacy with his elder daughter. (Later it would be said that King Henry had slept with Boleyn's wife as well.)

And what of his other daughter Anne, the one who had blossomed so unexpectedly in France? Henry and Wolsey had plans for her future, and Boleyn, eager as he was to accommodate his masters, was waiting impatiently for these plans to mature.

4

"When it chanced the Lord Cardinal at any time to repair to the court, the Lord Percy would then resort for his pastime unto the queen's chamber, and there would fall in dalliance among the queen's maidens, being at the last more conversant with Mistress Anne Boleyn than with any other; so that there grew such a secret love between them, that at length they were insured together, intending to marry."

If Anne was to be of use to her family, then she must marry, as quickly and as gainfully as possible. In 1520 a husband had been proposed for her. He was James Butler, a young Irishman raised at the English court and kept there as a glorified hostage, a pledge of his dreaded father's good faith. Uniting the houses of Butler and Boleyn was meant to achieve three convergent purposes: the enrichment of the Boleyns, the political furtherance of the Howards and the aggrandizement of Henry VIII's power in Ireland. The contentment of the prospective bride and groom were left out of consideration.

In 1520 English sovereignty in Ireland was more shadow than substance. English law, in theory, held sway there, the English lord lieutenant was nominally supreme over the "mighty men of Ireland"—the great chiefs—whose power in their own feudal "countries" was all but absolute. Yet in practice English paramountcy was maintained by pitting chief against chief—in particular, by supporting the house of Butler, holders of the earldom of Ormond, against the prepotent Geraldine house of Kildare.

Sir Piers Butler, "the Red," a murderous warlord who in his bloodthirsty ambition did not scruple to assassinate his own relatives, currently wielded the Butler power, and had his eye on gaining the highest post open to any Anglo-Irish lord—the post of lord deputy. He was the best candidate to hold it, for the always unstable peace was growing increasingly fragile and a number of chiefs had coalesced around Butler's leadership. Clearly the English needed to preserve his loyalty, particularly if King Henry's stated policy of keeping the peace in Ireland "by sober ways and persuasions, founded in law and reason, and not by violence," was to succeed.[1]

No one was more keenly aware of the need to keep Butler firmly allied with English interests than Thomas Howard, Boleyn's brother-in-law and present lord lieutenant of Ireland. Howard knew that his own success depended on preventing the "disorder and wilfulness" among the chiefs which the king deplored, and to do this he relied on Butler. Yet two things threatened to weaken their rapport. One was that Butler wanted the return of his son James from the English court. The other, a more longstanding grievance, had to do with the earldom of Ormond and the Ormond lands, which were claimed—in Butler's view presumptuously—by the Boleyns.

Five years earlier the last earl of Ormond had died, leaving his title and his lands—extensive areas of Tipperary and Kilkenny in Ireland and more than seventy manors in England—to his heir or heirs. But who were they, exactly? The late earl's two daughters, Margaret Boleyn (Thomas Boleyn's mother) and Anne St. Leger, or his illegitimate kinsman Piers Butler, whose claim depended for its entire force on the fact that there was no legitimate male heir and that he, Butler, had been administering the late earl's Irish lands for nearly twenty years and considered three quarters of them as indisputably his own? The dispute dragged on unresolved, with Butler calling himself "earl of Ormond" and acting as if he were master of the Irish estates, and with the two women in control of the English manors. (Margaret Boleyn turned her share over to her son Thomas to administer for her; he in turn sold one of the manors to King Henry, who was so taken with it that he expanded its already palatial proportions and rechristened it "Beaulieu.") Meanwhile both sides were unsatisfied; their grievances rankled.

Then in 1520 a proposal was made—perhaps by Howard—to resolve the feud by marrying Butler's son James to Thomas Boleyn's daughter Anne.[2] The Ormond wealth would be absorbed into the newly united family, allowing all parties to save face and avoid litigation. It was a good example of the king's policy of "sober ways and persuasions"—assuming that the two stubbornly self-seeking fathers could be persuaded to agree. Henry asked Howard to "ascertain whether the earl of Ormond is minded to marry his son to the daughter of Sir Thomas Boleyn." For his own part he would undertake to "advance the matter with Sir Thomas."[3]

A year later the matter had been no further advanced, however. Anne was still in France, and James Butler still, to his father's increasing impatience, in England. Butler had achieved another of his desires, though, and had been appointed lord deputy of Ireland—which gave the question of his son's marriage an added dimension. Butler was, in a sense, trapped by his own success. Before returning his son to him, Wolsey advised the king, it would be wise to wait and see how Butler performed as deputy. "No doubt, his son being in England, he will do all the better in order to get him home the sooner." But as long as there was a chance that the proposed marriage might be arranged, James Butler could be kept in England indefinitely, as it offered "a good pretext for delay."[4]

Wolsey wrote in November of 1521. Presumably when Anne came to England early in 1522 the situation remained unchanged, with the match still considered politically desirable and also advisable as a way to settle the issue of the Ormond inheritance, but with no agreement yet reached as to its exact terms. Anne was no doubt expected to wait in submissive anticipation until the outcome was reached, however long it might take.

Never mind that, after several years, there was no conclusion in sight, or that her young charms were withering with every passing month. Never mind that the prolongation of this matchmaking might result in lost opportunities for her to marry elsewhere, or that, God forbid, she might find herself incompatible

45

with the chosen bridegroom or he with her. Had Wolsey not judged him to be "right active and discreet," and displaying much "towardness"? Clearly he was vigorous, competent, able to make a good impression on men in high positions. What more could any young woman want?

Besides, it was universally understood, if not always accepted, that marriage was not an institution of the heart but of the properties. Land married land, and fortune fortune; from childhood on every sensible young woman took that for granted. Marriage was an entrepreneurial undertaking, sons and daughters were commodities to be bartered by parents who owned them, as surely as they owned their houses and furnishings. The suitability of the bride and groom for one another was of necessity a minor consideration which ought not to be allowed to stand in the way of a successful negotiation. Thus girls of thirteen were wed to gouty widowers of sixty, and callow youths to crusty dowagers, because however the spouses might be mismatched, the family holdings were well suited.

But what of love, that wayward force which "troubled and tossed all things upside down," as one sixteenth century writer put it, and sabotaged the careful arrangements made by parents for their children? Moralists agreed that romantic love was an unfortunate disease to be warded off by the preventive medicine of religious devotion and filial piety. Love of God, it was thought, helped to drive out the baser love of the flesh, as did dutiful reverence and submission to one's parents, who knew far better than their children who was deserving of their love.

To let so dangerous an urge as romance interfere with so serious a matter as matrimony was reckless, for love disordered the wits, driving the lover to madness. People in love were constantly wailing, sighing, groaning and complaining, now elated with excitement and now beside themselves with pain. Like madmen they lost all reason, wrote Juan Luis Vives, a Spanish humanist whose works were much read at the court of Henry VIII. They followed blindly wherever love led them, even when it led along dark paths toward illness or violence. Vives told of pale young girls, deserted by their faithless lovers, who wandered the streets begging their bread until they fell ill and died in brokenhearted wretchedness. And of cruelly disappointed maidens who, having loved passionately, learned to hate with equal passion and stabbed their fickle lovers to death.

To fall in love was bad enough, but to marry for love was simply inexcusable. Beyond unsoundness of mind it showed lack of good breeding, bad judgment, and a defiance of tradition and family propriety. It was, in a word, immature. And what was infinitely more dangerous, it was disobedient.

It is nearly impossible for us to imagine now the sheer power that parents, chiefly fathers, exerted over their children in the early sixteenth century. They were not only masterful, they were godlike, Olympian figures glaring down at their quaking offspring in wrathful splendor. And not only glaring down, but lashing out, physically, to wound and bruise and often draw blood. Girls were slapped until their skin glowed an angry red, or pinched until they were black and blue all over. Even the mildest uncooperativeness brought beatings, while serious defiance could be fatal. For backtalk or angry looks a girl could be struck so hard that she bled from the nose or mouth, her head "broken" in several places, with the punishment repeated several times a day. For being forward with a man, or sexually wanton, she could be killed. Vives wrote of how "many fathers cut the throats of their daughters" for unchastity—and so absolute was a father's control over his children that such crimes carried little risk.

Anne's course was clear, then. She must wait submissively while her elders negotiated her marital fate, telling herself that marriage was a business matter and that love, that destructive emotion, had no place in it. And she must always keep in mind the awesome force of her father's authority over her, and be careful not to arouse his wrath.

Such were the expectations. But such, surprisingly, was not what happened. The wayward force of love arose despite all, and Anne, high-spirited and self-impelled as she was, found it irresistible.

Among the eligible young men at court was Henry Percy, an impetuous, hotheaded young aristocrat of about twenty whose father was the earl of Northumberland. Percy was among the highborn young retainers living in the household of the powerful Cardinal Wolsey, and when Wolsey came to court Percy came with him.

"When it chanced the Lord Cardinal at any time to repair to the court," recalled Wolsey's gentleman usher George Cavendish long afterward, "the Lord Percy would then resort for his pastime unto the queen's chamber, and there would fall in dalliance among the queen's maidens, being at the last more conversant with Mistress Anne Boleyn than with any other."[5] The impetuous youth and the spirited, dark-eyed girl who in Cavendish's words "did excel all other" in her "excellent gesture and behavior" fell in love. Overlooking—or sabotaging?—the discussions between the Boleyns and the Butlers, and heedless of the interests of her relatives Anne became more and more "entangled" with Percy, and he with her, though he too was ignoring an engagement made for him by his father the earl. Percy was pledged to marry Mary Talbot, daughter of the earl of Shrewsbury, and had been since childhood. It was a purely pragmatic match, whose aim was to align two border families with similar interests and responsibilities, and young Percy had no love for Mary Talbot—rather, as it turned out, the reverse. But for him as for Anne, family honor required that the commitment made on his behalf be kept, and in paying court to Anne he breached that honor, with predictable results.

The erotic attachment between the two was no secret, and in time, according to Cavendish, King Henry heard of it and was "much offended." As Percy was in Wolsey's entourage the king asked the cardinal to intervene and separate the lovers, which he proceeded to do.

Cavendish recalled in great detail the events that followed. Calling Percy into his presence, Wolsey criticized him with an icy logic that reduced him to tears.

"I marvel not a little of thy peevish folly," the cardinal began, "that thou wouldest tangle and insure thyself with a foolish girl yonder in the court, I mean Anne Boleyn. Dost thou not consider the estate that God hath called thee unto in this world? For after the death of thy noble father thou art most like to inherit and possess one of the most worthiest earldoms of this realm."

In his most sonorous clerical manner Wolsey reminded his young protégé of his responsibilities to his father and, most important, to his king. He ought not only to have asked his father's permission before speaking to Anne but should have "submitted all his whole proceeding" to King Henry, who would have found him a much more nobly born girl than Anne Boleyn, one who "matched his estate and honor." By not approaching the king, Wolsey warned, Percy had not only brought down on himself considerable royal displeasure but had forfeited the "high estimation" in which he might otherwise have been held.

"But now behold what ye have done through your willfulness," the cardinal went on, warming to his subject. "Ye have not only offended your natural father but also your most gracious sovereign lord, and matched yourself with one such as neither the king nor yet your father will be agreeable with the matter." Wolsey informed the trembling Percy that he intended to send for his father the earl, and that when he arrived the king would instruct him either to put an end to his son's agreement with Anne or disinherit him. As it happened, Wolsey explained, King Henry was just at the point of making quite different arrangements for Anne—the betrothal to Butler—and so her indiscretion with Percy was doubly inopportune.

Here he paused, and Percy, "all weeping," instead of submitting, made a surprisingly defiant response.

"Sir, I know nothing of the king's pleasure therein (for whose displeasure I am very sorry). I considered that I was of good years and thought myself sufficient to provide me of a convenient wife whereas my fancy served me best, not doubting but that my lord my father would have been right well persuaded." Though Anne was only "a simple maid," the daughter of a commoner, he said, still she was related to the ducal houses of Norfolk and Ormond, and thus of equal descent—here Percy stretched a point—to his own. He ended in startling fashion by insisting that he "could not deny or forsake" what had passed between him and Anne, and asking Wolsey to intercede for him with the king, so that by his "princely benevolence" the situation might be left as it was.

Wolsey's reaction was swift and furious. "Lo, sirs," he cried to the servants who stood in attendance nearby, "ye may see what conformity or wisdom is in this wilful boy's head! I thought that when thou heardest me declare the king's intended pleasure and travail herein, thou wouldest have relented and wholly submitted thyself and all thy wilful and unadvised fact to the king's royal will and prudent pleasure to be fully disposed and ordered by his grace's disposition as his highness should seem good."

"Sir, so I would," Percy answered, "but in this matter I have gone so far before so many worthy witnesses that I know not how to avoid myself nor to discharge my conscience."

The prickings of Percy's highborn conscience, Wolsey's references to the "unadvised fact," or act, committed by the two young people, the "worthy witnesses" who were present, indeed the whole tenor of Cavendish's account are meant to convey the weightiness of the situation.[6] Clearly, we are meant to infer, the lovers exchanged vows, making an agreement to marry. In the eyes of the church this was a binding pledge, tantamount to marriage, valid even without the presence of a priest or witnesses.

Such an agreement was bound to have far-reaching consequences, especially when made between a man and a woman already promised to others. But given Anne's later marital history the exact nature of her dealings with Percy take on the gravest significance. Yet precisely because of this, the evidence is clouded by self-interested lies and self-serving omissions, as well as by the intricacies of canon law and the ingenious wits of canon lawyers. The truth, whatever it may have been, remains elusive and we are left with educated conjecture.

Most likely the simplest and most natural reconstruction of the story is closest to what actually happened. Anne, headstrong and impatient with the inconclusive negotiations over the betrothal to James Butler—and possibly not finding either him or his future in backward Ireland to her taste—flirted, became infatuated, and finally chose to cast her lot with Percy. It was an intelligent choice as well as an emotional one; above all it was independent, self-determining. The lovers were, one suspects, no more chaste than they were discreet; like many another rebellious couple of the time they may well have considered themselves married and consummated the marriage, as witnesses long afterward claimed.[7]

To be sure, the witnesses may have been lying. Yet the self-willed natures of the lovers, Anne's erotic French background and the increasing promiscuity of English court life argue in the direction of a sexual as well as romantic bond. Not many years after this the dowager duchess of Norfolk, Anne's great-aunt, came upon Anne's cousin Catherine Howard and her lover kissing "after a wonderful manner, . . . kissing and hanging by their bellies like two sparrows," and after slapping them and shouting in her anger she asked sarcastically "whether they thought her home was Henry VIII's court?"[8]

Cavendish's account of the escapade makes no mention of Thomas Boleyn's reaction to his daughter's rash behavior, but he must have left her in no doubt of his heated disapproval. Slaps, kicks, blows may have punctuated his storm of angry criticism. Anne had disgraced herself, thrown away her good repute, possibly ruined her chance to marry well. She was a witless, defiant girl, a foolish girl, as Wolsey had said, light-headed and wilful. Tudor fathers were brutally stern, and most likely Boleyn acted in character. Yet at the heart of his fury was a calculating logic. Clever, resourceful man of affairs as he was, he must have weighed the situation with his usual opportunistic detachment. Here he had a disobedient, prideful daughter, whose passions ran high and whose attractions were evident. Beyond her spoiled, sulking rebelliousness he may have caught a flash of great temperament, a dazzling, magnetic fire given to few women. And, too, it may by this time have become evident that the Butler match might never be concluded, the volatile politics of Ireland having moved into a different configuration from the one they had held when the alliance was first proposed. All in all, Thomas Boleyn may have thought, his younger daughter's indiscretion, though risky, was not irremediable, and on the whole it put her in a new and more interesting light.

Wolsey got nowhere with Henry Percy until he called the boy's father to court. The earl came at "quick speed," alarmed and infuriated that his son should have acted so childishly as to rouse the anger of the king. Wolsey explained the situation to him, and then, sitting on a bench in one of the long galleries of Wolsey's palace, Northumberland spoke to his son.

"Son, thou hast always been a proud, presumptuous, disdainful, and a very unthrift waster," he began, as Cavendish recalled the conversation. "Therefore what joy, what comfort, what pleasure, or solace should I conceive in thee?" Percy had shown utter disregard for his father, his king and his patrimony. He deserved no leniency, though by the king's extraordinary grace he was to be forgiven, provided he never went near Anne again, on pain of King Henry's "high indignation."

Yet the ramifications of Percy's "entanglement" with Anne remained to be dealt with. It was not a simple matter, but after "long debating and consultation" the pledges made were "infringed and dissolved"—by exactly what means, and whether Anne was a party to any of the proceedings, Cavendish did not record—and to put Percy permanently out of harm's way he was married off to Mary Talbot in accordance with his father's original intentions.

As it turned out, Percy was to pay a heavy price for his involvement with Anne. He did eventually inherit the earldom (though his father had threatened to disinherit him), but his clash with Wolsey coupled with the loss of his love and a miserably unhappy marriage destroyed his health. Fevers and stomach disorders made his life a torment, while his continuing fear of the mighty cardinal and of the king played havoc with his nerves.

And in truth, though he was severed from Anne he was never to be free of her while she lived. Time and again, as Anne became more and more prominent and her past associations more and more of interest, Percy was called upon, as Anne was, to lay bare all that had passed between them. No doubt he came to regret ever having met her, and to curse the rash impulse that had brought them together.

And Anne, humiliated, her passion and her will thwarted, saw in the wrathful, commanding cardinal the incarnation of her misfortunes. It was Wolsey, the king's omnicompetent minister, who spied out her private designs and intervened to block them. It was Wolsey who bore down on Percy with his fierce intellect and reduced him to tearful submission. Fleshy and heavy-jowled with advancing age and dissipation, it was the corrupt cardinal who snuffed out her young love and separated her from her beloved. The pain of her loss mingled with a mounting desire for vengeance.

"Mistress Anne Boleyn was greatly offended," Cavendish recalled, "saying that if it lay ever in her power she would work the cardinal much displeasure." To complete her disgrace she was ordered to leave the court and stay in the country for a time under her father's supervision. It was a blow to her pride and ambition—and it put marriage, if marriage was yet to be possible, still further off. She cried, she frowned, no doubt she cursed her fate in rich French curses. And after a time her inner turmoil curdled into a calculating design to avenge herself on the fat, red-robed prelate who had shattered her ardent desires.

5

*"After that all these troublesome matters of my
Lord Percy's was brought to a good stay, and all
things finished that was before devised, Mistress
Anne Boleyn was revoked unto the court, where
she flourished after in great estimation and
favor."*

Most likely Anne's exile from court was brief. According to Cavendish she went "home again to her father for a season," and that season was probably a matter of months rather
than years. To be sure, Anne's name does not appear prominently in the surviving court records for the next several years,
but it would be a mistake to assume, as her earlier biographers
have tended to do, that this must imply a prolonged absence
from court.

In all probability Anne's stay in the country was no longer
than that of any other courtier who managed to incur the king's
disfavor. King Henry commonly banished those who displeased
him, then recalled them a few months later. They returned to
court chastened beings, heartily sorry for all their offenses and
eager to bask once again in the scorching sun of the royal presence. Anne too returned, eager though not chastened, and before long she not only had regained her former status but was
being drawn into greater prominence than before.

There was no further talk of marriage for her—or at least
there is no record of any—and the carefully fabricated plans to

unite the Boleyns and Butlers through the union of Anne and James Butler seem simply to have melted away.[1]

But if marriage was remote, romance was not. The evidence suggests that Anne had several lovers in the years following her involvement with Henry Percy, and that in these years she acquired a reputation for unchastity.[2] Who her lovers were no source records, except for one—the tall, handsome, golden-haired Thomas Wyatt.

"Nature made Wyatt tall with powerful muscles/And sinews strong; adding thereto a face/As beautiful as any," wrote John Leland in his eulogy of the poet. Wyatt's superb physique made him a fit companion for the king and his athletic favorites Brandon, Francis Bryan and Henry Norris on the tiltyard, and he took part in the "challenge of feats of arms" staged at court in the Christmas season of 1524–25. His agility in the lists was only the most conspicuous of a galaxy of accomplishments. Wyatt was a scholar, an able courtier with appointments as clerk of the Jewel House and esquire of the body to the king, and a poet—the most outstanding poet of his generation, in fact, though to contemporaries his political capabilities stood out more sharply than his aesthetic gifts.

He was in his early twenties when he became attracted to Anne, an intensely attractive figure himself with his balance of robust vitality and lyric sensitivity, virility and intellect. Unlike Percy, whose callow boldness had led him to disaster, Wyatt had depth of character, he had promise. Yet Anne was, or ought to have been, beyond his reach, not only because her Howard ancestry put her far above him in status but because he was not free to court her. He was irrevocably, and miserably, married.

At the age of seventeen Wyatt had married Elizabeth Brooke, daughter of Thomas Brooke, Lord Cobham, and had fathered a son. By the time he began his advancement at Henry VIII's court, however, the couple had become estranged as a result, it seems, of the wife's adultery. For the next decade and more they maintained a rancorous separation, sharpened by quarrels over maintenance and by Wyatt's provocative public comments about his guilty wife, which infuriated her family. Meanwhile the poet had long since begun to woo other women, among them the ensorceling Anne Boleyn.

"Coming to behold the sudden appearance of this new beauty," Wyatt's grandson George wrote long afterward, relying on the authority of Anne Gainsford, one of Anne Boleyn's maids, Wyatt "came to be holden and surprised somewhat with the sight thereof, after much more with her witty and graceful speech, his ear also had him chained to her, so as finally his heart seemed to say, 'I could gladly yield to be tied for ever with the knot of her love.' "[3]

A poem of Wyatt's played on the name "Anna," and has been thought to refer to Anne Boleyn:

> *What wourde is that that chaungeth not,*
> *Though it be tourned and made in twain?*
> *It is myn aunswer, god it wot,*
> *And eke the causer of my payn.*
> *A love rewardeth with disdain,*
> *Yet it is loved. What would ye more?*
> *It is my helth eke and my sore.*

That she rewarded his love with disdain seems confirmed by George Wyatt's account. Anne, he wrote, finding that Wyatt was married, "rejected all his speech of love, but yet in such sort as whatsoever tended to regard of her honor she showed not to scorn, for the general favor and goodwill she perceived all men to bear him, which might the rather occasion others to turn their looks to that which a man of his worth was brought to gaze at in her, as indeed after it happened."

Anne may well have reasoned that Wyatt's interest in her would make her appear more attractive to other men, but there was considerably more to their involvement than this. Wyatt himself, the evidence suggests, later admitted either to the royal Council or to the king himself—or both—that Anne was a woman of light morals, as he had good reason to know.[4] Given her temperament and his, her early sexual awakening and the sensuous climate of the court, a love affair between them seems more likely than not.

The famous sonnet Wyatt wrote about Anne—adapted from a sonnet by Petrarch with highly subjective alterations—evokes her as a tamelessly desirable creature, with a fey singularity about her that led him to describe her as a fleeing deer, an elusive quarry in an enchanted forest:

> Who so list to hount, I knowe where is an hynde,
>   But as for me, helas, I may no more:
>   The vayne travaill hath weried me so sore.
>   I am of theim that farthest commeth behinde;
> Yet may I by no means my weried mynde
>   Drawe from the Diere: but as she fleeth afore,
>   Faynting I folowe. I leve of therefore,
>   Sins in a nett I seke to hold the wynde.
> Who list her hount, I put him owte of dowbte,
>   As well as I may spend his tyme in vain:
>   And, graven with Diamondes, in letters plain
> There is written her faier neck rounde abowte:
>   Noli me tangere, for Cesars I ame;
>   And wylde for to hold, though I seme tame.[5]

Yet one senses that it was more her spirit that eluded and wearied him than her physical self. What was untouchable about her, what evaded possession and proved "wild for to hold" was her inner being, that part of her personality that remained firmly within her own control (or at any rate successfully hidden and beyond reach) no matter how intimate she became with a lover.

Wyatt carried on his wearying suit amid a setting of courtly magnificence and continual, often strenuous merrymaking. Both he and Anne were caught up in a kaleidoscopic whirl of courtly pastimes: ceremonies, celebrations, rituals and revelry that filled most of their waking hours.

As members of a royal court populated by upward of a thousand servants of all degrees of rank and stature, from the king's councillors to the principal household officials to the greasy kitchen boys, they had their assigned roles in the intricate human mechanism surrounding the king. They waited on him when he rose early in the morning and again when he retired late at night; they attended him while he dined, and formed a retinue to escort him when he processed from his private apartments to the palace chapel for morning mass and again for evensong. They cleaned and warmed the rooms he lived and worked in, prepared his food, washed and brushed his garments, looked after his dozens of horses and dogs and falcons. And they did these things according to elaborate procedural rules centuries old, which made of each simple task a time-consuming, all but sacred ritual whose component parts were shared among many pairs of hands.

Attending to King Henry's personal needs was only the beginning of the courtiers' function. Beyond this they were expected to keep him company when he exercised on the tiltyard, ride with him to the hunt, follow at his heels when he went walking, dance when he danced after supper and then play cards and dice with him until the early hours of the morning. They were expected to form an appreciative audience when he performed on the virginals or recorder, and to share his enjoyment of the music his minstrels played. And then, in the intervals between these duties, the more exalted personnel of the court was on display in the presence chamber where the king gave audiences and in the dining hall where he entertained his guests. Christenings and weddings too made demands on their time, not to mention such family matters as matchmaking, litigation and settling the estates of relatives recently deceased. Here personal interests overlapped with those of the professional man or woman of the court, for as in the case of the Boleyns, preferment in the royal household was often linked to advantageous marriages, usually with the sons or daughters of other ambitious servants of the king.

Taking part in revels and disguisings was among the courtiers' chief pastimes, and at the court of Henry VIII the revels were frequent and the pageantry splendid. Almost any extraordinary event served as the occasion for revelry—the seasonal festivities at Christmas and New Year's and other church feasts, the birth of a prince or princess, the making of peace or even of war, the visits of foreign envoys or royalty. A theme was chosen, one of the court poets was assigned to write the text to be spoken and sung and one of the court musicians chosen to compose the music. The revels master planned the setting and costuming, hiring carpenters and painters and gilders to decorate the hall or banqueting house where the revels were to be staged and ordering quantities of "revels stuff" from the large rented storerooms where it was kept.

Then when the preparations and rehearsals were concluded, the masquing unfolded. The richly costumed dancers moved back and forth against a backdrop of antique pillars or gilded arches, threading their way through artificial gardens whose lifelike trees and flowers were fashioned from silk and taffeta. Disguised as mysterious beings from faraway lands, turbaned or crowned or swathed in veils and jewels, they danced in a dream-world, figures from a medieval romance come to life.

There was outdoor make-believe as well. One May Day the entire court trooped up to Shooter's Hill behind the palace at Greenwich, the king and the two hundred archers of his guard attired in Lincoln green velvet. One member of the company, dressed as Robin Hood, invited all present to "come into the greenwood, and see how the outlaws live," and the others followed him to a rustic banquet chamber deep in the woods. Cut boughs had been woven into a walled chamber festooned with flowers and scented with sweet herbs. Here the king and queen presided over a meal of venison and wine, and afterward enjoyed a parade of decorated floats and bands of musicians "sounding the trumpets and other instruments."

As one of Queen Katherine's maids of honor Anne played her part in the spectacles, clad in luxurious gowns and elaborate headdresses, partnering the king and the men who were his favorites and so had the privilege of joining him in the revels. With the other maids she attended the queen, walking behind her or standing near her when she sat down. The maids were expected to do little but honor the queen and enhance the court with their loveliness, and Anne's actual duties were light. According to one visitor to King Henry's court the "sumptuous appearance" of Katherine's waiting maids made the queen herself look quite plain, and this, when added to the king's propensity for choosing mistresses from among the young women who attended his wife, must have made the position of maid of honor to the queen a desirable if stressful one.[6]

To keep up a sumptuous—or even a reasonably presentable

—appearance amid the dirt and disorder of the royal household must have been a sizable challenge. Nothing in the palace was ever really clean, not the flea-infested bedclothes or the carpets that covered the tables, not the heavy, ornate, unwashable gowns or even the layers of underclothing that grew grimy between infrequent launderings. Everywhere Anne stepped her satin slippers encountered the foul-smelling rushes that covered the unswept, bespattered floors; everything she touched, from the soiled tapestries to the smudged table linen to the smoke-darkened walls, was coated with the thick residues of age and use.

Anne and her companions in the queen's apartments were allowed a daily ration of bread and ale and wine, which they no doubt shared among themselves in private, but they took their main meals amid the pandemonium of the common dining hall, where the general commotion caused by hundreds of milling servants was augmented by the presence of hundreds more unsavory "boys and vile persons," vagabonds, prostitutes and "mighty beggars" who found their way unbidden to the king's table. Dogs roamed under the long benches scavenging for food, and from time to time a servant would rush through the room cracking a whip and ringing a bell to frighten them away. Nor was the squalor confined to the common areas of the palace. Even in the relative gentility of the queen's apartments the maids were crowded together, usually two to a single narrow bed, in one room under the often lax supervision of the Mother of the Maids. Here they talked, joked, and quarreled late into the night, their boisterous noise disturbing the senior household officers who slept—or tried to—in quarters nearby.

If any of the maids of honor, or anyone else in the royal entourage, for that matter, set down his or her impressions of Anne Boleyn in these years their words are lost. Wyatt's evocation of the fey, elusive beauty he sought in vain tells nothing about the headstrong girl with French tastes who was thrown together with perhaps half a dozen other young women—all of them of higher birth than herself—in Katherine of Aragon's austere chambers. Whether Anne was admired, envied, scorned or perhaps ostracized by the others cannot now be discovered, but her status, combined with her strong personality and personal attractiveness, may well have provoked dislike.

What was Anne after all but a commoner's daughter, dark as a gypsy and with an unseemly growth on one of her fingers? Her father was an important man, her sister too had a certain salacious prominence, but apart from her obvious ability to attract men Anne herself was not really in a class with the fair-skinned, well-bred daughters of the nobility. She had tried and failed to marry above her station (and the story of her abortive love affair with Percy may have been told and retold often behind her back), and no man had come forward to offer her marriage. Her future was uncertain, but she did not seem destined, as most other young women of the court did, for amiable obscurity.

As to Queen Katherine's reaction to her graceful, dark-eyed maid of honor their temperaments were so dissimilar that the queen could hardly have taken to Anne. As it was, Katherine must have associated Anne with her sister, and her sister with King Henry, the unfaithful husband she adored and obeyed despite the disturbing state of their marriage. There were even rumors about Anne's mother and the king. Anyone named Boleyn would have been an unlikely candidate for the queen's favor; Anne, with her self-assurance and self-will, was especially unlikely.

Still, she did not owe her appointment as maid of honor to Queen Katherine's favor, but to her father's expanding role in government and in the inner circle of power surrounding the king.

Thomas Boleyn, far from being content to stop at becoming household treasurer, was reaching far higher, while amassing new offices and honors every few months. Each of the stewardships, keeperships and other minor offices the king granted him brought him little in itself, but in the aggregate they were worth a good deal while serving also to extend his influence as the leading gentleman of Kent. The various positions served to strengthen and reinforce one another. As steward of the royal manor of Tunbridge and holder of other offices in the town he collected the rents and taxes due to the king—at considerable profit to himself; as household treasurer he disbursed funds to himself in his other capacities to refurbish the manor and repair the town bridge, adding to their value and hence to his own income.[7]

He had long since eclipsed his Kentish neighbors and fellow courtiers, the Poynings of Westenhanger, the Wyatts of Allington, the Brookes of Cobham. He was on terms of intimacy, or of intimate animosity, with such court luminaries as William Compton, a commoner fabulously enriched by King Henry and appointed to his privy chamber, and Charles Brandon, the royal alter ego and Boleyn's jealous rival. Boleyn's brother-in-law Thomas Howard succeeded to the ducal title of Norfolk on his father's death in 1525, a boost for all the Howards and those with Howard connections. Boleyn had meanwhile become a knight for the body in 1523, and was shortly afterward made a baron and summoned to Parliament. His diplomatic duties abroad lessened; clearly the king found him indispensable at home.

A letter from Wolsey to King Henry in the spring of 1525 reveals how intimate was Boleyn's role in the everyday process of ruling. King Henry relied on his chief minister Wolsey to do much of the hour-by-hour groundwork of reading dispatches, writing letters and drafting documents; the king and the minister communicated at intervals during the day, as papers and messages went back and forth between them. In April of 1525 Wolsey was away from court, at one of his houses. Henry sent Boleyn to him as his personal messenger, carrying a gift and verbal instructions. Wolsey sent word back thanking the king for his "gracious token" and adding, somewhat curtly and no doubt with some resentment of Boleyn, that for the "speedy execution" of royal business there was no substitute for the royal presence itself. In other words, rather than sending the indispensable Boleyn the king should take advantage of Wolsey's hospitality and come in person.[8]

Yet Wolsey's sour disapproval did nothing to halt Boleyn's upward progress. Soon he and his wife Elizabeth were among that handful of courtiers and royal relatives allowed to lodge at the palace, instead of renting quarters nearby.[9] Boleyn's account book reflects his advancement: there were payments to family members and for Anne's expenses, bills for the costly fabrics required for court costumes and for the embroidering of them, payments for costs resulting from moving back and forth between Hever and the capital, and, funding it all and more, payments to Boleyn from the bailiffs who collected his rents and sold the animals and foodstuffs produced on his lands.[10]

Anne's brother George rose in prominence and fortune along with his father, receiving offices and fees that, in conjunction with the annual income he enjoyed as "one of the cupbearers when the king dineth out," allowed him to afford to keep his place at court.[11] Quick-witted, arrogant and a talented poet, George Boleyn drew no lasting comment from his contemporaries, and whether he showed the same reasonable attachment to his other relatives as he seems to have to Anne is unknown.[12]

In enriching Thomas Boleyn and providing for his son in the early 1520s King Henry was laying a foundation for the future. Titles brought with them exceedingly high costs, and the king meant to ensure that, if and when he ennobled Boleyn, the new peer would be prepared to bear the expense. To be sure, he had the share of the English Ormond inheritance passed on to him by his mother, not to mention his own patrimony and the incidental income brought in by the lumber mill he owned and the ransom money he extorted from the families of certain Breton merchants whom he "took prisoner at sea" on one of his voyages abroad. But his inherited lands and ordinary income would hardly have sufficed to pay the enormous taxes imposed on a peer, or to enable him to afford a large and luxurious household. Hence the shower of royal endowments and the elevation that shortly followed them.

The ceremony that took place at the new royal palace of Bridewell on June 16, 1525 had as its focus the symbolic designation of King Henry's bastard son, six-year-old Henry Fitzroy, as heir to the throne. But several others were honored at the same time, and at the very end of the long ritual "Lord Boleyn was created Viscount Rochford."[13]

It was a hot and dusty day, and the crowd that gathered to watch the spectacle came solely to catch a glimpse of the king's little son, who was usually kept out of sight, and to talk in hushed tones about the momentous implications the proceedings held for the succession. Nine-year-old Princess Mary, until now the king's official heir despite her sex, was no longer her father's clear choice. In granting to his son by Bessie Blount the title he himself had held as a boy, the title duke of Richmond, King Henry was proclaiming a new preference. Mary, and her mother Katherine, whose lack of sons had led to this state of affairs, were being displaced. It was not exactly a palace revolution, but it clearly represented a shift in expectations, not to mention an alteration in England's attitude toward the queen's nephew Charles V.

A fanfare was sounded and a company of lords entered the presence chamber where King Henry stood waiting under his golden canopy, a throng of dignitaries to his left and right. Behind the lords came Garter Herald, bearing the first of young Fitzroy's patents of nobility, and behind him followed the earl of Northumberland with the boy's ceremonial sword. Last came young Fitzroy himself, wearing the robes of an earl and flanked by the earls of Arundel and Oxford. Invested by his father with his earldom—for he had to be made an earl before he could attain the higher honor of duke—the boy processed out of the chamber and then returned to repeat the entire procedure, this time wearing ducal robes of crimson and blue velvet and invested by his father with the ducal cape and circlet.

After this the other elevations were an anticlimax, particularly the last creation. A hardworking royal servant, Thomas Boleyn, was being rewarded with a title—the Butlers' title of Rochford. (The barony of Rochford had fallen vacant with the earl of Ormond's death; Henry revived it for Boleyn, but made him Viscount, not Baron, Rochford.) No doubt the overheated onlookers yawned and wished the tedious ritual over. But for Boleyn the creation marked a watershed in his career, his passage into the ranks of the privileged. Few men achieved what he had; of those few who amassed wealth far fewer gained titles. It was one thing to carry messages between the king and his chief minister, to have a voice in the royal Council; it was another to be called Milord Rochford, to wear the fur-trimmed robes of a nobleman and to dine, as only noblemen were allowed to do, on many courses at dinner and precede all those below the rank of viscount whenever the rules of precedence were observed.

Boleyn was not yet fifty, and was in better than average health. With his brother-in-law Norfolk and the king's powerful friend Brandon (like Boleyn, a commoner elevated to the peerage) he might yet gain more influence with King Henry, opposing the cardinal and perhaps, slowly, supplanting him. He had come this far, why not still farther? Especially now that the queen, always before one of her husband's valued advisers, was being so pointedly demoted.

By the summer of 1525, most likely, Mary Boleyn had yielded place as royal mistress to some other woman, or to a variety of pleasing but fleeting sexual liaisons. The king's heart, it seems, was unengaged. Yet he was an amorous man, a man who could be influenced by a woman. Why not Boleyn's other daughter Anne?

Perhaps he had already noticed her, admiring her striking coloring, her style, the way she stood out among the other maids who attended the queen. She was one among many nubile young women at court, and not the handsomest. But Wyatt had written charmingly of her, and her black eyes were remarkable. And now, of course, she was the daughter of a peer of the realm.

Among the ships in King Henry's flotilla was the *Katherine Pleasance*, named for the queen and used on important occasions. In the fall of 1523 the *Mary Boleyn* was on the list of the royal ships, a sound, newish craft with a crew of seventy-nine sailors. In 1526 the military accounts show a payment to Thomas Boleyn, Viscount Rochford, for a ship for the royal navy called the *Anne Boleyn*—a vessel whose fate and import no one but King Henry then knew.

6

*"The king began to kindle the
brand of amours . . ."*

Amongst those who were esteemed to honor Anne Boleyn two were observed to be of principal mark," wrote George Wyatt, relying on the memory of Anne's maid Anne Gainsford. "The one was Sir Thomas Wyatt the elder, the other was the king himself."

The king himself—that manly paragon whose towering presence so dominated his court and age. If George Wyatt's Elizabethan account is to be believed, King Henry courted Anne at the same time as Wyatt did, and the two clashed over which had possession of her loyalty and affection. The account tells how the poet, engaging Anne in conversation, ". . . in sporting wise caught from her a certain small jewel hanging by a lace out of her pocket or otherwise loose, which he thrust into his bosom, neither with any earnest request could she obtain it of him again."[1]

Wyatt treasured Anne's jewel on its length of lace and wore it around his neck under his doublet, hoping that in time either she would offer to let him keep it or, at least, he could use it as an excuse "to have talk with her, wherein he had singular delight." Anne made no particular effort to get it back, according to her biographer's informant. Despite the misleading implication that the trinket was a love token she had given Waytt, the jewel itself was not worth taking trouble to recover. So Wyatt kept it, and kept on wearing it, all the while trying to ingratiate himself with Anne.

The king, noticing how Wyatt was hovering around Anne and how she kept aloof from him, felt emboldened to declare his own feelings for her. He tried to seduce her, but finding her careful of her honor he spoke of marriage, and took one of her rings from her, wearing it afterward on his little finger. According to this account, it looked to others as though this was merely "an ordinary course of dalliance," but King Henry took it much more seriously than that, as the result showed.

A few days later he was playing bowls with several of his favorites, among them Wyatt. Henry was in good spirits—"more than ordinarily pleasantly disposed"—and when he insisted that one of the casts was to his advantage, he playfully "pointed with his finger whereon he wore her ring," looking at his rival and saying,

> "Wyatt, I tell thee it is mine," smiling upon him withal. Sir Thomas at the length casting his eye upon the king's finger, perceived that the king meant the lady whose ring that was, which he well knew, and pausing a little, and finding the king bent to pleasure, after the words repeated again by the king, the knight replied, "And if it may like your majesty to give me leave to measure it, I hope it will be mine."

With that Wyatt took the lace from around his neck and used it to measure the cast. As soon as he saw the jewel hanging from the lace Henry recognized it as Anne's, and at once his temper flared. He picked up the bowl and hurled it away angrily. "It may be so, but then I am deceived," he spat out, and then stalked off, "breaking up the game."[2]

This anecdote, recorded as it was long after the fact by a man eager to restore Anne's good name and to put her chastity and propriety beyond question, can hardly be taken as a faithful record of events. It shows an overwhelming bias in favor of Anne, and it begs the question of why, if she refused the attentions of the married Wyatt, she consented to talk of marriage with the king, who was still wed to Queen Katherine at the time. Very likely the account conflates into a single series of episodes wooing that may, at least in Wyatt's case, have gone on over several years—and of course, it leaves out the sexual dimension of that wooing (except in the backhanded way meant to vindicate Anne's character) entirely.

Yet for all its dramatic fictions the story as George Wyatt told it rings true in one respect. In that it portrayed the king as volatile, hot-tempered and prone to believe himself the victim of betrayal, it exactly mirrored his humor at the moment when Anne Boleyn entered his life.

In the mid-1520s the king was in his mid-thirties, handsome and virile, glowing with health and strength. His "quick and penetrable" gray eyes seemed to take in everything, his agile mind was everywhere at once, darting from military affairs to improvements to his palaces to problems of theology or church law. Nothing was outside the scope of his vast interests: not the names of his ship captains, not the exact number of mercenaries in the employ of Francis I or Charles V, certainly not the latest designs in tilting armor. He conversed volubly, knowledgeably, incessantly about these and a hundred other things, projecting himself easily into situations and locations remote from his own. There was a wide-ranging, roaming alertness about Henry, a sense of restlessness, of sublimated activity that clung to him even when he was at rest. He was a man, an observer once remarked, who "wanted to have his feet in a thousand shoes."

His days were filled with bone-shattering exercise—breakneck riding, tireless hunting, wrestling with the more athletic of his companions and long brisk walks. His nights were often even more frenetic. When there were no banquets at the royal palace Brandon, Boleyn and others of the wealthy and influential entertained the king in lavish fashion at their luxurious London houses, or Wolsey showed him princely hospitality at his palatial residences of York Place and Hampton Court. During the course of these long evenings Henry made several grand entrances, robing and disrobing each time, sometimes taking part in the masques and disguisings put on for his enjoyment, sometimes merely seeking to vary his own magnificence. After the formal entertainments were over he danced, vigorously and continuously, leaping and bounding with the abandon of a young stag, his exuberant, almost belligerent physicality a marvel to everyone who witnessed it. He went on without rest for hours, ending fresher and more bright-eyed than he began, then retired to restore himself with a few hours of sleep before beginning the energetic day ahead.

"When he moves the ground shakes under him," a visitor to Henry's court wrote early in his reign. At thirty-four he was still a groundshaking presence, hurling himself through his days and nights with almost superhuman vigor.

And in superhuman splendor as well. To his subjects the king looked more like a divinity than a man, his outsize, powerful body encased in shimmering satins and thick, glowing brocades, his fingers gleaming with jeweled rings, his entire person aglow with gold. Golden ornaments in the shape of roses or teardrops or love knots hung from his velvet caps and embroidered doublets and hose, sparkling in the sunlight, and it gave him pleasure to pluck them off and throw them to his waiting admirers.

When he stood in all his glory under the high canopy of golden cloth that hung over his gilded throne, the effect on observers was awesome. To say that he was kingly seemed a gross understatement: he was imperial, sovereign, without earthly peer. Surrounded by his courtiers in their own brilliant finery he was an exquisite being, remote and, save for the current of all but uncontainable nervous energy that pulsed through him, marmoreally sublime.

Yet splendid as he was Henry's kingly energies were thwarted. By 1525 he had arrived at an impasse in his reign, a dark turning which left him frustrated and baffled. It was this that lay behind his moody reaction when Wyatt showed him Anne's bit of lace and jewel, this conviction that much of what he had achieved in the first decade of his reign was collapsing into disarray. Rule was yielding ground to chaos all around him; the distinction he had won for himself and England among the European states was beginning to decay.

The decay was all the more painful in that the king had once been so exalted. As a boyish ruler of twenty-two King Henry had launched a massive invasion into France, capturing towns, performing feats of personal daring and, for one glorious moment, chasing the fleeing French knights from the field at the Battle of the Spurs. These exploits and his widespread reputation for chivalrous treatment of his enemies won him the epithet Great Harry; his admirers compared him to his brilliant predecessor Henry V, who had won the great victory of Agincourt in 1415 and gained the crown of France.

Nothing short of the conquest of France, in fact, would satisfy the bellicose young king, who was said to be "as eager for war as a lion" and who was perpetually engaged in either preparing or recovering from or planning another invasion attempt. He called it his "Great Enterprise," the grandiose dream of conquest that, more and more, took possession of his ambitions. As he entered his thirties the dream expanded—though the military campaigns he launched ended in disaster—until, by 1525, it reached completely unrealistic heights.

Henry hoped to lead one final, invincible invasion, with the aid of his ally and in-law Charles V. But in aspiring to restore England's medieval hegemony over France Henry could not have been more out of phase with the logic and direction of European affairs, whose character was Machiavellian, not medieval and whose chief locus of competition was not France but Italy. While King Henry was dreaming of his Great Enterprise, his presumed ally Charles V was defeating the French at the Battle of Pavia—and capturing King Francis—and in the aftermath of this significant victory Charles was less inclined than ever to join his hotheaded uncle in an anachronistic military escapade.

Meanwhile Henry's subjects, drained by years of extraordinary taxes to support his futile campaigns, exploded into near rebellion when taxed once more to pay for the Great Enterprise. Knots of angry villagers gathered to protest the "Amicable Grant," as the new tax was ironically called, assaulting the royal commissioners sent to collect their money and organizing themselves to resist the armed soldiery they knew would inevitably arrive to punish them. Everywhere the reports were the same: ugly refusal to cooperate, coupled with loud criticism of the king and his hated minister Wolsey. Brandon, commissioner for Suffolk, encountered mobs hundreds strong, while Boleyn, collecting in Kent, was set upon and forcibly prevented from carrying out his duties.

The two blows struck Henry almost simultaneously. His subjects, once loyal and full of praise for Great Harry their king, had become disaffected and rebellious. And his nephew Emperor Charles, the man he had taken to be his staunchest friend and ally, the ruler to whom he had lent nearly half a million crowns so that he could carry out his own military ventures, was betraying him. Charles informed Henry that, if he insisted on pursuing his Great Enterprise, he would have to pursue it alone.

The breach with the emperor, like the true character of diplomatic and military affairs on the continent, could have been foreseen. Imperial interests in England had been deteriorating for some time: exchanges of ambassadors between the two realms had been allowed to lapse, the generous pensions once paid by the imperial government to key figures at the English court (among them Thomas Boleyn) were no longer forthcoming, and Wolsey, who had been accustomed to receiving the most generous pension of all, was so thoroughly alienated that he was among the emperor's worst enemies.

Yet the gravity of the rift was unforeseeable. It was more than a rupture between states exacerbated by a personal quarrel, it was a major shift in England's diplomatic alignment. From now on the realms of Charles V—Spain, the Low Countries, the German-speaking lands—would be England's adversary and France, Henry's dreams of the Great Enterprise apart, would perforce be her friend.

More than any other single issue on King Henry's troubled mind the break with the emperor brought to a head the problem of his marriage. By the mid-1520s it was a marriage in name only; Henry no longer shared his wife's bed and had to struggle inwardly with the bitter certainty that he would never have a legitimate male successor.

And in the light of England's worsening relations with the empire, Katherine's role was radically altered. Like all royal wives who were foreign princesses, she had always had two functions—to produce sons, and to serve as a living link between her father's court (now her nephew's) and her husband's. Now that it was clear that she would never succeed in bearing a son, her diplomatic function became dangerously conspicuous. Katherine of Aragon was a Spanish matron whose spoken English, though fluent and often eloquent, was heavily accented. She prayed, confessed and conversed with the Spanish women who were her most intimate friends and servants in their common native tongue. She taught Spanish to her little daughter Mary, and surrounded herself with an entourage of Spanish chaplains and physicians. She was in every way a foreigner, ill at ease in her English clothing and full of the proud gestures and mannerisms—some called them "Castilianisms"—of the homeland she had not seen for decades.

Throughout her years in England Katherine had always performed her diplomatic function vigorously, and with as much professionality and more perspicacity than many an ambassador. She had at times actually taken the place of an ambassador, sending long and informative dispatches in cipher to the Spanish court and serving as a shrewd observer of English affairs. Though she had not been formally called upon to do this for some time she still thought of herself as her nephew's special representative in England, a permanent outpost of Hapsburg interests at the Tudor court. She wrote to Charles assuring him of her continued "readiness for his service" and encouraging him to send her instructions about how to be of use to him.[3] Wolsey accorded Katherine the same treatment he gave foreign ambassadors, placing informants among her servants and reading every letter she sent and received. Soon after the arrival of the imperial ambassador Mendoza he put a further constraint on Katherine's freedom. She could not hold any private conversations with the Spaniard, he informed her. He, Wolsey, would have to be present whenever they met.[4]

No doubt Henry's searing repudiation of his faithless Hapsburg nephew scorched his wife as well. His wife, his helpmeet she might be, but she was also the blood relative of his newest enemy, the woman whose Spanish was immeasurably better than her English and whom Wolsey strongly suspected of being an active imperial agent. Whatever else Katherine was, she was also her nephew's loyal ally, and given King Henry's present mood this made her a disloyal, not to say treasonous, presence at his court.

Katherine's shifting marital role was exceedingly unsettling to Henry, particularly as it was becoming inseparable from a deepening crisis in his view of himself and his life.

That his marriage was barren of sons was tragic enough in itself, but that through inadvertence he might have brought the tragedy on himself was a realization almost too harsh to be borne. There were rumors, whispers, mutterings in taverns to the effect that the king's marriage was accursed. Incest and murder befouled it; God was punishing Henry for these grave offenses "by not suffering [his] issue to prosper." The incest arose when Henry married his late brother Arthur's widow (Katherine had been married to Henry's older brother Arthur for five months in 1501–2; the marriage ended in the prince's death.) As for the murder, it was recalled that before Arthur and Katherine were married a leading Plantagenet claimant to the throne, the earl of Warwick, was executed to prevent a possible challenge to Arthur's title. His sacrifice tainted the marriage, it was in a sense "made in blood," and so was blighted, first by the almost immediate death of Prince Arthur and then by Henry and Katherine's lack of sons.

The whisperings worked on Henry's overexcited mind, awakening his fears and deepening his feeling of unease. In marrying Katherine he had sinned against divine law, he was being punished for his sin. What was more, he would go on being punished for the rest of his life, unless he could find a way to purge himself of his inadvertent transgression.

The intellectual in Henry too wrestled with the idea of a curse on his marriage. Time and time again he turned in his mind a quotation from Leviticus: "If a man shall take his brother's wife, it is an impurity: he hath uncovered his brother's nakedness; they shall be childless."[5] They shall be childless, he told himself. It could hardly have been more plain. The warning had been there all along for him to see, and in failing to heed it he was worsening his plight through his own blindness.

Was there no way out for him? He discussed the problem with the theologians at his court, hounding them for a solution, seeking the answer in the works of the Church Fathers and in the classic texts of canon law. He badgered his confessor John Longland. How could he rid himself of his tainted union with Queen Katherine? And if he did not succeed in ridding himself of it, how could he endure the prickings of his scrupulous conscience? Beginning in 1522 or 1523, the king "never left urging him," Longland said later, "until he had won him to give his consent."[6]

To make of his psychic torment an intellectual puzzle quieted the king's fervent imaginings somewhat. But behind all the textual scrutiny and abstruse discussions was the driving force of fear, the insistent thirst for release from an implacable destiny.

As the sinister influences gathered in around him—the receding of his achievements and hopes as king, his betrayal by Emperor Charles, the erosion of his subjects' loyalty and esteem, his sadly transmogrified marriage, the overarching specter of a divine curse—Henry faltered, then for a time gave way to irritable dejection. He felt defeated on all fronts, and with each new setback his dejection deepened. To his subjects he appeared enfeebled, and they attributed his loss of his powers to further malevolent forces. His advisers were using dark magic on him, it was said. Wolsey and Brandon joined in occult collaboration to "meddle with the devil," and through him to "keep their master subject." Filled with a sense of defeat, his Promethean energies chained, Henry allowed heavyheartedness to overcome him. He withdrew into relative inactivity, his buoyant physicality and tireless appetites in eclipse.

It was during this fallow season of his life that Henry was, to use his phrase, "struck by the dart of love."

Exactly when and how he became infatuated with Anne Boleyn is a mystery. She had been there, sweeping in and out of his presence, for a long time, slender and graceful and much admired. The sight of her abundant black hair and captivating dark eyes, the richness of her skin, even the sound of her voice and her laugh must have been familiar, if somewhat indistinct. Unless they were remarkably unalike Henry no doubt saw much of her sister Mary in Anne; it is even possible that at first he saw little else.

Yet there must have come a moment, a magic pause in time, when he saw her afresh—saw her, and loved her. Then, caught up in a tangle of desire and excitement and giddy exhilaration, he was taken out of himself, his dark mood swept aside completely and his vision of the world irrevocably changed.

To King Henry, enmired as he had been in despondency, Anne was much more than a vital, desirable girl who roused his passion. She was an elixir of hope. The jumbled fragments of his disordered life fell into place once again around her. The expectation he had of winning her love regenerated him to renew his kingly triumphs, and to avenge himself on those who had betrayed him. He felt stirring within him the puissance and mastery that had once moved his subjects to awe. Great Harry was reborn with the birth of a great love, and Great Harry could overcome anything—the obstacle of a tainted marriage to a worn queen, the urgent need for a son to succeed him (surely Anne could help him there), even the long shadow of divine vengeance.

That Anne seemed to bring Henry new life and hope immeasurably strengthened his bond to her, so that to the powerful force of sexual attraction was added the alchemy of gratitude and of a profound sense of release. The new enchantments of love drove out the old sorceries that had enchained Henry, putting him forever in his beloved's debt and putting her forever, in the list of his loves and mistresses, in a class by herself.

The object of the king's grand passion could hardly have known anything of the personal upheavals which preceded it. Anne may have been aware that for some time the king's boisterous energies had seemed subdued, his moods uncharacteristically withdrawn or irritable. Certainly she knew (as who at court did not?) that the succession was dangerously unsettled and that the royal marriage had become a mere politeness. But of Henry's desperation, his predisposition to love magnificently and lastingly, she knew nothing at all, and when he made his passion known to her she must have taken it at first to be a mere seduction.

She resisted—or at any rate she did not melt in trembling surrender. The honor, the opportunity represented by becoming the king's current sweetheart were vastly appealing, not to mention the challenge of the role itself. Bold and wilful as she was Anne cannot have held back out of timidity, nor out of simple coquetry. Pride, ambition, the allure of royalty itself all would have drawn her toward her lover, his power a strong aphrodisiac and his passion sparking an elemental, if not a romantic or personal, response in her.

Yet flattered and gratified as she must have been by his interest she was not moved to love him in return, and in any case she could not afford a spontaneous reaction. Henry's long relationship with her sister, the son born to them, the semifamilial tie their relationship created must have made it awkward, at the very least, for Anne to consider Henry as a lover—unless of course she welcomed the chance to compete with her sister and if possible to surpass her.

Two things, most likely, held Anne back. First, the man who was wooing her was no ordinary man, no ordinary king. Henry VIII was a unique creation, larger than life and with a unique capacity to inspire dread. His outsize manliness was clearly as dangerous as it was attractive, especially when combined with his unlimited authority as ruler. In his desires and appetites he was close to insatiable, and while this might delight an ardent lover it gave Anne pause.

Beyond this, and overriding all, was the probability that Thomas Boleyn guided his daughter's response to her royal admirer, and Boleyn saw clearly what that response must be. Anne, he reasoned, must react to the king's wooing with maidenly unavailability. Whatever gossip said about her, she must feign modesty—without abandoning liveliness—and allow Henry's passion for her to expand.

"Fainting I follow," Thomas Wyatt had written of Anne, his elusive quarry. Now the king eagerly took up the hunt for the tameless hind, the fleeing deer who resisted capture. He was a tireless hunter, his strength renewed by his ardor. But Anne too was practiced in the chase, and the farther she ran, the more she seemed to leave the mighty king panting breathlessly behind.

7

"The king waxed so far in amours with this gentlewoman that he knew not how much he might advance her."

The king was giddy with love. He thirsted for the sight of his beloved Anne, he longed for her as he had never before longed for any woman. She was his lure, his charm, the force that drew him and that made him forget everything but that he loved and desired her. The power she exercised over him was, or so he would recall later, a power beyond seduction—a power so great, causing in him a love so deepgoing and so compelling that he felt himself bewitched.

He was not only giddy with love—he was giddy with hope. Everywhere he looked he saw, not intractable dilemmas, but solutions to his problems, ways out. As his passion arced upward his hopes also rose, so that what had been unattainable now seemed within his reach—indeed within his grasp.

A change came over him in the fall of 1526, a change in attitude, in approach. He became decisive and aggressive once again, throwing himself vigorously into the thick of affairs with a purposiveness that contrasted with his former withdrawn bafflement. His transformation came soon after he lost his heart to Anne, and followed even more immediately events in Italy which threatened indirectly to disrupt plans he had begun to make to alter his private life.[1]

He had made up his mind to end his marriage to Katherine, and as marriage was a sacrament governed by church law, to end it he needed the cooperation of Pope Clement VII. But Pope Clement owed his election to none other than Katherine's nephew Emperor Charles, and what freedom of action he retained was threatened in September of 1526 when allies of the emperor broke into the papal palace in Rome and ransacked it. Clearly his person was at risk.

Henry's reaction was swift and bold. He sent Clement the generous sum of thirty thousand ducats to support the anti-imperial Italian League, a coalition of Italian states which though largely ineffectual was symbolic of unified opposition to the emperor. And he began, with Wolsey, to draw closer to his ancient enemies the French.

The meaning of these initiatives was clear, or seemed clear, to the community of royal servants and court officials who were continually alert to every shift in the king's mood and purpose. Henry had finally made up his mind to put aside his queen— though precisely how and when he meant to do this remained uncertain. A major alteration in the power structure of the court was imminent, and this meant new alignments among the courtiers, new opportunities for advancement and, of course, new rivalries and new dangers.

Gossip about the approaching downfall of the queen—gossip not entirely unmixed with sympathy for her—gave way to secret plans and furtive calculations. Who would benefit by Queen Katherine's displacement? Who would be pulled down along with her? How could the uncertain situation be best exploited? The ceaseless scheming swirled through the court, sweeping councillors, officials, eager patron seekers and hungry relatives and hangers-on into its turbulent vortex.

Self-interest demanded that the ambitious attach themselves to those most likely to prosper under the new order. Chief among the probable beneficiaries was the king's bastard Henry Fitzroy, already heir in all but formal title and steadily increasing in honors and importance. He was said to have the household and income "to keep the state of a great prince" and was in fact referred to as "the prince" in discussions with foreign ambassadors. Recently Henry had appointed him lord high admiral, lord warden of the Marches and lord lieutenant of Ireland—and there was even talk of giving him unprecedented authority as king of Ireland, an appointment which appeared to elevate him to higher rank than his legitimate half-sister Mary, princess of Wales. English diplomats empowered to arrange a marriage for the boy with a continental princess were told to hint that Fitzroy might soon be "exalted to higher things"—i.e., that he might soon be designated heir in preference to Mary.[2]

If Fitzroy seemed bound to prosper, Wolsey's fortunes were less certain. Though for many years all powerful in Henry VIII's government the lordly cardinal now faced growing opposition from Norfolk and his Howard faction, including the fast-rising Boleyns. What role Wolsey played in aiding the king to achieve his objectives where his wife was concerned would determine his degree of influence over Henry and his government in the future. The courtiers were divided: not all continued to fear him, and some threw in their lot with the Howards and Boleyns, taking particular note of the fact that Thomas Boleyn's daughter Anne was the king's current sweetheart.

"Thy niece, thy cousin, thy sister or thy daughter," Wyatt wrote cynically, "if she be fair, if handsome be her middle,/If thy better hath her love besought her,/Advance his cause and he shall help thy need." This, surely, was what the predatory Norfolk and his shrewd, self-seeking brother-in-law Thomas Boleyn were doing. They were encouraging the gallant, womanizing king in his attentions to Anne, just as they had encouraged him to take her sister Mary as his mistress six years earlier. (And just as, rumor had it, they had not interfered when the king had slept with Lady Boleyn at some unspecified time in the past.)

King Henry, the courtiers reasoned, had been enticed into a liaison with yet another Boleyn female. For the time being, for as long as she managed to continue to amuse him, she would be among those sought-after few who controlled access to the king's person—and therefore controlled the flow of his gifts, his patronage. "It was therefore judged by and by through all the court of every man," wrote Wolsey's gentleman usher George Cavendish, "that she, being in such favor with the king, might work masteries with the king and obtain any suit of him for her friend."[3] Anne's friends multiplied—as did those of her father and her uncle. She became an object of interest, flattery, solicitation. Her aid was sought on any number of matters, large and small, and those who sought it were all the more urgent in their appeals in that they expected her period of usefulness to be relatively brief. Before long, no doubt, the king would discard Anne for a new favorite, and her value as a conduit of benefits would be lost.

This expectation, though it proved to be wrong, was nonetheless understandable. Henry was an amorous man, his flirtations and casual sexual attachments probably as numerous as they were unexceptional. The relatively sparse surviving evidence about his extramarital love life should not mislead us into thinking him restrained or even moderate in his passions. Probably he was not a sexual glutton; certainly he was romantic, and romance may have served at times to deflect lust or to overshadow it. But Henry lived robustly, with ardent physicality, and in an age which took men's erotic recreation for granted. So far as is known Henry's tastes were uncomplicated and strictly heterosexual—and therefore accepted by his contemporaries as natural and unremarkable. Certainly no one thought him lukewarm in his appetites. The slander that Wolsey was "the king's bawd, showing him what women were most wholesome and best of complexions" was injurious not because it insulted the king in any way but because it accused Wolsey, archbishop of York and cardinal of the church, of immorality.[4]

Through the summer and fall of 1526 Anne suddenly found herself to be the object of considerable attention, first from the king and soon afterward from the personnel of the court as well. Much as Henry might have preferred it so this was no private wooing: his comings and goings were much too significant to go unnoticed or unremarked, and word spread quickly that he was visiting Thomas Boleyn's daughter very often and staying late and long. Like it or not, her status changed because of him, and because of the speculations that arose from his visits to her.

How she felt about the change, whether she had done her best —at her relatives' urging—to attract Henry or had merely become the focus of what one ambassador called "the king's great appetite" by doing little or nothing we cannot now discover. No letters from or about Anne, no impressions of her behavior or demeanor during the early months of King Henry's fascination with her survive. No one set down in writing what she said or did—or at least, no such writings have been preserved. Many years afterward Cavendish, writing with a strong bias against Anne, recalled that "after she knew the king's pleasure and the great love that he bare her in the bottom of his stomach, then began she to look very hault and stout, having all manner of jewels or rich apparel that might be gotten with money." "Hault and stout" denoted arrogance and superiority; Anne was never known for her humility and very likely her newfound distinction brought out all her hauteur. Apparently it also brought out her sense of style, her ability to dress strikingly and with exquisite taste, so that her clothing and jewels had a strong impact on those who saw her and made her memorable. More than any other indicator dress signified status at the Tudor court, and in spending lavishly on her wardrobe and adornments Anne was anticipating the rank she hoped to achieve. Or rather, her father was anticipating it for her, since it was his wealth that went to adorn her and at his command that the silkwomen and embroiderers and purveyors of velvets and gems came often to attend on his daughter.

Highly strung, her nerves taut and her fiery nature keyed up to meet the challenge of her new role, Anne must have felt a shiver of fear from time to time. King Henry was a lordly, masterful thirty-five, she a girl in her early twenties, possibly even younger. No matter how confident her manner her youth must at times have betrayed her; for a fleeting moment the mask of arrogance must have dropped, revealing a tremulous uncertainty in her voice and a momentary hesitation in her bold gestures. But if so it only enhanced her charm, and served as a reminder that no matter how dazzling her vivacity and Gallic sophistication Anne was still an English maiden, her future entirely unsettled because she was not yet betrothed.

That she was still without a fiancé was the overriding fact about her, however her status might be changing in other respects. Both her sister Mary and her brother George were married; her sister had borne several children. In the ordinary course of things Anne would have been married long before this. Yet it seemed to be Anne's fate to live outside the norms of her time: where other wellborn English girls were raised in England she had been raised in France; where other girls accepted as husbands the men chosen for them Anne had chosen for herself, and unwisely, a man already pledged elsewhere. Her peers were all wives by now, settled and secure in their young matronhood while Anne pursued her eccentric life path alone.

To her relatives, though, Anne was not a young girl possessed of an errant destiny, she was a useful commodity to be bartered in the political marketplace, her value enhanced a hundredfold by the king's infatuation for her. The fact that she was still unwed was to them a great advantage, for King Henry was about to unmarry himself from his queen and the last thing Anne's father and uncle wanted was for her to be tied down inconveniently to a husband or a fiancé.

But had she tied herself down, in fact, some years before? Though Anne had no real husband she did have the ghost of one, young Henry Percy. Their involvement threatened to tarnish Anne's availability, as it had already tarnished her reputation. If, as seems likely, Anne and Percy had exchanged vows and, feeling themselves married, had slept together then she was not free to align herself to anyone else without first obtaining a dispensation to do so from the pope. It may have been in an attempt to clarify just what had gone on between them—or for some related reason—that Thomas Boleyn late in 1526 sent one of his servants on an errand to Windsor, "to Master Percy."[5] What message the servant carried, or what report he brought back, is now beyond discovery.

In February of 1527 envoys of the French king arrived in England, the delegation headed by Gabriel de Grammont, bishop of Tarbes. They came to negotiate the terms of a new treaty of alliance between the two realms, and their arrival was eloquent evidence of the closer Anglo–French relations the king was so actively seeking. So extensive were the preparations for their coming that word spread through the capital that King Francis himself was on his way to England, to take part in grandiose peace discussions affecting "all Christian princes."

King Francis was not in fact coming, but he probably would have been willing to do so had he thought that it would promote smooth agreement on treaty terms. He needed the English. Ever since the defeat of his army at the Battle of Pavia two years earlier Francis had been at the mercy of Emperor Charles. First he had been the emperor's prisoner, then, as part of the price of his release, he had been forced to relinquish his two sons to the emperor as pledges of his good faith in fulfilling the remaining conditions under which he had been allowed to go free. The royal children were still being held in captivity, and Francis counted on the support of the English in obtaining their release. Beyond this, it was evident that unless England and France made a unified effort to decrease Hapsburg power there would be no stopping the emperor in his bid for European hegemony. Both sides had compelling reasons to reach a new accord, and after two months of hard bargaining, they did so.

By the terms of the treaty signed at the end of April Henry and Francis agreed to declare war on their mutual enemy unless he acceded to their demands, among which were that the emperor release the two French princes and pay the sizable debts he owed to his uncle Henry. To the military alliance was added a dynastic one: Princess Mary was to wed Francis's second son —or, if war indeed broke out, Francis himself. Nothing was said about the substantial debts Francis owed his English brother monarch, but as a final token of amity the treaty called for the French to pay an additional fifteen thousand crowns a year into the English treasury.

Henry and Wolsey had driven a hard bargain, wearing out the patience and diplomatic ingenuity of the French envoys by their carefully calculated negotiating tactics and exasperating them by their abrupt shifts of tone. Now conciliatory, now adversarial, they led the French to the brink of agreement, then yanked them back from it by becoming argumentative and insisting on impossible terms. Through it all, however, the king was careful to preserve the polite vocabulary appropriate to honorable men of rank. Both he and King Francis, his words implied, belonged to the knightly fraternity, indeed they were its natural leaders. Sordid bargaining was beneath them. Would that they were mere private gentlemen and not kings, Henry told one of the French ambassadors. Then they could meet frequently, as comrades and friends. As it was the best they could do was to promise to meet again as kings, in the manner of their fabled meeting at the Field of Cloth of Gold seven years earlier, though this time the encounter ought "not to be so pompous and costly as the former one."[6]

A solemn mass was sung amid particular splendor in the chapel at Greenwich to celebrate the signing of the treaty. Afterward there was jousting in the tiltyard, and despite the heavy rain the sport went on for upward of three hours and was notable for the number of solid hits scored by the opponents with their rebated lances. The trappings of the jousters represented a symbolic commentary on the accord between England and France. Swords and pens and coins were embroidered on their garments and horse cloths, along with the motto "By pen, pain nor treasure, truth shall not be violated."

As the gray afternoon wore on servants lit the candles and torches in the imposing banqueting house at one end of the tiltyard. Built specifically to entertain the French envoys, the vast structure was over a hundred feet long and thirty wide, its interior lavishly gilded and painted and hung with bright tapestries. Tall cupboards filled with a display of gleaming gold and silver loomed over the guests, while high above their heads stretched a ceiling of purple canvas painted with flowers and fruit.

The opulent setting, the music and gaiety and splendid entertainments, the order and overall harmony of the celebrations were meant to convey the impression that all was well at the court of Henry VIII, and certainly within the royal family. The queen occupied her accustomed place at her husband's side, smiling graciously and with the same intelligent animation that had always characterized her. Surrounded by her ladies and maids—among them, conceivably, Anne Boleyn—she sat in her pavilion on the tiltyard, cheering on the king who still jousted in her honor. She presided over her own table at the banquet, and took her seat as always on her throne under her gold canopy of estate.

Katherine was still queen; her daughter Mary was still heir to the throne. At least, every effort was made to have it appear so. The frail little blond princess, small for her eleven years and noticeably pale, was accorded the reverence of a sovereign, or future sovereign, as she stood regally at her father and mother's side. She was richly dressed and adorned with jewels, her retinue was large and impressive, her attainments were those of a child destined to take on worldly, if not exactly royal, responsibilities. The French envoys had been instructed to discover as much as they could about Mary, and what they saw of her convinced them that she was an exceptional child. She spoke fluent Latin, French, Italian and Spanish. Her intelligence was remarkable— indeed astonishing in a girl. She was a beautiful child, with her father's fair hair and gray eyes and his small and delicate features. And she had been carefully trained by her mother in the womanly arts of modest deportment, grace and refined behavior.

Physically, however, Mary left a good deal to be desired. One of the Frenchmen found her to be "thin, spare and small," and judged from her appearance that she would not be ready for marriage until she reached fourteen or even older. Though spirited and strong-willed she had the fragile look of a perpetually sickly child, one who would grow up to be a weak woman. Very likely she would not be robust enough for childbearing, and this, combined with the probability that Henry would soon put aside Mary's mother and seek to beget a male heir by marrying a new wife, diminished Mary's significance considerably.

There must have been something pathetic about her as she took part in the masque staged for the entertainment of the French visitors. Her thin little body was encased in trailing golden robes and loaded down with sparkling necklaces and chains more appropriate for a grown woman than an undersized child. She danced, with a child's earnest awkwardness, dances choreographed for adults. But this role, like the role of princess of Wales, was in actuality beyond her capabilities. King Henry might be very fond of his charming blond daughter, whom he called his "pearl of the world" and showed off proudly to the members of his court, but she could not be the son he needed, and the older she grew, the more obvious her inborn inadequacies became.

No doubt the astute French envoys, like most others present, paid far less attention to the princess than they did to the beguiling young women who adorned the court and in particular to those who seemed to gain the king's special notice during the long nights of celebration. Who were these beauties, they asked one another, whose radiance outshone the brilliance of the torches and made them seem like angels? And which of them was likely to become the king's next favorite?

More important, whom would he marry once he had freed himself from his queen? Many presumed it would not be a woman of the court but Renée of France, a cousin of King Francis. She was an obvious choice, and the match would be a very sound one from the political standpoint. Wolsey was known to favor it, and Wolsey still had the king's ear. But every faction had its candidate, even the imperialists. Oblivious of the insult to his aunt Katherine, Emperor Charles was attempting to subvert the French alliance by means of certain women known, or presumed, to have influence over Henry.[7]

And then there was Anne, Thomas Boleyn's dark, bewitching daughter, who was still, interestingly enough, the object of much attention from the king. The French envoys knew Anne, of course; she was as much a product of their court as of King Henry's. They remembered her as the younger sister of the great courtesan Mary Boleyn, now grown more prominent and, in her unique way, perhaps more beautiful than Mary and destined to become more influential than her sister had ever been.

Anne had audacity and allure, and she evidently knew how to please the king. Her father and uncle were rising swiftly to preeminence at court, only Wolsey now surpassed them. Whomever King Henry eventually married, the Frenchmen may have thought to themselves, she would clearly have Anne Boleyn as a strong rival for her husband's desire.

8

*"Ye may perceive that what thing so ever a man
purposeth, be he prince or prelate, yet notwith-
standing God disposeth all things at His will
and pleasure."*

On May 18, 1527, shortly after the French envoys left
England, a number of churchmen and experts in canon law
gathered quietly in Cardinal Wolsey's palace at Westminster.
Besides Wolsey himself the archbishop of Canterbury, William
Warham, was among them, along with other bishops and ecclesiastical authorities. There was no fanfare; the greatest secrecy
was observed. Wolsey had summoned his colleagues for a grave
and solemn purpose: to pronounce on the validity of the king's
marriage to the queen.

King Henry was at last doing what had for so long seemed
unavoidable. He was taking steps to separate himself from the
wife whose bed he no longer slept in, the mother who was barren
of sons, the Spanish queen who was a Hapsburg spy. Several
things, among them his deep desire for Anne and for the unbur-
dened life she represented, along with the definitive diplomatic
shift toward France, finally impelled him to undertake what he
had clearly been contemplating for a very long time.

The immediate impulse, though, seems to have come from
Wolsey, who suggested a procedure which promised to extricate

King Henry from his undesirable marriage without having to place reliance on the cooperation of the pope. Wolsey was not only archbishop of York and a cardinal of the church, he was papal legate, with wide-ranging powers enabling him, in effect, to act with papal authority. In his capacity as legate the cardinal was expected to oversee the moral virtue of the souls in his jurisdiction—which was all of England. Should he hear of a serious transgression it was his duty to summon the transgressor to a special legatine court where evidence could be brought against him or her and sentence passed.

King Henry, the legate had reason to believe, had transgressed divine law in living with his late brother's widow. Therefore he must be made to answer the charge and to renounce his sin.

The scheme was masterful in that it placed Henry in a defensive rather than an offensive position. Instead of following the usual procedure in such cases, that of bringing suit himself against Katherine in an ecclesiastical court, Henry avoided all the scandal, risk and notoriety by attending Wolsey's court as a defendant. He became the accused, not the accuser; the trial was secret, definitive (or nearly so), and, most important, the burden of proof was on the legate and not on the royal sinner who came before him. It would all be over in a matter of days, at most weeks. The king would be found guilty of living in sin, and ordered to leave the woman he had erroneously believed to be his wife. By the time the sentence was made public there would be no way to overturn it. The king would be free.

As to the canon law issues involved, Wolsey felt he was on secure ground. He had only recently brought a marital suit similar to King Henry's to a successful conclusion. Charles Brandon, duke of Suffolk, had a complex marital history which threatened to cause difficulties in his current marriage to the king's sister Mary. The validity of a papal dispensation was at the heart of the trouble. Wolsey made his ruling on the dispensation; the pope confirmed this decision and censured anyone who questioned the soundness of Brandon's present marriage to Mary Tudor. News of the papal confirmation had only just arrived. Wolsey was understandably confident that what he had been able to do for Brandon, he could do for Henry. The legatine court assembled without delay.

It must have been a faintly ominous scene in the room of Wolsey's palace, with the king called to judgment before the magisterial cardinal in the presence of mitred prelates and men of law. King Henry was easily overawed by sacred things, and even though this trial was to a large extent staged and its findings would presumably be a foregone conclusion he must have felt a chill of reverence pass through him as Wolsey intoned his admonitory words.

It was common knowledge, Wolsey began, that Katherine of Aragon, for eighteen years acknowledged in the realm as the king's wife, had earlier been married to the king's brother Arthur. She had lived with Arthur as his wife, and the marriage had been consummated. Thus, Wolsey warned, when the widowed Katherine married Henry both parties were breaking the law of the church, which prohibited marriages between relatives. The pope had granted a dispensation allowing them to marry, the cardinal went on, but not everyone believed that dispensation to be sufficient to countervail divine displeasure at the marriage.

Here the message turned portentous. The accused King Henry, Wolsey said, ought to feel the sharp prick of conscience and to fear the vengeance of God. That vengeance might take some time to manifest itself, yet it would surely be severe when it came.

The weight of the cardinal's accusation was unmistakable. The vengeance he alluded to had already taken the form of the king's lack of a son. Even worse punishments might loom ahead. Wolsey confessed to being troubled by a profound concern for the salvation of King Henry's soul.

Despite all the precautions taken to keep the legatine trial secret Queen Katherine knew of it within hours, and so did the imperial ambassador Mendoza. Katherine, in fact, had seen something of this kind coming for months, though she did not know what form it would take. In March she had sent her physician Dr. Victoria to the emperor, with instructions to inform him that King Henry was laying the groundwork for the dissolu tion of their marriage. Wolsey had been busy for quite some time sounding out the opinions of experts in canon law and probing the recollections of elderly clerics who were at Henry VII's court when young Prince Henry and his widowed sister-in-law Katherine became engaged. Probably Katherine guessed the reason for these inquiries and drew the obvious conclusion that a legal proceeding was imminent.

Her treatment also gave her warning that she was becoming expendable. Restrictions on her movements and conversations were increased, her women were mistreated and in some cases sent away, her dignity and authority in many ways affronted. She was cut off from the ordinary business of the court almost completely, and had to rely on informants to find out what was going on. What information she was given by Wolsey or other representatives of the king she knew to be unreliable, and the fact that she knew she was being lied to redoubled her insecurity even as it made it all the harder for her to find out where she actually stood.[1]

All that spring, aware that she might at any moment be confronted with a legal maneuver intended to deprive her of her position as Henry's wife and queen, Katherine went on as she always had done, in appearance at least the same proud, regal woman she had always been. To be sure, she was looking older, her figure thick and shapeless, her face careworn and lined. The religious austerities which won her the respect and love of her servants and many of her subjects did nothing for her looks. The pouches and dark circles under her eyes came from night after night of broken sleep. Like a nun she roused herself several times during the night to pray, kneeling on the cold stone floor without allowing herself the luxury of a cushion. It was the rigorous, uncompromising piety of an embattled woman, but though it increased Katherine's inner strength it drained her physical resources and made her look worn out and unappealing. Compared to her youthful, fresh-faced maids of honor the queen was old, certainly too old, observers thought, for her strong young husband.

During the months of negotiations with the French Katherine had been only too conscious of the anomaly of her position. She was still the royal consort, her symbol, the pomegranate, was still intertwined with the Tudor rose on the painted ceiling of the banqueting hall. Yet gossip stigmatized her; already many of the courtiers saw Renée of France occupying the queen's throne —while Anne Boleyn, they added in a whisper, lay in her husband's bed.

The Frenchmen, as accomplished diplomats, had showered Katherine with hypocritical gallantry. But even as they bargained over the terms of her daughter's dowry they shook their heads over Princess Mary's future. A thin, undersized girl who was often ill was not likely ever to rule England—if she lived long enough to try. Her bastard half-brother Henry Fitzroy, they told one another, was at present the likely heir, as his father's growing attention to him made plain.

And to Katherine's dismay, they bargained over Fitzroy as they did over Mary, proposing to betroth him to King Francis's daughter when Mary was pledged to his second son. Nor was this the only royal marriage discussed for the son of Bessie Blount. English diplomats were exploring the possibility of marrying Fitzroy to a daughter of King Christian II of Denmark, or to an Italian heiress. One of Henry's envoys in Rome even suggested that an illegitimate daughter of the pope might make the perfect match for Fitzroy, bringing the king and pope closer together and possibly smoothing the way for papal approval of Henry's divorce from Katherine.

None of this made Katherine easy in mind about her daughter or herself. But she kept her peace, by and large, deriving some comfort from Mendoza's presence—though the two were not allowed to talk freely—and hoping that all-out war between England and the empire could be avoided. Everything might, after all, work out well. There was a small chance. Except for one thing: the unaccountable interest Henry was continuing to show in Anne Boleyn.

This, linked as it seemed to be with the upturn in her husband's spirits, was the unlooked-for danger that had begun to alarm Katherine more and more. This was the unpredictable element in the situation, volatile and beyond control. There was nothing she could do to lessen what was clearly an overmastering passion; she had simply to let it run its course. To complain or try to intervene could only do harm. According to Cavendish, Katherine hid her anxiety behind a gracious exterior.

"It is no doubt but good Queen Katherine," he wrote, having "both heard by report and perceived before her eyes the matter how it framed against her," showed no "spark or kind of grudge or displeasure" toward either her husband or Anne. She accepted the attraction between them "in good part," and wisely decided to be patient and pretend that she had nothing to worry about. Instead of avoiding Anne she went out of her way to show increased regard for her "for the king's sake," countering injury with honeyed courtesy.[2] Meanwhile she looked for help to her powerful nephew, especially after Wolsey convened his legatine court.

Katherine could not communicate directly with Charles V, but she could and did delegate others to speak for her. Mendoza, writing in diplomatic cipher, passed on to his imperial master not only Katherine's urgent pleas for help (conveyed to him through third parties) but a general impression of her state of mind and of the seriousness of her plight.

She was extremely apprehensive, he wrote, both because of the peril inherent in the threatened divorce and because she feared that the king's proceedings against her were about to come out into the open—unless he could be convinced that what he was trying to bring about through the legatine court was futile.[3] She hoped that, if Charles secretly informed his ambassador in Rome of what was being done in England, the ambassador could alert the pope, who would circumvent Wolsey's efforts. Above all she feared to force her husband's hand. If word of her own efforts should leak out, Henry might throw caution to the winds and brave the humiliation and scandal of a full-scale ecclesiastical trial after all.

With war looming this could be disastrous, Mendoza insisted. The English people, strongly attached to their queen, were "greatly excited at the rumors of war" and would react with fury to any assault on Katherine's position. This in turn would inflame the king against her and, given her relative helplessness, could put her in grave danger. Pressure must be brought to bear,

Mendoza urged, but cautiously, without putting Katherine too much at risk. Much depended on swift and tactful diplomacy. "All her hope rests, after God," he warned, "on the emperor."

Over the next two weeks Wolsey's court continued to sit, convening and adjourning covertly in the cardinal's palace. The king, called upon to defend himself against the accusation that he was living in sin with Katherine, produced the papal bull of dispensation issued by Pope Julius II in 1503 and presented it as his justification. This gave Wolsey the opportunity he sought to expose the canonical weaknesses in the bull—and therefore to assert the invalidity of the marriage.

The objections brought forward were as numerous as they were recondite. The dispensation was faulty because it had been obtained under false pretenses, or because it was not written in the customary form, or because the monarchs who originally requested it, Henry VII of England and Isabella of Spain, were no longer living. Or it may have been in force for a few years, but lost its validity when Prince Henry, as an adolescent, had made a formal legal protest against his betrothal.[4] Wolsey's lawyers found objection after objection, heaping up arguments any one of which would have been sufficient to challenge the efficacy of the dispensation.

On substantive issues it seemed there would be no difficulty in establishing the faultiness of the royal marriage, but procedurally Wolsey was on less certain ground. And it was proving to be impossible to maintain secrecy. Word of the trial leaked out, and spread rapidly and widely. Mendoza was able to learn so much about what was going on in the clandestine hearings that he could infer the nature of the inquiry and project that it would be fairly lengthy and that Katherine need not fear being called before Wolsey's tribunal for several months or more.[5] What the imperial ambassador knew, Katherine no doubt knew—and the knowledge enabled her, with what legal advice she was quietly able to obtain, to assess the consequences of her husband's activities and to begin to do what she could to protect herself against them.

Abruptly on May 31 Wolsey adjourned the legatine court, and set no date for future resumption. His stated reason was that there were legal difficulties requiring him to solicit additional opinions from lawyers and theologians before going ahead, but in fact he had come up against a seemingly insurmountable problem. From the outset Wolsey had realized that for his proceeding to succeed it had to remain secret. He was aware that the queen had the right to appeal any decision he and his colleagues arrived at, and to request that the papal court in Rome nullify his hearing and declare it meaningless. But Katherine would do this, he reasoned, only if she found out what was going on, and he counted on keeping her in ignorance. Once word of the trial began to spread, however, its value was lost and by the end of the month not only the queen but everyone at court had heard of King Henry's efforts to discard his wife.

Besides this, the case against the royal marriage no longer seemed as strong as it had. On certain vital legal points there was no unanimity among the experts. John Fisher, bishop of Rochester and among the most learned men in England, pointed out to Wolsey that the writings of the great canon lawyers contradicted one another on whether or not it was a sin to marry one's dead brother's widow—and it was precisely men such as Fisher, conservative and erudite, whose opinions the king would be relying on if he went further with his legal efforts.[6]

Overshadowing all this, though, were the first shocking, astounding reports from Italy, reports describing the capture and destruction of Rome, the Holy City, by the soldiers of Charles V.

Shortly before he adjourned his court Wolsey received word that the imperial army, fighting in central Italy against the combined troops of the pope, the French and the Venetians, had become mutinous and had overrun the papal city. Starving, rebellious and virtually leaderless, the imperial mercenaries swarmed through the narrow, ancient streets intent on plunder. All the wealth of Christendom was in Rome, it was said; the Catholic Spaniards among the emperor's troops hated and resented the fat, self-indulgent higher clergy who lived there in splendor just as much as his Lutheran German soldiers did. Anticlerical rage spurred them on to insult and humiliate the abbots and cardinals they seized before torturing them and forcing them to disgorge their treasure. A long-felt contempt for iniquitous Rome found release in the despoiling of altars and the smashing of precious relics of the saints.

But anticlericalism alone hardly seemed sufficient to account for the atrocities and sacrilege witnesses wrote of. Priests were murdered in cold blood as they stood before their altars, monks dragged from their cells and beheaded, nuns, young and old alike, beaten and raped. Day after day the orgy of brutality went on, until even the holiest places in the sacred city were befouled by mangled limbs and headless corpses. *"Sangre, sangre, carne, carne!"* shouted the frenzied Spaniards as they laid about them —"Blood, blood, flesh, flesh!" So savage was their lust for carnage that nothing, not even the body and blood of Christ, seemed able to atone for it.

With the sacking of Rome the spiritual citadel of Christendom was breached. The Eternal City symbolized the eternal church, the eternal faith. The ruin of Rome was to contemporaries the ruin of that universal belief that had bound Europe for a thousand years and more. Papal authority too was dealt a blow. Pope Clement VII fled across the Tiber to the Castel Sant'Angelo when the massacre began, powerless to save his city. He wept and begged for peace on any terms the invading soldiers asked, but no one heeded his entreaties. The pope himself was spared physical harm, but his claim to be leader of Christendom was hollow. He was a frightened old man surrounded by his enemies. From now on he would do as they told him.

King Henry saw as clearly as his chief minister did what the Roman debacle meant for him personally. It would now be impossible to obtain papal confirmation of the findings of Wolsey's court—even if the case against the validity of the royal marriage was strong, which it appeared not to be. Meanwhile the church was in peril and Wolsey, as one of its leading figures, had begun to see himself as its savior. Before taking any further measures against his wife, Wolsey advised Henry, he ought to make certain he had the support of his ally King Francis, with whom he might soon be going to war against the emperor. Wolsey could be instrumental in this. He would journey to France, meet with

Francis, and while there summon the cardinals of the church to an emergency meeting to decide what must be done about Pope Clement's captivity.

In the first days of June, as the weather turned warm and the grass grew green and waist high in the fields, the king rode out every morning to the hunt. He was a vigorous hunter, pursuing his quarry with tireless energy and leaving his companions and huntsmen far behind as he urged his mount on at a breakneck pace. Henry routinely tired several horses in a long day of hunting, and brought down as many deer as several less tenacious sportsmen. Hard riding tempered him, and he was greatly in need of calm.

Not for the first time, his plans had gone awry. Wolsey had convinced him that he could be free of his marriage, and Wolsey had been wrong. He was now worse off than he had been a month earlier, for now he had tipped his hand, and his wife— no, she was not his wife, he must learn not to call her that— would try to see to it that he would never succeed. He was angry at Wolsey, angry at Katherine, angry at himself for falling victim once again to someone else's misjudged tactics. Wolsey was in any case more intent on his own aggrandizement just now than on solving his master's marital conundrum. He had always wanted to be pope; he might now succeed.

The reports from Rome continued to reach England, full of accounts of barbarity and destruction. Having looted the city's wealth and murdered its citizens the imperial soldiers had begun to loose their bloodlust on one another. The putrid corpses bred plague, disease killed those who escaped violent death. The pope and his supporters in the Castel Sant'Angelo had not been able to hold out for long, and had been taken prisoner.

The royal secretaries brought news to the king's hunting lodge several times a day, but by remaining out in the fields or in the depths of the forest Henry avoided hearing it, as he avoided all business, and made his servants and messengers wait until late at night to see him and bring him their dispatches. It had been this way, during the summer and fall hunting season, since the start of his reign. And ever since then Katherine too had adapted to his schedule, accompanying him to his hunting lodges and staying there with him until he moved on to the next site in his itinerary.

She was ready to go on traveling with him, waiting for him, supervising the preparation of his meals and attending to his comfort just as if nothing had happened between them. But he could hardly allow this. He must make a break with her—or else risk affirming by his actions that he did not share the legate's concern for the salvation of his soul.

On June 22 Henry confronted Katherine. His words, as she relayed them to Mendoza afterward, were harsh and blunt.

For eighteen years, he said, they had lived together in mortal sin. They had never really been married in the sight of God. In God's eyes, rather, their union had been an abomination. He had not arrived at this opinion on his own, Henry went on, but had been convinced by the many canon lawyers and theologians he had consulted. Knowing what he now knew, his conscience would not allow him to live with her a moment longer. His mind was made up. From now on they would live in separate places, just like any two unrelated people, just as if they had never called each other man and wife. Which royal residence would she prefer to retire to? Henry asked Katherine.[7] And then he paused, for she had burst into tears.

She wept bitterly, painfully wounded to learn that the man she had loved with a wifely love for eighteen years now dismissed those years with a breath, hurt immeasurably more by his unemotional announcement itself. She knew how emotional he really was, how volatile his moods; no doubt she realized, even in the midst of her own distress, that his apparent lack of feeling was a mask, a protection for himself.

She could not begin to think about his question, much less give him an answer. She continued to weep, her tears all the more affecting in that they were the tears of a proud, strong and normally self-composed woman. Henry was moved—to condescension.

All should be done for the best, he told her awkwardly, knowing full well that what was best for him could never be anything but worst for her. Her tears unsettled him. Katherine rarely lost command of herself. What if she became hysterical? He tried to be consoling, meanwhile begging her not to say anything to anyone about what he had told her. He knew as well as anyone what affection she inspired, what awkwardness she could cause him if she broke down under the impact of his message. He had no desire to rouse her servants, or anyone else.

Apparently the interview ended quietly, but the court was full of talk of Queen Katherine and divorce. And it was noted with the greatest interest that King Henry was no longer on cordial terms with his wife.

9

*"The long hid and secret love between the King
and Mistress Anne Boleyn began to break out
into every man's ears."*

Though King Henry tried to suppress it word of his efforts to dissolve his marriage soon became common knowledge—"as notorious as if it had been proclaimed by the public crier," in Mendoza's evocative phrase. Scandal was loosed. From the rumor-swept court the story spread outward to the capital, the countryside, and across the Channel to the ports of the Low Countries and France.

Everywhere tongues wagged, people hissed and murmured and grumbled their harsh disapproval of the king's most recent misadventure. The marriage might be cursed, and childless, but that was beyond any earthly remedy. For the king to strike out so wickedly against his good and saintly queen was almost too outrageous, too shameful, to be true. Wolsey, the evil genius whose sharp animus against the emperor was well known, must be the author of this current wickedness.

Partly because of his inherent lordly offensiveness, partly because of his undeniable authority second only to that of King Henry himself, and partly because it was somehow comforting to make him the scapegoat rather than the king, people blamed Wolsey for many of their present woes. Wolsey's taxes, in particular the hated Amicable Grant, impoverished them. Wolsey's love of the French and hatred of the emperor and his subjects made their livelihoods uncertain by threatening England's vital trade with the Low Countries. Wolsey's belligerence brought war nearer, and his insufferable self-aggrandizement led him to dream grandiose and dangerous dreams of attaining greater power.

Londoners watched Wolsey take his departure for France early in July, riding from Westminster through the City in his red cardinal's robes, his tall silver crosses and heavy silver pillars carried aloft before him, a vast army of gentlemen and yeomen attendants arraying themselves before and behind. His coming was heralded by harbingers wearing his livery who parted the crowds in the streets and shouted orders to make way for the lord cardinal. After these followed the carts and carriages and pack animals loaded with his baggage, which made an imposing retinue as they clattered across London Bridge on their way toward the coast and the Channel ports.

As usual, they told one another through clenched teeth, milord cardinal was sweeping all before him. As he made his lordly way through the streets, displaying his incalculable wealth in the thick gold chains his servants wore and the priceless trappings of his mount, he incurred their renewed hatred and suspicion. They knew that he was bound for France, where they believed he intended to pave the way for King Henry to marry Princess Renée just as soon as his divorce from Queen Katherine could be obtained. For years, people said, Wolsey had been forcing the king to do his bidding, relying on the black arts to sway his mind. And for years the queen had disliked and distrusted Wolsey—an enmity sharpened by the cardinal's pro-French policies. If, as hardly seemed credible, the king was taking steps to dissolve his marriage then the cardinal must be the originator and prime mover of the undertaking. There was no other explanation for it.

Or was there? In August the imperial ambassador Mendoza

first reported what the queen may have suspected for months: King Henry's intended bride was none other than the brazen commoner many said was already his mistress, Anne Boleyn.

The inappropriateness, the sheer incongruity of it made Henry's preference for Anne even more incredible than his desire to divorce Katherine. A girl without a royal lineage, with nothing but herself to offer, a dowerless girl who brought no political benefits—what could the king be thinking of? Or rather, given what he evidently was thinking of, Anne's sexual favors, why bring marriage into his plans?

Because, of course, he needed a son, preferably several sons. But Anne was unfit to bear a king's sons. She might, like Bessie Blount, be unobjectionable as the mother of a royal bastard but never as the mother of a prince. It could not be, it was unthinkable. This went beyond any ambitious scheming of Wolsey's, and in any case Wolsey and Anne's Howard relatives were bitter enemies. Madness though it was, this scheme had to have come from King Henry himself.

King Henry, who was spending his summer hunting in the countryside, missed his sweetheart. It was not enough that he was constantly in the company of other Boleyns, Thomas and George, and of Norfolk. He missed Anne, and nuisance though it was for him to write, he put his pain into words. He began to write her love letters.

"Ma mestres et amye," he wrote in his even, rounded hand, "Moy et mon ceur remestet en vos mains que suppliant les avoyre pur recomander a votre bonne grace . . ." "My mistress and friend, I and my heart put ourselves in your hands, begging you to recommend us to your good grace and not to let absence lessen your affection."[1] To be apart from her hurt him "more than he could ever have thought possible," he told her, and then added somewhat pedantically, "reminding us of a point in astronomy, which is that the longer the days are the farther off is the sun and yet the hotter; so is it with our love, for although by absence we are parted it nevertheless keeps its fervency, at least in my case and hoping the like of yours."

Though the king's letter, like all his letters to Anne, is undated it sounds as though it might have been written in July of 1527, near the start of the season when Henry had no fixed court but moved from one country house to another. He anticipated a long separation from Anne, and the time stretched away before him in imagination, unendurably prolonged. "For myself the pang of absence is already too great," he confessed, "and when I think of the increase of what I must needs suffer it would be well nigh intolerable but for my firm hope of your unchangeable affection."

"Seeing that in person I cannot be with you," he concluded, "I send you now something most nearly pertaining thereto that is at present possible to send, that is to say, my picture set in a bracelet with the whole device which you already know; wishing myself in their place when it shall please you." He signed himself "votre loyall serviteur et amy"—"Your loyal servant and friend, H. Rex."

The king's anxiety at being separated from his beloved was not apparent to those who encountered him that summer. After seeing the sort of establishment he kept in the country, with dozens of servants working to maintain the luxury and pomp of court life amid the rural setting, and after watching him gallop off into the forest, his huntsmen and companions riding along behind, visitors remarked on his cheerfulness and vitality. He was "merry and in good health," one of them wrote, keeping "a very great and expensive house." "He daily passeth the time in hunting," added another. "He suppeth in his privy chamber . . . [and] there suppeth with him the dukes of Norfolk and Suffolk, the marquess of Exeter and the lord of Rochford."

The lord of Rochford was more in evidence than ever at the king's side. With Wolsey away in France his work was done by the coterie of noblemen who hoped to oust him: Boleyn, Norfolk and Charles Brandon, duke of Suffolk, who though he was no lover of the Boleyns was willing to join with them in supplanting the cardinal. With Anne paramount in the king's hopes and plans it was only natural that he should spend more time than ever with her father, and that Boleyn, who was already in the front rank among the councillors, should move up still higher.

There was a synergy at work of the sort which gave Tudor politics its volatile character. The more important Anne was to her royal admirer the more likely he was to advance her influential father to greater responsibilities. And the more important Boleyn became the more he was able to encourage the king in his aspirations to marry Anne, especially with Wolsey out of the country. Father and daughter promoted one another's interests assiduously, with Norfolk adding his political weight and his authority as family patriarch.

Now that there was to be (or so King Henry hoped) a family tie between the Boleyns and the Tudors personal and political interests converged to cement them in a peculiarly firm bond. When Anne became queen Boleyn would become his sovereign's father-in-law; George Boleyn would become his brother-in-law. A new dimension was added to their camaraderie, and though the king was always the king, fearsome in his life and death power, he was now being drawn into the finely spun web of familial loyalties and familial obligations. Invisible yet strong, the threads of this web would in time ensnare him to an extent he could not foresee, just as his passionate attachment to Anne was to lead him into hidden toils.

He was writing to her again, for what meager news he had had of her ("the time seems to me very long since having heard of your good health and of you") had left him both amazed and in despair.

"To my mistress," he began, writing in French as before. "The great affection I have for you persuades me to send this messenger the better to ascertain your health and wishes; and because, since our parting, I have been advised that the opinion in which I left you has been wholly changed, and that you will not come to court either with madam your mother or in any other way."[2]

Evidently she had told him she would come to court, then sent word to the contrary. Enamored as he was, and tortured by his separation from Anne, this was a harsh blow. The already unbearable separation was to be prolonged. His spirits sank, he was baffled.

Anne's response, "if true, I cannot enough marvel at," Henry wrote, "sure as I am that I have never there placed you in a false position, and it seems to me a very small return for the great love I have for you to be kept at a distance from the presence and person of the one woman in the world whom I most esteem."

He was chiding her, yet this was at the same time a cry of the heart. Anne, or those who directed her, was toying with him. He was not yet sure of her love; far from it, in fact. Confused, he chose to interpret her change of mind in the time-honored fashion of suffering lovers. She was playing the disdainful mistress; he must adopt the tone of the imploring, adoring servant.

"If you love me with such good affection as I hope," he went on, "I am sure that the estrangement of our two selves must be a little wearing to you, though at the same time this pertains not so much to the mistress as to the servant. Ponder well, my mistress, that absence from you is very grievous to me, hoping that it is not by your will that it is so; but if I understood that in truth you yourself wished it I could do no other than complain of my ill fortune while abating little by little my great folly."

In closing the letter Henry begged Anne "to believe what the bearer will say to you from me," and signed himself her "entire servant, H. Rex."

Possibly the bearer of the letter was instructed to ask Anne whether in fact her decision not to come to court was her own, or whether it had been forced on her by others. Possibly she sent word back to Henry through him that she did indeed return his love, however appearances might indicate the contrary. Or she may have sent a cryptic reply, intended to baffle the king still further. Or, worse still, she may have sent no reply at all.

If there was inconsistency in Anne's responses to the king—aside from the deliberate caprice that was intended to keep his own emotions off balance—it should come as no surprise, for Anne, bold and hardy as she was, had been subjected to more sudden personal upheavals over the past year or so than any other young woman of her generation.

First had come the king's admiration for her, then his reckless love. And then, before she had fully adjusted to the love of this awesome colossus—with all the family pressures, goads, restraints and general tensions that accompanied it—Anne had become aware that Henry hoped to make her his queen.

In only a few short months her fortunes had been transformed twice over: first when she glimpsed the possibility of becoming his mistress, and second when she first understood that he intended to marry her.

Anne had no doubt daydreamed about marriage to the king for a long time, and if we are to believe Cavendish she went far beyond daydreaming: she was at the head of a secret cabal to dislodge Wolsey, dethrone Katherine, and set herself up as the leading figure at Henry VIII's court. But however Anne may have wished for rank and influence, and however she may or may not have sought actively to achieve it, nothing can have prepared her completely for the shock that came once she realized fully that her king desired to share his throne with her. Amid the politicking, much of it petty and ignoble, that swirled around her the grandeur of that vision—of the resplendent king reaching down to lift a mere commoner's daughter up beside him—must have floated through Anne's dreams, asleep and awake.

Now more than ever, her future was linked with his. Unless she displeased him, or lost him to another woman, or unless he was unable to set his marriage to Katherine aside, she, Anne, would become queen. The die was cast. There was no way out for her. If she should have second thoughts, if she should try to escape the future that now loomed ahead of her, her father and uncle would prevent her escape.

It was settled, then. The king, everyone said, had made his choice. But between the lovers themselves there was still uncertainty and doubt. In her letters to Henry Anne was sometimes forthcoming, sometimes she held back. It was a paradox that the couple the world took to be passionately, sinfully united were in reality not yet a couple at all (always assuming, of course, that the undated love letters which give this impression were written in the summer of 1527 and not earlier). Henry was in greater torment than ever. He decided to bring matters to a head.

"In debating with myself the contents of your letters I have been put to a great agony," he wrote to Anne, "not knowing how to understand them, whether to my disadvantage as shown in some places, or to my advantage as in others.[3] I beseech you now with all my heart definitely to let me know your whole mind as to the love between us; for necessity compels me to plague you for a reply, having been for more than a year now struck by the dart of love, and being uncertain either of failure or of finding a place in your heart and affection."

In what he wrote next there was no hint of marriage; rather the king seemed to be trying to persuade Anne to become his official mistress. He had hesitated to name her his mistress, he explained, "since if you only love me with an ordinary love the name is not appropriate to you, seeing that it stands for an uncommon position very remote from the ordinary. But if it pleases you to do the duty of a true, loyal mistress and friend, and to give yourself body and heart to me, who have been, and will be, your very loyal servant (if your rigor does not forbid me), I promise you that not only the name will be due to you, but also to take you as my sole mistress, casting off all others than yourself out of mind and affection, and to serve you only."

Now, the term mistress could denote a chaste lover as well as a bedmate; it could also be taken to refer simply to the dominion Anne held over Henry's emotions, as it did when he called her mistress of his heart. But here, the reference to giving herself to him "body and heart" and the phrase "si vous le plet de faire loffyce de ung vray loyal mestres et amye," which could be translated "if it pleases you to fill the office" as well as "to do the duty" of a mistress, imply that Henry wanted Anne to share his bed and perhaps to be his "maîtresse en titre," or official mistress—a rank which Anne was thoroughly familiar with from her years at the French court but which had never before existed in England.

Without making too much of this, it is at any rate evident that when he wrote this letter the king was still the ardent if exasperated wooer hoping (by no means confidently) to make love to the woman he desired. Had there been an understanding of any sort between them—certainly an agreement to marry—he would have written very differently.

Between this letter and the next one, it seems, Anne (or those who dictated her letters) composed such a masterful response that from then on relations between Henry and Anne were on a completely new footing. So delicately yet persuasively did she assure him of her love and fidelity that his doubts gave way to certainty. So chastely did she express herself that his eagerness to possess her was replaced by gentlemanly restraint. He no longer made demands on her, or felt the need to remind her that there might be other women with claims on his attention. Instead he rededicated himself to Anne alone, and alluded, in his reply, to his "unchangeable intention"—quite probably, the intention to marry her.

"For a present so beautiful that nothing could be more so (considering it as a whole) I thank you very cordially, not only for the handsome diamond and the ship in which the lonely damsel is tossed about, but chiefly for the fine interpretation and too humble submission which your kindness has made of it."[4]

Was the gift she sent him an allegory of Anne's own tempest-tossed life? Probably so, and in choosing this particular image Anne no doubt recalled her dangerous adventure at sea, when as a child she was nearly shipwrecked during the stormy Channel crossing. Then as now she was in the grip of forces far stronger than herself, then as now she felt that she ultimately faced them alone.

Henry was as much moved by the eloquence of the giver as by the gift. "The demonstrations of your affection are such, the beautiful words of the letter so cordially couched, as to oblige me ever truly to love, honor and serve you, begging you to continue in the same firm and constant purpose, assuring you that so far from merely returning your devotion I will out-do you in loyalty of heart were that possible."

As for lovemaking, that would wait until, with God's aid, Anne became Henry's wife. ("If at any time I have offended you," he asked, "give me the same absolution as you yourself demand.")

"Henceforward my heart shall be dedicated to you alone, with a strong desire that my body could be also thus dedicated, which God can do if he pleases; to whom I pray every day to that end, hoping that at length my prayer will be heard, wishing brief the time and thinking it long until we meet again." He signed the letter "Written by the hand of the secretary who in heart, body and will is your loyal and most assured servant HR." At the bottom of the sheet the king's initials are woven into a design that also includes Anne's initials enclosed in a heart and the motto "seeks no other."

At last there was harmony of purpose between Henry and Anne. The couple whom the world had long taken to be lovers had finally pledged themselves to one another, he eagerly, she, it seems, in some distress, feeling herself buffeted by contrary winds and sensing the high price of her acquiescence.

It was no wonder Anne chose to represent herself to Henry as a girl alone in a storm-tossed ship. She was embarking on trackless waters, with no one save herself to steer her course. To be sure, there was no lack of demanding voices all around her, telling her how and where to go and at what speed. But they could not be relied on, these voices that clamored in the wind; if she followed them she might come safely into harbor—or she might be dashed onto the rocks.

Anne was a bold mariner, yet it would take more than sheer audacity to surmount the rough waters of court intrigue. Strong opponents stood ranged against her, chief among them the proud, stubborn queen and the domineering cardinal who had destroyed her marital hopes once before. But then, Anne may have thought to herself as she looked at the gift she was sending him, the girl in the ship was not really alone. For the king stood with her, and as long as she had him for her helmsman and protector she could ride out any storm.

10

*"Then began other matters to brew and take place
that occupied all men's heads with divers imag-
inations, whose stomachs were therewith fulfilled without any perfect digestion."*

When Cardinal Wolsey, attended by his ostentatious retinue of twelve hundred servants and guardsmen, disembarked at
Calais he was given a princely reception. The soldiers of the
garrison arrayed themselves in orderly ranks to welcome him,
and the English citizens of the town, much as they hated the
cardinal and resented his cordiality toward the French, turned
out in the streets to greet him, though few were heard to cheer
him as he rode by in his rustling silks. At Boulogne—like Calais,
under English rule—the burgesses of the town erected pageants
in Wolsey's honor, much as they would to honor visiting royalty,
and paid exaggerated deference to his self-appointed role as savior of the imperiled church.

In one of these pageants a nun, representing the church, was
violated by three Germans and three Spaniards—an allusion to
the rape of the papal city by the armies of Charles V—and a
cardinal rescued her and set her on her feet again. In another
the pope was knocked off his throne while the emperor sat mag-
isterially above him, dominating him; a cardinal pulled the emperor off his pedestal and set up the pope in his place. And in a

third a cardinal made peace between the kings of England and France—something Wolsey ardently hoped to do, taking great satisfaction from the epithet the French bestowed on him, "Cardinal Pacificus," Cardinal Peacemaker.[1]

Peace was, in fact, Wolsey's principal objective, for if he could somehow bind England, France and the empire in a treaty of universal peace then the pope would be freed and the crisis in the church would automatically be brought to an end. And with that crisis over and Pope Clement released from his captivity King Henry's divorce could proceed without hindrance, since the pope would no longer be so beholden to Emperor Charles that he could not grant King Henry what he asked.

Should the universal peace elude him Wolsey meant to fall back on his second plan: to summon all the cardinals to Avignon and from there, with their concurrence and support, to take over headship of the church, acting on Pope Clement's behalf. This too would enable him to take action to end King Henry's marriage. Whatever happened, the king's interests would be served.

But the grandiose plans went awry. Not only was the emperor unwilling to cooperate in any peacemaking effort but, knowing what he knew of his relative Queen Katherine's troubles, he was determined to thwart Wolsey's efforts in every way possible. Thus when the cardinal sent representatives to Pope Clement to persuade him to issue a document bestowing his authority on Wolsey for as long as he was confined in the Vatican the pope, with the emperor's envoy at his elbow, declined to do so. And when the cardinals were summoned to Avignon, Clement forbade them to go, so that in the end only four of them came to Wolsey's phantom conclave—far too few to legitimize the leadership role he coveted. It was soon clear that Cardinal Peacemaker was to be the savior neither of the church nor of the peace, and instead of spreading harmony he turned to making the divisive suggestion that Charles V be deposed.

The withering of his aspirations was galling to Wolsey, but he had been out of England only a short time when personal worries of a more immediate kind began to nag at him.

Through informants he learned that King Henry was falling

more and more under the influence of the Boleyns and their faction. Incredibly, Henry had in mind to elevate Anne Boleyn to the status of queen, Wolsey was told; his desire for her fired his energies and made him more impatient than ever to obtain his freedom from Katherine. Wolsey had made his journey in part to arrange for that freedom, yet he had failed, just as he had failed a few months earlier when he tried to declare the royal marriage invalid in his legatine court.

Wolsey's well developed political instincts told him that a dangerous situation was brewing. Anne, who had an old score to settle with him, had managed to bemuse the king and make him offer her the throne. Where Anne went, her relatives naturally followed, and so Thomas Boleyn now stood next to Henry, whispering in his ear, planting doubts in his mind about his chief minister. And not only Boleyn but Norfolk too, and all those who clung to them for patronage.

This was the way it happened, the way favor was won and lost. Without being there to defend himself against the accusations of his enemies, Wolsey knew, he could not prevent the slow erosion of his place in the king's estimation. The longer he stayed away the more he was bound to slip in status, to sink deeper and deeper in a quicksand of malicious insinuations, blame, and subtle attacks. King Henry was highly suggestible, and would be predisposed to believe whatever Anne told him. And Anne would have little good to say about the man who had once parted her from her lover Henry Percy.

Furthermore, Wolsey was more vulnerable now than he had ever been. He was no longer the wonder-working, indispensable diplomat and minister he had been a few years earlier. His rapport with the French, while valuable to King Henry, was hardly unique. Thomas Boleyn too was at home at the court of Francis I—who paid him an exceptionally large pension to ensure his good will—and had just returned from an ambassadorial mission there shortly before Wolsey left England.[2]

All in all, it looked as though Wolsey was likely to be in serious trouble unless he returned home soon. But he chose to stay in France, perhaps hoping that he might yet find a way to serve his master and so redeem himself, perhaps realizing that it was already too late to salvage his influence at Henry's council table. Then, while still in France, he learned that the king was in a sense betraying him, by pursuing his divorce on his own, behind Wolsey's back.

Henry, surgent and energetic now that he and Anne were in agreement, could not wait for the cardinal's unwieldy methods to mature. All on his own he thought of a new way to achieve his objective. If the problem lay in setting aside his marriage to Katherine—if that was all that stood between him and marriage to Anne—then he would circumvent the problem by asking the pope to grant him a dispensation allowing him to have two wives. It was brilliantly simple, if unorthodox, and either he or a trusted clerk drew up the draft dispensation and arranged for his secretary Dr. Knight to travel to Rome and deliver it to Pope Clement.

When Wolsey found out about this brazen maneuver Henry abandoned it, but he soon had another tactic in mind. He drafted another bull for Knight to take to Rome, and then a third, pouring out his hopes in a letter accompanying this final version and telling Knight that nothing was more important to him than the papal acquiescence which would pave the way for his marriage to Anne. ("For that is it which I above all things do desire," he wrote.)[3] As significant as Henry's bold initiative itself was the fact that the messenger who carried the letter to Knight was Boleyn's chaplain John Barlow, whose wisdom and diligence the king praised and whose discretion he relied on.[4]

Even more indicative of the swift changes that were taking place at court was the reception the cardinal was given when he finally returned from France. By custom the king, when informed of Wolsey's return, would ordinarily have summoned him to a small private chamber for an intimate discussion. This time, however, the messenger who brought Henry the news of Wolsey's return found Anne beside him—more handsome, voluble and self-assertive than ever. To the man's amazement she presumed on the king's indulgence so flagrantly that she did not hesitate to speak for him.

When should the cardinal come for his audience, Wolsey's messenger asked, and where?

Before the king could answer Anne spoke peremptorily, her dislike for Wolsey evident in her voice.

"Where else is the cardinal to come?" she snapped. "Tell him that he may come here, where the king is."

No doubt the messenger, startled by Anne's forwardness and by King Henry's bland tolerance of her outrageously disrespectful behavior, looked to the king to see what he ought to make of her words. But Henry merely confirmed them, adding nothing further, and so the man left.

Wolsey, who had a violent temper, was "extremely annoyed" by the incident and even more angry over the fact that he was returning from his prolonged and exalted mission emptyhanded. He had now to regain what standing the Boleyns had wrested from him, while at the same time inventing some fresh strategy to achieve his master's purposes and so win back his benevolence. For in allowing Anne to treat Wolsey's messenger impudently Henry was conveying his own displeasure with the cardinal, and even as he burned with anger Wolsey no doubt felt a momentary tremor of fear.

He disguised these feelings, though, as in the following weeks he opened his commodious palace of Hampton Court to a crowd of French diplomats whose visit to England was meant to consolidate the amity Wolsey was working so hard to maintain between the two realms. Nearly three hundred dignitaries and their servants had to be accommodated, but so great was the cardinal's wealth and so expert were his household officers that the monumental effort of hospitality went smoothly. Wolsey himself went out of his way to appear the insouciant host, his "loving and familiar countenance" betraying no sign of the strain he was under. Laying formality aside he allowed his French guests to sit down to their dinner one night without him. Then, after they had eaten the abundant first course and were admiring the second—made up of more than a hundred "dishes, subtleties and curious devices"—he suddenly made his entrance in the great hall, "booted and spurred" in his riding apparel instead of in the costly robes of a great prelate. He "called for a chair and sat himself down in the midst of the table," Cavendish recalled, forgoing the raised dais and chair of honor his rank warranted, "laughing and being as merry as ever I saw him in all my life."

His merriment was cut short, though, when he found that he had aroused the king's jealousy. Ordering his household staff to devise feasting and entertainment that surpassed Wolsey's, King Henry staged a remarkable spectacle for the Frenchmen at Greenwich. The spacious banqueting house in the tiltyard was splendidly arrayed, the gleaming golden cups and bowls and flagons of the royal plate put out on tall cupboards, the long banqueting tables set up and covered with fine linen. While they dined the visitors watched in disbelief, as "lusty gentlemen in gorgeous complete harness" jousted on horseback in their midst, thundering up and down the length of the hall and splintering their lances against one another's armor with loud reports.

Following the jousting a group of exotically costumed masquers performed an interlude, and then there "came in such a number of fair ladies and gentlewomen that bare any bruit or fame of beauty in all this realm, in the most richest apparel, and devised in divers goodly fashions that all the cunningest tailors could devise to shape or cut to set forth their beauty, gesture, and the goodly proportion of their bodies." Was Anne among these fair ladies? Or did her high if ill-defined status as the king's intended wife put her so far above the other young women of the court that she would not have been included? Included or not, present at the banquet or not, Anne was more than ever in the forefront of everyone's thoughts. Her striking looks and sharp tongue, her elegant dress, and the "amorous affection" the king showed her made her a dark celebrity; she stood apart, occupying no definite place in the stratified ranks of the royal court. She was morally disreputable, yet without peers or superiors (save for the king) to control her or punish her. Anne was a glamorous anomaly, an embarrassment—and a power to be reckoned with.

The Boleyn march to preeminence continued. It was rumored that, having made the commoner Thomas Boleyn a viscount, the king was about to create him duke of Somerset, an elevation that would have made him the equal of his brother-in-law the duke of Norfolk and of the third member of the striving trium-virate in the royal Council, Charles Brandon, duke of Suffolk. The elevation did not take place, but the way was cleared for Boleyn to exchange his present rank for a higher one when at long last the jurisdictional tangle over the Ormond lands was definitively settled. With the conspicuous aid of Wolsey—who no doubt enjoyed heaping coals of fire on his enemy by serving as the handmaiden to his advancement—a settlement of the long-standing dispute between the Boleyns and the Butlers was worked out. The lands in Ireland were divided between the two families, and Piers Butler received an Irish earldom and relin-quished his claim to the English earldom of Ormond—which, in February of 1528, was conferred on Thomas Boleyn.[5]

Anne was now an earl's daughter, though for her own part she was still a "lady of the chamber," and nothing more. In spite of all that had happened to alter the plans and expectations of Anne, Henry and Katherine their formal relations were essen-tially unchanged from what they had been six years earlier when Anne first came to the royal court. The king was still the queen's husband, and, despite his earlier pronouncements to the con-trary, visited her at prescribed times in her apartments as cour-tesy demanded and as had been his custom throughout their marriage. Anne was still an unmarried lady of the chamber, part of the queen's household and owing her deferential obedience. Apart from all the gossip, and the besotted look in King Henry's eyes—and, of course, the ongoing attempts to dissolve the royal marriage—there were no outward signs that Anne was about to take Katherine's place.

In private, however, Anne's peculiar situation was unmistak-able. In the early spring of 1528 one of Henry's chamber gentle-men, Thomas Hennage, recorded in a letter to Wolsey what was taking place at Windsor, where Henry was staying. The king went out hawking or walking in the fields every day, Hennage wrote, and attended to business at other times. Anne and her mother were both at the palace, and were accustomed to receiv-ing special attention. Hennage himself brought them food from the king's own table, and carried messages to and from them, humoring them in their requests and fulfilling their particular wishes. A servant of Wolsey's named Forest had just arrived at the palace that day with news for the king; Hennage informed the cardinal that Anne and her mother noted Forest's arrival and that Elizabeth Boleyn had asked the servant to request a "morsel of tunny" from his master for her. She repeated the request to Hennage as well. As for Anne, she was affronted that Forest had not come to pay his master's respects to her, and perhaps bring her a gift. The oversight was significant, she felt sure, and she complained to Hennage about it, "saying she was afraid Wolsey had forgotten her, as he sent her no token." Hennage tried to make amends, telling Anne that the message Forest brought was so important that in deputing him to carry it Wolsey had forgotten all about sending gifts.

But Anne was not to be put off with excuses. That night when Hennage brought Anne her share of the king's supper she asked him to stay and eat with her, and while they ate she told him she "wished she had some good meat from Wolsey, as carps, shrimps, or other." Though it embarrassed him to have to pay serious attention to such a request Hennage passed it on to Wolsey in his letter. "I beseech your Grace, pardon me that I am so bold to write unto your Grace hereof," he wrote apologetically. "It is the conceit and mind of a woman."[6]

That Anne expected Wolsey to acknowledge her with tokens of respect went hand in hand with the increasing optimism she felt about the king's divorce. After six months of captivity in Rome Pope Clement had fled the city in December of 1527 and taken refuge in Orvieto, where there were no imperial troops to harass him—though they were not far off—and where, in his humiliated and anxious state, he might be expected to give a more sympathetic hearing to King Henry's request.

With luck Henry could now obtain what he wanted by the simplest and most infallible means: the pope, in the fullness of his authority, could declare Henry's marriage to Katherine to be no valid marriage, while at the same time granting the king a dispensation to marry Anne. No lengthy proceedings, no abstruse argumentation were required, merely a just decision by the vicar of Christ, and his signature on one or two carefully drafted documents.

Emissaries were sent to Orvieto to persuade, convince and, if all else failed, to bully Clement into cooperating. And though he did not prove immediately cooperative there was still every reason to think that in time he would be, especially now that the military situation in Italy had begun to turn against the imperial forces.

Encouraged and, at first, backed up by the English, a French army swept into Italy and began pushing Charles V's mercenaries southward. By the spring of 1528 the French had driven the imperialists out of Rome and held them at bay in Naples. Pope Clement, his fears allayed somewhat by the triumph of the French and the defeat of the emperor's armies, ended his procrastination and handed the English envoys the documents they had been waiting for.

Two cardinals, Wolsey and a colleague (Cardinal Campeggio, a worldly-wise prelate with strong English connections, who was expected to be well disposed toward King Henry), were to be authorized to hear in England arguments for and against the marriage and to make a judgment as to its soundness on behalf of the Holy See. Should they decide it was unsound then Henry and his erstwhile queen would be free to take other spouses—and, relying on a new bull of dispensation, Henry would be able to marry Anne. Most important of all, Clement stipulated that once the two cardinals, acting as papal legates, reached their decision no appeal would be allowed against it.

The proceedings envisioned in the bulls Clement had drawn up had all the advantages of Wolsey's legatine court—an expeditious hearing, with the outcome influenced by a preponderance of English theologians and legists, a setting in which King Henry, instead of bringing suit, would be seen as the passive object of others' legal scrutiny. But unlike Wolsey's abortive hearing this one would be definitive, and public. Indeed Henry would have every reason to make it public, so that the arguments raised against his marriage and the legates' formal pronouncement would be given the widest possible publicity.

Word of the favorable events in Rome reached England in May of 1528, and Henry, overjoyed, at once called Anne to come and hear the news. The way was finally open for them to surmount the obstacles that had lain in their path for so many months. For a full year now Henry had been making serious efforts to gain his freedom from Katherine. There would be one more delay, while Cardinal Campeggio made his way from Italy to England, but once he arrived, the final solution to all the king's difficulties would be at hand.

Over the next several weeks, as the warm spring days lengthened and the men and women of the court spent their leisure hours strolling along the riverbank and through the hilly grounds of Greenwich Palace, Henry and Anne must have felt an unfamiliar sense of peace and calm. There was no lull in governmental affairs—quite the contrary, in fact. England's brief entrance into the warfare on the continent (an English herald had actually declared war on the emperor at Burgos in Spain) had led to a public outcry from King Henry's war-weary subjects, and ultimately to a hurried truce. Yet the cessation of a state of war did not bring to an end the clamor against Wolsey, who was as usual blamed for the hostilities, or to the rioting that broke out in the regions most dependent on the Netherlands trade. But in the wake of the optimistic turn of events in Rome the popular dissatisfaction seemed less pressing, and the pleasures of spring more enticing than ever. The palace gardens were full of flowers, the fields were covered in new grass and on Shooter's Hill, where the court went maying, the woods were cool and inviting, full of the scent of green boughs and blooming hedges.

So seductive were the courtly pastimes, the long afternoon walks, the hunts and picnics in the open air that it was possible to overlook, at first, the disturbing news from London.

The earliest deaths, in April, had been dismissed as predictable harbingers of the changing of the seasons. There was always mortality in the spring. But then the numbers of the dead and dying began to grow so rapidly, and the dread of an epidemic to spread with such urgency, that before long the royal household downriver at Greenwich was in an uproar. For the sweating sickness had come again.

The reports from the capital were terrifying. Everywhere there was panic, with people shutting up their shops and boarding up their houses and fleeing into the country, taking only what they could carry. Some collapsed even as they fled, others as they made plans to get away. Even the luckiest of the citizens, those who somehow managed to avoid infection, were caught in the macabre web as relatives, friends, colleagues and associates were carried off, leaving their goods and responsibilities to the living.

Ordinary life was suspended as the city gave itself up to death and the fear of death. Within days thousands died, and the ceaseless tolling of church bells, ringing for the dead, the carts that rolled through the streets, piled high with corpses on their way to common graves, the fires burning at streetcorners to purge the foul air that hung over the city all gave warning of the pestilence. "We saw them thick as flies," wrote the French ambassador Du Bellay of his visit to London at the height of the epidemic, "rushing from the streets and shops into their houses to take the sweat whenever they felt ill. I found the ambassador of Milan leaving his lodging in great haste because two or three had been suddenly attacked."[7] Wolsey had come to the capital on business but had no sooner arrived than he "immediately bridled his horses again," and rode back the way he had come.

A sense of overwhelming apprehension was often the first symptom of the sweating sickness, it was said—yet hardly anyone in the vicinity of London, including the royal courtiers, was without fear by the first week of June. Three times before the sweat had scourged England's population, and each epidemic had brought more fatalities than the one before. It was the Lord's Visitation, the people said, a punishment for sin. That was why the strongest and most vital men and women in the population, those in the prime of life, were the first to be struck down. This was no ordinary disease, it was an inescapable sign of a wrathful God. As such it was feared with a blind, unreasoning fear—even though fear itself marked the onset of infection.

"It is a most perilous disease," Du Bellay wrote. "One has a little pain in the head and heart; suddenly a sweat begins; and a physician is useless, for whether you wrap yourself up much or little, in four hours, sometimes two or three, you are dispatched without languishing."[8]

"A physician is useless." It was the incurability of the sweat which made it so frightening. That, and the swiftness of its spread. And it spread, that first week in June, to Greenwich, where suddenly the servants in the king's household began to clutch their heads and groan in pain, their bodies reeking, sweat pouring from their heads and armpits and groins.

Before the huge royal establishment could rouse itself to leave the palace the deaths began. The kitchen servants, one of the apothecaries, one of the royal masons, even the servants in the king's own chamber were all dead or dying. Suffolk's son and heir was dead, Norfolk came close to death. No one could count on being spared; the doctors did what they could, but the priests were far busier, rushing from one sickbed to the next to administer the last rites and often arriving too late.

Children, great ladies, men of all ages, within hours hundreds in the king's vast household were carried off. So far the king himself had come to no harm, and his heir Henry Fitzroy, who was safe in an isolated lodging far to the north of London, had also been spared. Princess Mary too was unaffected, as were her mother (did Henry, in that season of mortality, wish her dead and himself an eligible widower?) and a number of her ladies.

But the Lady Anne did not escape. First one of her maids was infected, then Anne felt herself overtaken by the chilling fear, the severe headache and chest pains, and the deadly perspiration. Her chaplain may well have been with her in her suffering —or he may have been attending her brother and father, who had also succumbed to the disease—and no doubt those of her servants who were not yet ill did what they could to save Anne's life. But Henry, her protector and future husband, the one man who might have been expected to care most whether she lived or died, was not at Anne's bedside. Devoted as he was to her, he was still the king, and the king's health could not be placed in danger.

Henry had in fact put some distance between himself and the woman he loved.[9] Having arranged in advance to leave for Waltham, where the sweat had so far made no appearance, on June 16 Henry went ahead with his departure on the scheduled day even though it meant leaving Anne behind in her sickbed. Dreading infection he dislodged in great haste once he learned of her illness, and with a small party of healthy companions rode as hard as he could for the north.

11

"Long was the desire and greater was the hope on all sides expecting the coming of the legation and commission from Rome . . ."

Anne was gravely ill. She was swathed in blankets and carried by litter from Greenwich to Hever, where her father and no doubt many others in the household had already taken to their beds, some for the last time. Feverish, possibly delirious at times, bathed in her own reeking perspiration and anguished by the dread of imminent death Anne must have prayed earnestly that she might be spared. And that the king too might be spared, should he succumb—for without him her own survival would be, if not futile, certainly unenviable. If Henry died his widow would reign, as regent for her daughter, and Katherine's regency could only be harsh and punitive for Anne.

Wretched with pain, her head throbbing and her heart pounding, she may have suffered more from apprehension than from the torments of the sweat itself. What if her father died, or her uncle Norfolk? What wouldn't the mighty cardinal do then to turn the king against her? Wolsey's contempt for her, his seething hatred for Boleyn and Norfolk, his bias in favor of a French marriage for King Henry all would compound his enmity; devious as he was, he might even make common cause with the queen, or with Charles Brandon, duke of Suffolk, whose alliance with Boleyn and Norfolk was proving to be unstable.

But then these dark imaginings may have lifted, and in her fantasy Anne may have envisioned not the triumph of her enemies but their deaths: proud Wolsey felled, being laid in his ornate tomb, Queen Katherine too on her bier, surrounded with the pomp of a royal funeral. And the king, a joyous widower, soon a bridegroom.

Did Anne, amid her thoughts of mortality and bereavement, wonder at all about those she cared for? About Henry Percy, heir to the earldom of Northumberland, or about her relatives and in-laws or her sister Mary? Or were her feverish musings only a confusion of fearsome images and blind panic, too incoherent to shape themselves into thoughts at all?

The disease took a particularly dangerous course with Anne. Instead of flowing copiously and freely the toxin-laden sweat "turned inward," as contemporary physicians termed it, and became life threatening. The same danger arose with Thomas Boleyn. Very likely an apprehensive chaplain administered the sacrament to both father and daughter in their extremity, and possibly the last rites as well.

Ironically, it must have been at this juncture that a letter arrived at Hever for Anne from the king, who did not realize that she was seriously ill. After several weeks of moving from one country place to another, dodging the infection, Henry and his companions had come to rest at Hunsdon. Here, with the dying around him in abeyance, Henry settled in to wait out the epidemic and sent a message to his beloved.

"My uneasy qualms regarding your health have much troubled and alarmed me," he wrote (in French), "and I should have had no ease without certainty, but as you have not yet felt anything I hope and take for granted that it will pass you by as I trust it has with us; for when we were at Waltham, two ushers, two grooms of the chamber, and your brother, the Master Treasurer, fell ill and are receiving every care, and since then we have been well physicked in your house at Hunsdon, where we are well established and, God be praised, with no sickness."[1]

"It may also comfort you to know it is true," he went on

124

blithely, "as they say, that few women or none have this malady, and moreover none of our court, and that few elsewhere have died of it."

Always assuming that Henry's letter reached Anne at Hever, she must have heard his comforting words indistinctly, her consciousness clouded by fever. Sick or well, she did not share his philosophical turn of mind, and she may have found the remainder of his letter galling, despite its tenderness.

"Wherefore I beg of you, my wholly beloved," he wrote, "to have no fear nor to be uneasy at our absence; for wherever I may be I am yours, although we must sometimes submit to fortune, for who wishes to struggle against fortune is usually very often the farther from his desire. Wherefore, comfort yourself and be brave, and avoid the evil as much as you can, and I hope shortly to make you sing for joy of your return."

For his own part, Henry had ceased to struggle against fortune and made his peace with it. He made his confession, received absolution, revised his will (and whom did he name as his successor, Mary or Henry Fitzroy?) and heard mass several times a day. Being thus "armed toward God and the world," as he put it, he did his best to stay busy and active, while taking sensible precautions against coming into contact with the infection. For exercise he walked abroad in the garden, alone, in the mornings and practiced shooting with the crossbow between dinner and supper. He stayed away from the queen and ate his meals in isolation, his only companions his secretary Brian Tuke, his physicians and apothecaries. Even this proved to be risky; one of the apothecaries, John Coke, contracted the sweat and another of the king's familiar company, the messenger who carried his letters to Anne, died of it.

But if the threat moved closer, the king simply redoubled his precautions. To purge the air of its poisons he ordered that braziers of live coals be kept burning in every room, and the entire residence stank of vinegar, which was thought to be a purifying agent. He ate and drank sparingly, dosed himself with medicinal compounds, and cultivated an attitude of cheerful resignation. The advice the king sent to Wolsey was the prescription he was himself trying to follow: to "be of good comfort, and put apart fear and fantasies, and make as merry in such a season contagious your Grace may."[2]

Two things preoccupied him and helped to take his mind off the peril that swirled around him. One was his fascination with drugs and medicines. Henry had been an amateur apothecary for years, and was knowledgeable about the curative properties of plants and medicinal compounds. One cure for the sweating sickness was ascribed to him: a preventive made of herbs and ginger mixed in white wine and drunk for nine days, followed by a second potion of treacle and medicinal waters, followed by still a third treatment—if the first two had failed to ward off the disease—consisting of an herbal plaster applied to the skin to "draw out all the venom" and restore complete health. To apply his intelligence to the problem of the epidemic helped to give the king confidence, and in his isolation he made himself an expert in its symptoms and treatment. He talked volubly to his secretary Tuke about how the sweat struck its victims, what its onset was like and how easily it might be prevented if certain measures were taken. It was important, he insisted, to breathe only wholesome air, to keep to oneself except for a few servants and companions who were absolutely free of infection, to "use small suppers, drink little wine," and take "the pills of Rasis" once a week.

His other preoccupation was his "book"—a treatise he was composing on the merits of his case. Wolsey and his fellow legate Campeggio would soon be convening their court to sit in judgment on Henry's marriage to his queen; by the time this happened he meant to have set forth in writing all the arguments in his favor. He worked on the treatise with his customary fervor, sitting at his desk for hours at a time and concentrating so hard that his head ached. Along with marshaling the opinions of theologians and canon lawyers Henry was arming himself mentally —just as he was arming himself spiritually against the sweating sickness—for the coming combat. For just as he believed that an optimistic attitude kept disease at bay, so he believed that in convincing himself of the soundness of the case against his marriage he was improving the odds that he would prevail. When he wasn't actually working at the book he was talking about it. "His highness," wrote Tuke, "cometh by my chamber door, and doth, for the most part going and coming, turn in for devising with me upon his book."[3]

Into these absorbing and on the whole hopeful activities burst the news of Anne's severe illness.

"There came to me suddenly in the night the most grievous news that could arrive," Henry wrote her, "and I must needs lament it for three reasons: the first being to hear of the sickness of my mistress, whom I esteem more than all the world, and whose health I desire as my own, and would willingly bear the half of your illness to have you cured." The second reason was that Anne's illness threatened to prolong their separation from one another, and absence was ever his enemy. The third was much more serious. It was that Dr. Chambers, the king's chief physician and the one he relied on most, was not available to be sent to Anne's bedside. Instead Henry sent her Dr. Butts, "the only one left, praying God that soon he can put you in health again, in which event I shall love him more than ever. Praying you," he entreated Anne, "to be governed by his advice regarding your sickness, by doing which I hope soon to see you again, which will remedy me more than all the precious stones of the world." He signed himself "the secretary, who is, and always will be your loyal and most assured servant." At the bottom of the letter he drew a heart around Anne's initials and wrote his own, HR for Henry Rex, on either side of them.[4]

How Dr. Butts ministered to Anne when he got to her is impossible to say for certain, but chances are he used the king's poultice and some of his herbal potions as well, taking care to keep her awake—for to let a patient fall into a deep and coma-like sleep was invariably fatal. Some doctors starved their patients, and bled them from their arms or hands or from between their shoulders. Others wrapped them, burning with fever, in warm blankets and shut them in overheated rooms, following the ancient medical precept that like cures like, in this case extreme heat driving out extreme fever. Presumably Dr. Butts was enlightened enough to avoid this treatment, and presumably he avoided, too, the more arcane remedies of folk medicine and of spiritual healers—magical words, incantatory names or phrases from the Bible, mystical letters worn around the neck or inscribed on the body. Whatever he did, Anne was well again in July, and the king, informed of her symptoms and the course of her illness, pronounced her perfectly recovered and "past the danger." Her father too recovered, but more slowly; toward the end of July he was still too weak to return to court.

Whether Anne's natural vitality caused her recovery or whether, as the king believed, the sweating sickness was indeed kinder to women than to men, nonetheless Anne's return to health cannot have been taken lightly. She had come close to death, yet God had preserved her life, he had wanted her to live. In the sixteenth century such a recovery was invested with particular significance, and the king, who feared and revered the extraordinary, may have seen in it a divine message. Anne may have shared his view, and beyond that she must have felt a soaring sense of relief and joy.

It was at this portentous time, with the legatine trial in prospect and with Henry buoyant and confident of the strength of his case and the likelihood of a swift judgment against Katherine, that he and Anne moved to a deeper stage of intimacy and began to make preparations for their wedding.

The change was obvious, the entire court was aware of it. He caressed her as only the fondest lovers caressed each other, his eyes followed her with a passionate tenderness and lit with amorous delight when she smiled her response. Unspoken desire flowed between them, erotic and unmistakable, and the fact that they flaunted rather than concealed their eager yearnings meant that they saw no reason to restrain themselves, that they were confident of becoming man and wife very soon.

"Both the king and his lady, I am assured, look upon their future marriage as certain, as if that of the queen had been actually dissolved," Mendoza wrote to the emperor. He commented on the wedding preparations, and on the reckless passion the king showed for Anne.[5] For once the scandalous couple's public behavior went beyond what rumor said of them, or nearly beyond it. (Pope Clement was convinced that Anne was pregnant.) What the ambassadors saw left them in no doubt that Henry was "following his appetite," "giving the reins to his passion." The bond between them was strong and sexual, so strong that it made the king blind. His appetite was leading him headlong into marriage, by way of his mistress's bed. "Mademoiselle Boleyn was returned to court," the French ambassador Du Bellay reported toward the end of August. "The king is so infatuated that none but God can cure him."

Several of Henry's letters to Anne evoke the mood of this passion. "Mine own sweetheart," the king wrote, "These shall be to advertise you of the great elengenes* that I find here since your departing, for I assure you methinketh the time longer since your departing now last than I was wont [sic] to do a whole fortnight. I think your kindness and my fervencies of love causeth it," he went on, "for otherwise I would not have thought it possible that for so little a while it should have grieved me, but now that I was coming toward you methinketh my pains been half relieved, and so I am right well comforted in so much that my book maketh substantially for my matter."

His sharp depression and even sharper elation bespeak his "fervencies of love" more clearly than the explicit last phrases of the letter. "Wishing myself (especially of an evening) in my sweetheart's arms, whose pretty duckies [breasts] I trust shortly to kiss; written with the hand of him that was, is, and shall be yours by his will HR."[6]

Another letter, written as Campeggio was nearing England and the legal denouement seemed close at hand, blended excitement and anticipation.

"The legate which we most desired arrived at Paris on Sunday or Monday last past so that I trust by the next Monday to hear of his arrival at Calais, and then I trust within a while after to enjoy that which I have so long longed for to God's pleasure and our both comfort; no more to you at this present mine own darling for lack of time, but that I would you were in my arms or I in yours, for I think it long since I kissed you."[7]

"Within a while after"—such a brief time span separated them from the marriage they were now ardently counting on. Henry's desire for Anne leaped in him, Anne's desire to attain the wifely

* strangeness, loneliness

status her ambition drove her to consumed her. She was now hopelessly compromised; all pretense of modesty was ludicrous. In permitting Henry to fondle her in front of his courtiers and visiting ambassadors, in making arrangements for her wedding, in inviting scandalous insinuations Anne was gambling everything on the outcome of the legates' investigations. Or it may have been that, seeing how far her royal partner's rash desire could lead him, she expected him to marry her no matter what the outcome of their inquiry.

Come what might, marriage appeared to be within her grasp. Caught up in her delicious expectations, her lover wooing her as never before, she too was blind to the possibility of failure. Their time was finally at hand; no one and nothing could thwart them.

Not even Wolsey. In her elation Anne began to presume that the cardinal was genuinely working to promote her marriage to the king, or so it appears from a letter she wrote him.

"In my most humblest wise that my heart can think, I desire you to pardon me that I am so bold, to trouble you with my simple and rude writing," she began, adopting the self-abasing style courtesy demanded from a young woman writing to an eminent older man, "esteeming it to proceed from her, that is much desirous to know that your Grace does well, as I perceive by this bearer that you do. The which I pray God long to continue, as I am most bound to pray, for I do know the great pains and trouble that you have taken for me, both day and night, is never like to be recompensed on my part, but only in loving you, next unto the King's Grace, above all creatures living."[8]

The apparent love feast between Wolsey and Anne was all the more remarkable in that the two had only recently been at odds in an issue of patronage. The abbess of Wilton Abbey, Elizabeth Shelford, had died and Anne was promoting her in-law Eleanor Carey (the sister of Anne's brother-in-law William Carey) to replace her. Wolsey had promised to make Eleanor prioress—not abbess—when that office became vacant, and had given his word on this to William Carey. But after Carey died of the sweating sickness there was no one but Anne to defend her relative's interests—or, rather, Anne chose to take up Eleanor's cause as a way of asserting her leverage against the cardinal's. The battle lines were drawn: heedless of the wishes of the nuns, whose right it was in theory to elect as abbess whomever they chose, Wolsey put forward his candidate, the present prioress Isabel Jordan, and Anne supported Eleanor Carey—or Eleanor's sister who was also a Wilton nun. Either way a Carey must become abbess, Anne told Henry.

But Wolsey busied himself at once in thwarting Anne's scheme. He went to the abbey, questioned the nuns, and so intimidated the aging Eleanor Carey that she confessed "to have had two children by two sundry priests" and to have been the mistress of a third man as well, "and that not long ago." If her vitality was admirable, clearly Dame Eleanor's morals were not, and when Wolsey reported the results of his inquiry to the king the latter wrote a characteristically high-minded letter to Anne ruling her candidate out. "I would not for all the gold in the world cloak your conscience nor mine to make her ruler of a house which is of so ungodly demeanor," he said, "nor I trust you would not that neither for brother nor sister I should so destain mine honor or conscience." Out of fairness (and in an attempt to placate Anne) Henry decided to choose another nun entirely. "To do you pleasure," he told Anne, "I have done that neither of them shall have it; but that some good and well disposed woman shall have it; whereby the house shall be the better reformed."[9]

But this was not the end of the story. Wolsey went ahead and forced the conditional election of the prioress Isabel Jordan over the king's objections and in spite of his explicit displeasure. Anne was no doubt "aggrieved," as Henry told Wolsey she would be, but in the end the conditional election was transmuted into a binding one. Once again Wolsey had triumphed over Anne.

Yet to judge from her letter to him, her gratitude at his "great pains and trouble" on behalf of obtaining the king's divorce far overcame her pique at the outcome of the election. She loved Wolsey, next only to the king himself, "above all creatures living," she meant to reward him in time, she was beside herself with hopeful anticipation.

"My Lord, I do assure you, I do long to hear from you news

of the legate; for I do hope, and they come from you, they shall be very good. And I am sure you desire it as much as I, and more, and if it were possible, as I know it is not. And thus, remaining in a steadfast hope, I make an end of my letter, written with the hand of her that is most bound to be, Your humble servant, Anne Boleyn."

At the bottom of Anne's letter was a postscript. "The writer of this letter would not cease, till she had caused me likewise to set to my hand," Henry wrote.[10] He congratulated the cardinal on having escaped the sweating sickness, reminded him to "keep good diet," and alluded to the divorce—which he called "that trouble"—and to how he and Anne hoped by Wolsey's "diligence and vigilancy" soon to be "eased out" of it.

If there was breathless hope in Anne's words, there was warmth and magnanimity in Henry's. His recent scalding anger at his great servant and cardinal had melted away. With his beloved Anne beside him, coaxing him to add a word or two to her letter—really, of course, to add the weight of monarchy to her words—and with a happy wedding in prospect Henry was mellow, his frustrations at bay and all his ferocity abated. Anne made him glow with happiness, he radiated contentment as well as possessive desire. The joint letter reflected a halcyon moment, when the manifold setbacks and discomfitures the two had faced were counterbalanced by their surgent hopes.

The moment was brief. The legate Campeggio was on his way to England, far too slowly to satisfy Anne and Henry, but progressing nonetheless. By the last week in September he was at Calais, waiting to cross the Channel, and to avoid any appearance of impropriety Anne returned to Hever. There she would wait, fretfully, impatiently, until word came from London that Wolsey and Campeggio had concluded their investigation and pronounced a favorable judgment.

She would wait—but not idly, for the planning of a royal wedding was a tremendous undertaking, and one which the Boleyns were likely to have to undertake alone. There would at best be sullen cooperation in the ceremony from many of the courtiers, Anne knew, and undoubtedly some would refuse entirely to take part. The king would have to coerce them. He might even have to coerce the servants and officers who were in charge of determining protocol and procedure. They might balk at playing a part in making a commoner into a royal wife.

But more likely than not Anne put such thoughts aside with a toss of her head and a disdainful frown, and gloried in her fantasies—fantasies of herself adorned as a bride, superbly gowned and regal, attended by maidens and pages who carried her train. And of her incomparable groom, tall and massive and boyishly handsome with his red-blond hair and beard and alert gray eyes. Of the royal chapel, scented with incense and lit with bright torches, its walls covered with colorful hangings and its floor ankle-deep in sweet-smelling herbs and rushes. And of the crowd of common folk who would wait at the palace gates to catch a glimpse of the king's bride, and the crowd of nobles inside the chapel, respectful if not cordial in the presence of the woman who would soon become their queen.

Anne's fantasies, we may presume, did not include romance. But if she did not love him Anne must at least have begun to feel the fondness of familiarity toward Henry, and a certain confidence. She was a fixture in his life, not a passing infatuation. His heart was hers, she was his "great folly." Marriage would be her ultimate protection—marriage and a child, an heir. Once she was Henry's wife Wolsey could not touch her, should his present good will toward her evaporate, nor Queen Katherine, nor her father, nor her uncle, nor anyone else among those who wished her ill.

Once before Anne had been sent to Hever in connection with her marriage, that abortive union she had made with Henry Percy. Then she had been a wilful girl, banished to her father's house, forced to endure romantic disappointment and humiliation in angry solitude, her will thwarted. Since then, however, all had changed. Now she was a formidable, even powerful young woman, retiring to Hever of her own free will, proud of the triumph it would be to marry the king, her ambition fulfilled. Then Anne had dragged out her exile in bleak uncertainty, her future unclear. But now, with her future all but assured, she would wait out her temporary isolation with a high heart, "remaining in a steadfast hope."

12

*"Thus went this strange case forward from court
day to court day, until it came to judgment, so
that every man expected the judgment to be
given upon the case at the next court day."*

A buzz of voices filled the great hall of the monastery of Blackfriars in London. The legatine court, with Cardinals Campeggio and Wolsey presiding, was about to convene, and though it had been in session for several weeks today would mark the first time the king and queen would both be present.

The spectators had begun to arrive early, even before the personnel of the court—the officers and proctors, the theologians and ecclesiastics who advised the queen, the king's lawyers —made their appearance. They had a great deal to talk about, and the sound of their excited conversations rose and fell in the vast room as grooms and ushers came and went bringing in the furnishings for the participants. There were two thronelike chairs, upholstered in cloth of gold, for the legates and a long table draped with tapestries in front of them. Dominating the room, to the right of where Campeggio and Wolsey would sit, were a high canopy of gold brocade and under it, on a raised dais, a richly upholstered throne for the king. To the left of the legates' chairs was a smaller canopy and chair for Queen Katherine. Places were prepared for the archbishop of Canterbury,

Warham, and his colleagues and for the lesser figures in the coming drama, and all the while the murmuring continued and the onlookers watched nervously for the arrival of the king and queen.

That the king would come was beyond doubt. This was to be his hour of vindication, when after two years of obstructions sentence would at last be pronounced and—he confidently expected—his marriage to Katherine would be judged invalid. Over the many months between Wolsey's abortive secret hearing in May of 1527 and the convening of Campeggio's widely publicized tribunal the king had become as expert as any theologian or jurist on the canon law of divorce. He had written a long and thorough treatise on the issues pertinent to his own marriage, he had studied the writings of others with exhaustive finality. He was an expert, and his expertise boosted his self-assurance to a point far beyond the reach of logic. He was absolutely convinced that he was in the right, that he would prevail.

Only a few days earlier Londoners had seen him riding downriver in his barge, surrounded by a company of ladies and gentlewomen of the court, cheerful and high-hearted, pausing along the way at Thomas Boleyn's riverside mansion while he waited for the tide to change.[1] He was on his way to Greenwich, where he would stay until the day of his summons to the court session at Blackfriars. He was ready, and more than ready, to make his appearance.

But the queen was another story. Would she answer her summons? She had already appeared before the legates once, sweeping into the hall with "a great company" of female supporters and declaring, in her broken English, that Campeggio and Wolsey were not competent judges for her case and appealing to Rome for more impartial justice. She had displayed an awesome regality on that occasion, but at what cost those among her women knew who were witnesses to her sadly deteriorating relations with the king.

He not only humiliated her by making a shameful spectacle of himself with the strident commoner Anne Boleyn, he dishonored her by his outrageous accusations. He sent Archbishop Warham and another aged cleric, Bishop Tunstall, to interrogate her, and their questions were sharp and pitiless. Was it not true, they demanded to know, that Katherine had attempted to murder her husband? Was she not even now plotting to kill him, or possibly encouraging one of her Spanish servants to do it for her? They had reason to believe that she was conspiring treasonously with others in the realm; this, and her evident malice toward her lord and husband, made her a dangerous person—too dangerous to be allowed to see either King Henry or their daughter Princess Mary.[2]

Katherine was more than shrewd enough to realize what the king was doing, that his tactics were in one sense impersonal, intended simply to bully her into giving way and withdrawing from their marriage by entering a convent. But the fact that she understood his motives did nothing to make Henry's inhumane threats and insults less damaging to Katherine, in particular the cruel threat of separating her from Mary. She suffered under his persecution, her suffering made all the harder to bear in that, although she had scores of well-wishers at court—and thousands more in the country at large—none of them had enough influence to protect her.

It was this that had led her to seek out Cardinal Campeggio in advance of the date of her summons to his court and confide her worries to him. She was "very anxious and perplexed about her affairs," he wrote afterward. She had been expecting two imperialist lawyers from Flanders to take charge of pleading her cause, but they had not come, apparently because Emperor Charles was convinced that they would not be safe in England.[3] Consequently Katherine would have no advocates but those the king had appointed for her, and they could hardly be expected to be impartial. To be sure, Bishop Fisher could be counted on to speak out on her behalf, as he had ever since King Henry first began his assault on the integrity of the marriage. But Fisher, though eloquent, was one lone voice against many, and in any case he was a theologian and not a jurist; he could do little to save the queen from a judgment that was almost certain to go against her.

The murmuring of the crowd turned to whispering as one by one the dignitaries and judicial officers took their seats. Then came the legates, preceded by clerics bearing the heavy gilt processional crosses and axes that were the symbols of their rank. Campeggio drew most of the attention. He was a crippled old man, in obvious pain. The long, scraggly beard he wore made him look more like a hermit than like the learned canon lawyer he was. The cardinal had sworn to let his beard grow, the story went, because he was in mourning for the English church.

The queen made her entrance, tense but dignified, looking, one observer said, as careworn as a woman of fifty though she was in fact only forty-three. The king followed her, youthful and robust and in cheerful spirits. Standing in majesty under his shimmering golden canopy, King Henry was master of the vast room. Seating himself on his throne, he began the session by making a speech. He spoke of his tormented conscience, which alone had led him to seek the truth about his marriage and to put himself in the hands of the legates to receive their just judgment.

As he finished speaking the queen suddenly rose out of her chair and, to the amazement of everyone in the hall, walked boldly up to where her husband sat on his raised dais and knelt down at his feet.

"Sir, I beseech you for all the love that hath been between us and for the love of God," she began (as Cavendish, who was present, recorded her words), "let me have justice and right. Take of me some pity and compassion, for I am a poor woman and a stranger, born out of your dominion. I have here no assured friends, and much less indifferent counsel. I flee to you as to the head of justice within this realm."

Katherine's audacity broke the decorum of the court, her heavily accented voice audible in the startled silence.

"Alas, sir, wherein have I offended you, or what occasion of displeasure have I deserved against your will or pleasure? Intending, as I perceive, to put me from you, I take God and all the world to witness that I have been to you a true, humble, and obedient wife, ever confirmable [sic] to your will and pleasure, that never said or did anything to the contrary thereof."

For twenty years she had lived his life, Katherine told Henry, loving his friends and hating his enemies, contented to shape her will entirely to his, without once complaining or showing discontent. And she had borne his children, a number of them, and though only one of them had survived that was not her fault, but God's will.

"And when ye had me at the first (I take God to be my judge) I was a true maid without touch of man," she went on, defending both her honor and her veracity with heartrending candor, "and whether it be true or no, I put it to your conscience. If there be any just cause by the law that he can allege against me, either of dishonesty or any other impediment, to banish and put me from you, I am well content to depart to my great shame and dishonor. And if there be none, then here I must lowly beseech you let me remain in my former estate and to receive justice at your princely hands."

She continued, and the king made no move to stop her, though by this time he must have realized that she had no intention of keeping to her assigned role in the proceedings. She argued that her father King Ferdinand would never have pledged her to a flawed marriage, nor would Henry's father have consented to it, and that therefore on the face of it she was Henry's wife by the simple logic of the situation as it had been on their wedding day many years ago.

As to the current trial—a "new invention now invented against her"—it was manifestly unfair since she was unable to defend herself, having no advocates of her own.

"Therefore I most humbly require you," she concluded, "in the way of charity and for the love of God (who is the just judge) to spare the extremity of this new court, until I may be advertised what way and order my friends in Spain will advise me to take. And if ye will not extend to me so much indifferent favor, your pleasure then be fulfilled, and to God I commit my case."

And with those words she got to her feet, straightened herself to her full height and, making a curtsy to the king, walked out of the hall on the arm of one of her servitors, Griffith ap Rhys. The court crier called her back, but she walked resolutely on, and the king wisely did not interfere.[4] To try to coerce her would have appeared more churlish than regal, and her defiance, though moving, would in the end have no impact on the legates' decision.

The excitement and commotion Katherine's speech generated in the great hall was mild compared to the uproar that greeted her once she left it. A huge crowd was waiting for her, shouting approval and encouragement. "Good Katherine!" "How she holds the field!" "She's afraid of nothing!" And the queen, heartened by the boisterous show of support, smiled and nodded to the crowd in acknowledgment, sending the people into fresh outbursts of noisy congratulation.

The June weather and the carnival atmosphere—Londoners were preparing to celebrate the feasts of Saint John and Saint Peter with pageants and bonfires and "very fine entertainments" —brought people out into the streets in large numbers. They were restless with holiday spirit, and any London crowd was volatile and potentially dangerous. A dozen years earlier the truculent young apprentices of the town had overrun the for-eigners' districts and committed indiscriminate assaults on mer-chants, sailors, even the envoys of foreign courts in an excess of frenzied xenophobia on May Day. Now the unruly citizens were fired by their hotheaded sympathy for Katherine, and there was no telling how far astray their zeal for her cause might lead them.

The imperial ambassador Mendoza believed that the English were so outraged over their king's treatment of his wife—and his evident intention to deprive the princess of her right to the throne—that they would willingly go so far as to join the ranks of an invading army in the queen's defense.[5] He exaggerated the extent, but not the fervor, of the popular reaction. Campeggio and his retinue were "much pushed by the great crowd" soon after their arrival in England, and lost their shoes; they were lucky not to lose their limbs. The king was alarmed when, as he and Katherine were walking along a semi-public gallery connect-ing the palace and a neighboring building, "immense crowds of people" gathered and publicly wished her victory over her ene-mies, "so that this kingdom may be saved from utter ruin."[6] He ordered that the gallery be closed off at once.

The partisan feeling went very deep, and was linked to other issues besides the welfare and status of the beloved queen. In the fall and winter of 1527–28 the English wheat crop was so poor that London was threatened with famine. Wolsey promised to bring French wheat into the capital in large enough quantities to prevent mass starvation, but could not keep his promise. Instead the German merchants resident in London rescued the populace by arranging for shiploads of imperial grain to be brought in, which made the people vituperate Wolsey and the French and "love the emperor the better and all his subjects."

Of course, it was not only that they loved the emperor, and his aunt Queen Katherine: they hated Anne Boleyn.

Groups of angry women collected to protest the ascendency of the king's despised mistress in strident chorus. "No Nan Bullen for us! No Nan Bullen for us!" they shouted, and chanted the praises of "Good Katherine" at every opportunity. It was no good explaining to them, as Henry and his representatives often tried to do, that there were issues of conscience and canon law at the heart of the royal divorce; the people were convinced that lust alone motivated it, and that Anne had deliberately triggered that lust.

"The common people being ignorant of the truth," the chronicler Hall wrote, "and in especial women and other [sic] that favored the queen talked largely, and said that the king would for his own pleasure have another wife."[7] The legatine trial was only a sham, they insisted, an elaborate, hypocritical ruse to disguise sinful, shameful adultery.

Where Anne was during the trial we don't know, whether she remained out of sight at Hever or stayed in her apartments at Greenwich or possibly in her father's London house—the house the king visited shortly before attending the court. Her life cannot have been easy during the months between Campeggio's arrival in England and the actual convening of his court—nine months of continual delays during which the queen, her supporters and, distressingly, the legate himself had found one means after another to prevent the delivery of a judgment.

The "steadfast hope" Anne had held during the previous summer must have dwindled to a fitful prayer, then to stubborn perseverance. The king had assured her that Campeggio's decision would be rendered quickly, and that it would, of course, be favorable to him and adverse to Katherine. And he had told her repeatedly that, once the legate's judgment was pronounced, their marriage would take place. Yet after nine months there was still no judgment, and no certainty, save in the king's mind, that he would obtain the end he desired.

Anne was worse off than ever. She was widely—indeed all but universally—believed to be King Henry's mistress. "For some time past the king has come very near Mademoiselle Anne," Du Bellay reported. "Therefore you need not be surprised if they want to hasten [the legal proceedings]. For if her belly swells, all will be ruined!"[8] She had endured, and would continue to endure, the hostility and contempt this presumption led to in the expectation that she would soon be queen, and that as queen she would be able to force her enemies to smother their rancor. But she was not yet queen; the hostility toward her was increasing, and she must have realized that if she ventured out into the streets, particularly in the aftermath of Katherine's defiant speech, she would not be safe.

Until the long-awaited judgment was handed down, she would be in limbo, neither a respectable young woman nor a discreet courtesan nor a royal wife. It would have been an uncomfortable role for the meekest of women. For Anne, volatile and impatient, her ego roused by the king's promises and by his own excited expectations, it must have been intolerable.

It would have been infinitely more intolerable had Anne realized that the longer Campeggio's judgment was delayed, the less likely it was that he would rule in Henry's favor. Time and again the legate defeated Henry's sanguine expectations by one setback after another, until finally the limits of his leverage and England's began to be unmistakably clear. No matter how many envoys he sent to Rome, no matter how cleverly his attorneys argued, no matter how sincerely meant were his hints at withdrawing England's allegiance to the pope unless Campeggio gave satisfaction, his efforts were confounded by the subtleties of papal diplomacy. If a favorable judgment was to be rendered, it would be because Pope Clement willed it so—or rather, because the influence of the European sovereigns was such that he was obliged to will it so.

Inexorably the simple desire of a king without a male successor to wed a desirable new wife who could give him one was becoming something far more complex. What had begun by affecting Henry, Katherine and Anne had been swept into the vortex of continental politics and, in particular, into the conflict between Hapsburg and Valois on the Italian peninsula.

In the nine months that the cardinal had been in England the forces of Charles V had grown steadily stronger while those of Francis I, recently so victorious, fell back in defeat after defeat. Plague carried off nearly an entire French army, and the few survivors capitulated. Then a fresh offensive began, with the French invading northern Italy in the spring of 1529. This initiative too ended in failure when the French were crushed at Landriano. The defeat came as Campeggio and Wolsey were presiding over the court at Blackfriars, and unknown to them Pope Clement immediately undercut their authority by yielding to imperial pressure and revoking the case to Rome. Technically the revocation was nothing more than a change of forum. King Henry's case would be judged at the papal curia rather than in England. But in actuality the change of forum guaranteed an adverse judgment, since the curial court would be directed to rule in favor of Katherine.

Before word of the papal revocation reached England Campeggio, who had been told to postpone his decision by every means possible, adjourned the court in accordance with Roman practice, for the summer recess. It was not to meet again.

King Henry was furious. Wolsey, who knew that with the adjournment his last opportunity to retain power at the royal court was gone, felt intimations of despair. Katherine took heart. And Anne, we may assume, cursed Campeggio for his deceitfulness and her old nemesis Wolsey for being unable to prevent it.

Yet even as he formulated a new strategy—one which did not include Wolsey—King Henry was aware that he had to take a growing force into account, one which was increasing in strength rapidly enough to upset the traditional configuration of

European politics and to weaken both the papacy and the empire.

By 1529 the influence of Martin Luther was troubling the stability of Charles's German domains. Luther was not only a religious reformer who denounced the worldliness and corruption of the Roman church with uncompromising vigor, he was a popular hero. Lutheran princes and Lutheran cities were demanding political rights, and armed conflict with the Catholic emperor seemed likely. This threat, plus the westward advance of the Turks under Suleiman the Magnificent into Hapsburg lands, meant that the emperor's concern for Queen Katherine was not likely to result in an invasion of England. As long as the Lutherans remained strong, Henry could press for his divorce unhindered.

And there was another, larger shift in his strategy, one linked to the burgeoning secularization of Renaissance monarchy. If Henry could not obtain the cooperation of the pope, he might look to the English church without the pope. The ties between England and Rome—ties of ecclesiastical jurisdiction, church taxes, church law—were not sacrosanct. They could be broken, if need be, in the interests of securing the succession.

The court was adjourned at the end of July and the king gave orders for the preparation of a hunting progress. The harts were fat and the hounds eager for the chase, and in the deep woods and country meadows he could forget the tensions and exasperations that dogged him in the capital.

And in the country Anne would be with him. He ordered a sumptuous traveling outfit for her, with several saddles, harnesses and horse trappings in black velvet fringed with silk and gold. She was equipped like a queen, she rode in his company just as his queen ought to do. And the stout Spanish woman who still clung to the title of queen was nowhere in sight. Henry had commanded that she leave the palace and take up residence elsewhere.

13

*"The King commanded the Queen to be removed
out of the court and sent into another place. And
his highness rode in his progress with Mistress
Anne Boleyn in his company all the grease season."*

Anne stepped surefootedly into Katherine's place and
stayed there. She rode at the king's side with her queenly traveling retinue, or in her expensively upholstered litter. Her demeanor had all the arrogance, if not the graciousness, of
majesty; she expected to be obeyed. A chamber was prepared
for her in each of the great houses or hunting lodges where the
royal party stayed, and she carried with her the tapestries, embroidered cushions, furnishings and ornate bedclothes to make
it sumptuous. If not the title, she would have at least the setting
of royalty. The title would follow in time.

In temperament Anne was already a queen. Harsh and imperious when she believed she had been slighted or ill served, she
used her influence over the king as a weapon to keep her numerous opponents at bay. Subordinates were learning to be wary of
her anger, and to guard their words and actions "for fear of
Madame Anne's displeasure." Her insecure position may have
made her especially sensitive, for in spite of all the promises King
Henry had made to her she was in reality nothing more than
Lord Rochford's daughter and Lord Norfolk's niece. And unless

Anne Boleyn, painted by an unknown artist after her marriage to Henry VIII

Thomas Howard,
3rd duke of Norfolk,
Anne Boleyn's uncle

James Butler, earl of
Ormond, by Hans
Holbein. Negotiations for
a marriage between Anne
Boleyn and James Butler
went on for some time but
were never concluded.
The portrait was
previously identified
incorrectly as Thomas
Boleyn.

The young Henry VIII,
date and artist
uncertain, perhaps
c. 1520

Torrigiano's bust of the
young Henry VIII

Thomas Wyatt, by Hans Holbein

Cardinal Wolsey

Charles Brandon, duke of Suffolk,
by an unknown artist

Katherine of Aragon in middle age, by an unknown artist

Mary Tudor sketched as a
young girl, perhaps by
Holbein

Thomas Cranmer,
archbishop of Canterbury

Anna Bollein Queen.

Drawing of Anne Boleyn by
Hans Holbein. Until
recently the identification
of this drawing was doubted
by scholars, but it is now
thought to be Anne Boleyn.

Thomas Cromwell

Jane Seymour, who became
queen after Anne Boleyn's
death

Henry VIII, portrait
attributed to Joos van
Cleeve, conventionally
dated 1536.

there was a considerable change in the way the king went about obtaining his divorce, she might never be anything more than that.

Fortunately for Anne, there was a change in the offing—and according to Cavendish, she had a good deal to do with bringing it about.

There had to be a scapegoat for the disaster at Blackfriars, and inevitably, Wolsey was blamed. The mighty cardinal had been on the defensive for a long time; now, in the aftermath of his most painful and humiliating failure, his enemies crowded around like vultures eager for the kill. Or like crows, Wolsey himself might have said bitterly. He called Anne the "Night Crow," in unflattering reference to her dark beauty. In the past Wolsey had always relied on Henry's warmhearted friendship to overcome his anger; he had been in disgrace before, but by making an earnest personal appeal he had been able to break through to the underlying trust and affection the king had always felt for him. But now Anne stood between him and that affection, and whatever fleeting rapprochement he had achieved with her the summer before had vanished completely, replaced by implacable hatred.

As long as the king was in the countryside on progress, spending his days in the company of Norfolk and Suffolk and Boleyn and his evenings with Anne, Wolsey had little hope of gaining a personal audience with Henry. His enemies would be at their work, poisoning the king's mind against him and reminding Henry that it was the arrogant, lordly cardinal who had led him on in the false belief that his divorce could be settled in England. It was the rich, greedy cardinal who had turned Henry's subjects against him by imposing oppressive taxes to pay for disastrous foreign wars. And it was none other than the haughty, self-important cardinal who had led England into a diplomatic blunder so great that her standing among the European nations might be permanently lowered.

For grave though the collapse of the legatine court was, graver still was the fact that, while he had been devoting all his attention to the king's divorce, Wolsey had allowed a dangerous situation to develop on the continent. The defeated French were making peace with the imperialists; the next step would be an accord between the emperor and the pope. Shortly after Campeggio adjourned his court a peace treaty was signed at Cambrai between the two continental powers. England was abandoned by her French allies—the allies Wolsey had cultivated for so long —and all but excluded from the treaty.

This Henry could not excuse, and Wolsey knew it. He found his powers restricted. His enemies were taking over his responsibilities. He asked for a personal audience with the king, but was refused—until he found an undeniable excuse, the departure of Campeggio from England. When the Italian came to say his formal farewell to Henry at Grafton, Wolsey came with him, and Henry received him "with as amiable a cheer as ever he did and called him aside and led him by the hand to a great window, where he talked with him."[1]

It was Wolsey's last chance to redeem himself, and it may have been futile. But according to Cavendish (who "heard it reported by them that waited upon the king at dinner"), Anne was incensed that the king should receive the cardinal with such courtesy, when he deserved nothing better than to be turned away in anger.

"Sir, is it not a marvelous thing to consider what debt and danger the cardinal hath brought you in with all your subjects?" Anne was overheard to ask Henry as they dined together in her chamber.

"How so, sweetheart?" he asked her.

"Forsooth, sir, there is not a man within all your realm worth five pounds but he hath indebted you unto him by his means." She referred to Wolsey's ruinous taxes.

"Well, well," the waiters reported Henry as replying, "as for that there is in him no blame, for I know that matter better than you or any other."

"Nay, sir," she answered as boldly as she dared, "besides all that what things hath he wrought within this realm to your great slander and dishonor. There is never a nobleman within this realm that if he had done but half so much as he hath done but he were well worthy to lose his head. If my lord of Norfolk, my lord of Suffolk, my lord my father, or any other noble person within your realm had done much less than he, but they should have lost their heads or this."

Anne's effrontery was remarkable. No one else could have spoken this way to Henry and gotten away with it. Katherine never had, undoubtedly no woman had. Yet the king's answer, as Cavendish recorded it, was mild.

"Why then I perceive ye are not the cardinal's friend."

"Forsooth, sir, I have no cause nor any other man that loveth your grace. No more have your grace if he consider well his doings."

At this point the meal had ended and the waiters, after removing the table linen and dismantling the trestle table, left the king and his lady alone. What they said to one another then we don't know, but at some point it was agreed that they would ride together the next day to look over ground laid aside for a new hunting park.

After he left Anne Henry resumed his conversation with Wolsey, talking to him alone for hours and making Anne and her relatives apprehensive. But when Wolsey appeared to see the king the next morning Henry was already prepared to ride with Anne as arranged, so the two did not confer. Though Wolsey waited several hours for them to return he finally had to give up and go back to his own house, as the king had ordered him to do. King and cardinal were not to talk again. By Anne's "special labor," Cavendish explained, Henry was kept away from Grafton long enough to ensure that when he finally returned the cardinal would be gone.[2]

Unquestionably Anne was doing everything in her power to prevent a reconciliation between the two men, as no doubt her father and her uncle told her to do. But she was neither the cause nor the instrument of Wolsey's fall. Bad luck, King Henry's uniquely irresolvable marital dilemma and, at the end, sheer overwork and exhaustion felled Wolsey, as did more subtle historical forces. The mighty cardinal had become an anachronism, a great ecclesiastic wielding temporal authority in an increasingly secular age. The king preferred a chancellor who was not a cleric. Wolsey was ordered to surrender his seal of office and was replaced by Thomas More, an able and experienced lawyer and diplomatist who had achieved fame as a humanist scholar and man of letters. Wolsey was stripped of most of his wealth as well as his worldly power, and sent away. His enemies tasted their revenge.

Wolsey was barely out of office when Anne began to savor hers. She went with Henry and her mother to Greenwich, where all the costly goods that had formerly been the cardinal's were displayed. (He had lost no time in presenting them all to the king, knowing they would eventually be demanded of him anyway.) Since what was Henry's would become Anne's once she married him—and hers to use and enjoy even before that—she must have felt a proprietary excitement in examining the quantities of splendid furnishings laid out along the walls. There were dozens of tapestries, some frayed and faded, some new and jewel-bright, depicting hunting and hawking scenes, flowers and heraldic beasts, naval battles and pastoral landscapes. The cardinal had been renowned for the seemingly inexhaustible supply of hangings he owned, ranging from the magnificent sets he displayed on important occasions to the almost equally gorgeous ones used on "inferior days."

Beyond these, there were some sixteen costly beds, their wooden posts beautifully carved into columns or sculpted into other ornate shapes, adorned with canopies and curtains of velvet and cloth of gold. Chests and tables of exquisite workmanship, paintings and other art treasures, vestments studded with gems and gilded candelabras, chalices and monstrances were all Henry's for the taking. The chapel goods in particular—including the cardinal's heavy gold processional cross—would be melted down and minted into a fortune in gold coins. As for the plate, "such a number of plate of all sorts as were almost incredible," most of the bowls, pots and flagons would be absorbed into the royal plate; those set with rubies, diamonds and sapphires would be sent to the king's Jewel House for safekeeping.

It had been rumored that Wolsey's income was fully a third as large as the king's, and unlike the king, Wolsey did not have to use any of his to govern a kingdom. The array of treasures gave full proof of the rumor. Even Henry, who had been keeping an envious eye on Wolsey's wealth for more than a decade, was reportedly surprised at the extent and value of the cardinal's hoard. Anne and her mother may have regarded the immense exhibit as a sort of wedding present from Wolsey, a last gesture of good faith toward the marriage Anne held him responsible for preventing.[3]

Wolsey's cause was lost, yet for months he persisted in efforts to regain the king's kindness. He was fully aware that, like everyone else, he would have to go through Anne to reach Henry. He urged his servant Thomas Cromwell to work as hard as he could to persuade Anne to mediate for him, hoping that if her displeasure had abated somewhat Cromwell might just be able to move her. "This is the only help and remedy," Wolsey wrote. All possible means had to be used to attain her favor. He wrote to Anne himself, but though she sent "kind words" back to him through Cromwell she would not promise to speak to Henry on his behalf —and in fact, Du Bellay wrote in a dispatch, Anne had made the king promise her that he would not grant Wolsey a private audience. And the courtiers understood that anyone who took the cardinal's side in the presence of the king would gain the royal favorite's lasting enmity—something none of them took lightly.

The wheel of fortune had come full circle. Once Wolsey had been all-powerful, and Anne a powerless nobody. Then his large shadow had fallen across her path, he had crushed her hopes and robbed her of the future she had cherished as wife to Henry Percy. Now she was supreme, and he the broken, groveling supplicant. He begged for her pity, and was crushed in his turn. Her "kind words" must have stabbed him to the quick; how often had he glibly promised kindness while doing secret injury?

According to Du Bellay Anne's influence was extensive. Speaking of the restructuring of authority in the royal Council, he wrote that "the duke of Norfolk is made chief of the council, Suffolk acting in his absence, and, at the head of all, Mademoiselle Anne."[4]

In December of 1529 celebrations were held to mark the creation of new peers. Thomas Boleyn and several others, most of them relatives of Anne's, were to be honored. Seen from the standpoint of court politics, the new peers owed their elevation to the ascendency of Norfolk in the Council, but most of the courtiers, and others, presumed that Anne's family was being exalted in preparation for her own elevation to the rank of queen.

There was every reason to think so. Not only was Anne's father given precedence at the ceremony, being the first to receive his earldoms (he was henceforth to be both earl of Wiltshire and earl of Ormond), but the event was marked by festivities at which Anne herself was given prominence. On the day following the formal creation of the peers the king held a huge celebration in London. A number of women were invited to attend, including Norfolk's wife and widowed mother, both duchesses, and Suffolk's wife, who because of her first marriage long before to King Louis of France held the rank of queen. As if to signal that Anne was soon to be greater than these, though at present she was only Lady Anne Rochford, the earl of Wiltshire's daughter, Henry gave her the place of honor at his side, not lower down but on his level, "the very place allotted to a crowned queen." (Incidents such as this must have rankled with the great ladies of the court and made them resent Anne more than ever. Precedence was a jealously protected right. Though she sided with her in the divorce conflict, Norfolk's wife found it hard to forgive Queen Katherine for giving her mother-in-law the dowager duchess pride of place at one court function; such slights and insults rankled and led to bitter grudges.)

The celebration had the feel of a nuptial feast. The lavish food and great quantities of wine the guests consumed, the music and merrymaking suggested a wedding dinner, as did the "dancing and carousing" that went on far into the night after the dining tables were removed. "It seemed," wrote the recently appointed imperial ambassador Eustace Chapuys, "as if nothing were wanting but the priest to give away the nuptial ring and pronounce the blessing."[5]

Chapuys had been in England only a few months but already he was alert to the significance of such carefully staged demonstrations as this one. King Henry was sending a message to his entire entourage—and to the Londoners who watched the procession of notables come and go and paid attention to their boisterous celebrating. He meant them all to understand that despite the repeated setbacks he was encountering in his efforts to be free of his cumbersome marriage, he was determined not to be thwarted forever. Sooner or later he would have his way. He ordered the clerics who preached public sermons to support his position on the divorce. They were to explain to the people that Pope Julius's bull of dispensation permitting Katherine to marry Henry (the document on which Katherine's case rested) was meaningless because no pope had sufficient authority to set aside divine law—in this case, the law which forbade a man to marry his brother's widow.

It was a clever tactic, attacking the authority of the pope to an audience that was vociferously anticlerical. The English associated the pope, and the Roman church, with luxury and worldliness, with fat prelates such as Wolsey who taxed them and lived splendidly from the profits of the taxes. But much as they might despise the pope and the corrupt church, Londoners loved the queen, and would not abandon their loyalty to her merely because she relied on the support of Pope Clement. Moreover, whatever they were told, they persisted in believing that Katherine was the victim of a lustful, adulterous husband and his brazen mistress. They refused to accept Henry's assertion that he had parted from his queen for the sake of his conscience. If his conscience made him uncomfortable over Katherine and Arthur, they asked, why did it fail to torment him over his past liaison with Anne's sister Mary? To marry Anne would be to repeat the sin he had committed in marrying Katherine, the sin of taking as his wife a woman to whom he was bound, in the language of canon law, by ties of affinity.

Besides, there was the obvious evidence of Henry's sheer besotted amorousness to contradict his self-righteous assertions of conscience. His "passionate attachment" to Anne became more obvious every day, Chapuys reported. His desire to make her his wife consumed him, he thought of nothing else. According to Norfolk, he was so shameless that he would debase himself before the emperor, "becoming his slave forever," if only the latter would abandon his objections to the divorce.[6]

And as ever, his desire to marry Anne was not an end in itself but a means to achieve the paramount goal of assuring the succession. What Henry wanted was not just Anne, but Anne's son, preferably several sons. Until the marriage took place and Anne was safely delivered of her first male child, England would continue to remain in a vulnerable position, with only a sickly princess to inherit the throne.

To be sure, other solutions to the succession dilemma were forever being proposed. One of these was that Princess Mary take Norfolk's son and heir as her husband, thus assuring that if Henry died the country would have a king to govern it while his wife reigned. The queen's partisans favored this proposal, not merely because it made Anne superfluous but because it offered the opportunity to drive a wedge between Norfolk and his ambitious Boleyn relatives. The idea was "much spoken of" in late 1529, but nothing came of it.

Alternately, the king's bastard Henry Fitzroy could be formally designated heir to the throne—and, for good measure, betrothed to the princess as well. Fitzroy was ten years old, in good health and, according to one report, "a wonderful lad for his age." He had his father's good looks, and his tutors had been assiduous in making him precociously literate in Greek and Latin and in training him in courtesy and good manners.[7] Kept far from court ever since his elevation to the rank of duke of Richmond, Fitzroy was out of sight yet never far from the king's thoughts or those of his councillors. Should Henry die, or Mary, he would suddenly become a vital link in the chain of succession, precious and irreplaceable.

There were other proposals too, proposals which must have made Anne grit her teeth in exasperation whenever she heard them whispered. The pope could, if he chose, legitimize children born to Henry and Anne, even if they never married. What if Henry gave up his battle to free himself from his present marriage and struck a bargain with Pope Clement to obtain this concession? That way Anne could give him the son and heir that Katherine could not, but he would no longer insist on setting Katherine aside. The succession would be assured, international crisis averted. Anne would lose out, to the extent that she was counting on becoming Henry's wife, but then how important were her expectations compared to the larger issues at stake?

That Henry might in time be driven to abandon his long campaign in favor of a compromise unfavorable to Anne was an alarming, if remote, possiblity. For the time being, though he admitted to feeling perplexed beyond endurance by the stalemate with Rome, Henry was energetically trying a new tactic. "The king of England is making such efforts to procure the divorce as are enough to set the world on fire," one of the emperor's correspondents wrote him. English agents were dispatched to all the centers of learning not under Hapsburg domination to persuade, cajole, bribe or, if all else failed, to bully the scholars teaching there into writing opinions corroborating King Henry's position. Canonists and theologians were urged to subscribe their names to documents setting forth the arguments against the validity of the marriage; by the dozens they complied, though sometimes angry local bishops seized the documents and burned them, forcing the English to the labor of collecting the signatures all over again.

The universities of Bourges and Bologna—the latter representing the most distinguished legal faculty in Europe—issued sentences supporting Henry, as did a majority of the faculty in the University of Paris. (That the minority included some of the most learned members of the faculty mattered less than that the weight of numbers was on the king's side.) To be sure, the determinations made in Bourges and Bologna were offset by those of the universities of Salamanca and Alcalá, where the doctors ruled for Katherine, and in fact the entire procedure was invalidated by political pressure, tergiversation (some doctors declared themselves first for Katherine, then for Henry, allowing both sides to claim their allegiance), and blatant partisanship. But Henry rejoiced in his successes, and publicized them throughout the kingdom. They reinforced his own scholarly judgment, and his naive but sincere conviction that if only he could prove the overwhelming intellectual merit of his position, he would prevail in the end.

Anne was less sanguine, however. Probably she realized, as

Henry did in his darker and more cynical moods, that facts and legal opinions had little to do with their situation. And while Henry might enjoy the purely mental exercise of collecting and studying treatises, weighing arguments and authorities against one another and combatting his opponents with his subtle reasoning, for Anne it all meant more delays. He might have time for such games and stratagems, she did not.

She complained, criticized and finally turned to making tearful threats. She "wept and regretted her lost honor" ceaselessly, warning Henry that she would leave him and making him so fearful of losing her that he agreed to do almost anything she asked.[8] She was difficult to appease; she made him weep too, and beg her not to talk about separating from him. To see such a giant of a man, robust and in his prime, reduced to helpless tears must have given Anne a thrill of power. It was this power of hers, this ability to play on the king's emotions and deflect his purposes, that made Du Bellay write that Anne was "at the head of all."

Yet even as she sensed her force Anne was aware that it might prove ephemeral. The number of her enemies was increasing, and her chief enemy, Wolsey, still lived. Little formal authority was left to the cardinal, but the memory of his long service and ability lingered in the king's mind. Anne heard that Henry had begun to lament his loss. When his councillors displeased him he shouted at them in a rage "that the cardinal was a better man than any of them for managing matters," and left them. Unless Anne prevented it Wolsey might be reinstated, and then he would remember her refusal to help him in his time of trouble. The precarious balance of influence might shift again, leaving her much the worse for having failed to strike the final blow. She decided to strike.

There was damning evidence against Wolsey. He had recovered some of his former energies and was using them to send messages, in cipher, to continental courts, including the papal court in Rome. He was guilty of "presumptuous sinister practices" to restore his influence. He was a traitor.

With Anne insisting, in a storm of tears, that Wolsey be brought to justice a warrant was issued for his arrest and he was summoned to London to await trial and, inevitably, execution. He set out from his archdiocese at York, traveling slowly, impeded by illness. Before he could reach the capital he collapsed and had to take refuge by the roadside. Anne had her way, but at the last Wolsey cheated her of the pleasure of watching him die. Instead of facing the executioner and his axe the cardinal yielded up his spirit amid the peace of Leicester Abbey, as the monks were chanting vespers.

14

*"The Queen's ladies, gentlewomen, and servants
largely spoke and said that she so enticed the
king, and brought him in such amours, that only
for her sake and occasion, he would be divorced
from his Queen, this was the foolish communi-
cation of people . . ."*

Anne was visiting a manor house beside the Thames on
an evening in late September of 1531. King Henry was not with
her, he was staying elsewhere and was not within easy reach.
Quite possibly he was away in the country hunting, so that any
news from London would take hours to get to him, and he would
be unable to do anything about it quickly when it did.

Somehow word of Anne's whereabouts leaked out, and
reached London. A crowd of women gathered, the women who
thought of themselves as Queen Katherine's most tenacious defenders. So Nan Bullen was alone, was she? Nan Bullen, the
woman they liked to call a "goggle-eyed whore," the six-fingered
witch who had bewitched the king and turned him toward an
evil destiny. The crowd grew larger and noisier, the shouted
name of Nan Bullen drawing more and more women out into
the streets and making them agitated and volatile. Their hatred
drew them together, made them hungry for action. Thousands
collected, among them many men dressed as women (were any
of them assassins in the pay of the emperor?), and swarmed
toward the place where Anne was staying.

According to the account reaching France—who the informant was is unknown—there were between seven and eight thousand men and women in the mob that set out to seize Anne and kill her.[1] Even if the numbers were hugely exaggerated it must have been a frightening sight, a vast throng of skirted marchers, red-faced and hostile, armed, presumably, with knives and sticks and broom handles, converging on the riverside house. There was no peacekeeping force to stop them, only the soldiers of the king's guard quartered far away at the palace. Probably the crowd massed, incited itself, and began its march before anyone in authority sensed danger. It was only women, after all—or what appeared to be women. What harm could mere women do?

Somehow Anne was warned about the oncoming mob, either by someone riding swiftly from the city to tell her or, possibly, by the low rumbling sound made by thousands of boots and shoes on yielding earth as the multitude approached. Anne evaded her captors by slipping across the river in a boat. When they arrived at the house she was gone—and very likely all the other occupants of the house were gone too—and the throngs of Londoners, after venting their anger in some fashion or other, stomped sullenly back home.

Little was made of the incident. There were no reports of massive punishments, no record of any official inquiry. As "a thing done by women," and abortive besides, the attack was dismissed as inconsequential.

But to Anne it must have been the nightmarish culmination of more than four years of mockery and injury and threats of violence. Ever since the summer of 1527, when it became generally known that King Henry intended to break free of Katherine and marry Thomas Boleyn's daughter, the people had heaped abuse on Anne, calling her names and ridiculing her and dishonoring her in every way possible. At first she endured it without complaint, trusting in Henry's adoring love and promise of marriage, reasoning that when she was queen the people would not dare to persist in their mockery. But then the wedding had been postponed, time and again, and the popular vituperation worsened. The longer Katherine remained queen in despite of Henry's efforts to dislodge her, the more her subjects championed her cause—and hated her rival. Now they had come, an army of haters, to kill her. And Henry had not been there to protect her, or to order her protection. She had been proven vulnerable, the mob might come a second time. What was she to do?

The attack was particularly humiliating in that Anne had begun to take heart once again and to expect her long delayed wedding to occur in October or November at the latest. She was assembling a queenly entourage, with servants and household officers and an almoner of her own, and was asserting to anyone and everyone that her triumph was finally at hand.[2] Then came the terrifying, infuriating attack by the Londoners, and with it, no doubt, whisperings and sneering from the jealous courtiers, further infamy on the continent, where Anne was already notorious, and worst of all, gloating smiles from Katherine.

Katherine! After all this time she still stood in Anne's way, though how one matronly, powerless foreigner could evade and resist her powerful husband's will for so long was remarkable, not to say miraculous. Katherine was not only courageous, she was clever, she knew how to hide her adamant obduracy and sharp wits behind a gracious and yielding exterior. She was charming and utterly womanly, disarming the clerics and councillors who hounded her and made demands of her by greeting them sweetly, a skein of wool around her neck and her needlework beside her. Instead of acting the part of the outraged queen she played the role of patient, forgiving wife and mother, saying her prayers for her misguided husband and treating the tragedy of her shattered marriage like a minor domestic inconvenience. Her loyalty to Henry knew no bounds. To anyone who accused him in her presence of betraying her with Anne, she maintained "strenuously, that all her king and lord did, was done by him for true and pure conscience's sake, and not from any wanton appetite."[3]

He abetted this farce by treating her with courtly politeness in public, their mild-mannered conversations giving no hint of animosity or conflict. "They pay each other, reciprocally, the greatest possible attention," wrote the Venetian ambassador, "or compliments, in the Spanish fashion, with the utmost mental tranquility, as if there had never been any dispute whatever between them."[4] There were limits to the politeness, of course. Katherine was no longer called queen, but "Mistress Katherine," and many of her prerogatives were seized by Anne. But she still had a queenly household of some two hundred servants to wait on her, including thirty maids of honor and fifty grooms and ushers who served her dinner and stood, stiff in their velvet liveries, while she ate.

In private a battle of nerves went on between the king and Mistress Katherine. They had lived together for more than twenty years, and had known one another longer than that. They knew each other's vulnerabilities, sensed each other's weaknesses. They were drawn together by painful memories of their dead children, and by pleasant ones of their living daughter Mary, who in the last four years had matured from an angelic child to a delicately beautiful young woman. Henry knew that to upset Katherine he had to do nothing more than to threaten to separate her from Mary. Katherine knew how to disconcert him in return by arguing circles around him—something she was very good at—or by impugning his rectitude or assaulting his ever sensitive conscience. Katherine knew better than anyone else that in his heart of hearts Henry feared himself. He was ill at ease with the rage that boiled up within him and spilled out uncontrolled, with his secret greed for mastery and his secret worry that he might be in the wrong.

All this made for strain between Henry and Katherine when they were alone together—alone, that is, except for the servants who brought them dinner or the Spanish women who stood unobtrusively at Katherine's side.

He had made her endure the pains of purgatory on earth, Katherine told Henry one afternoon after they had dined together. His neglect was painful to her, and he knew it.

"She had no cause to complain of bad treatment," he replied, "for she was mistress in her own household, where she could do what she pleased." Of course he could not see her as often as she might have liked, but he had a great many things to do, as she ought to understand.

"As to his visiting her in her apartments and partaking of her bed, she ought to know that he was not her legitimate husband, as innumerable doctors and canonists, all men of honor and probity," were quick to maintain. He went on at length about how "many other theologians" were sending their written opinions—all favorable to him—to England to be assembled into one comprehensive dossier and forwarded to the pope. "And should not the pope, in conformity with the above opinions so expressed, declare their marriage null and void, then in that case he would denounce the pope as a heretic, and marry whom he pleased."

There was no need for any of that, Katherine answered tartly, for theologians or no theologians, Henry himself knew perfectly well that the principal allegation on which the nullity suit rested was pure invention. He knew perfectly well that he had found her to be a virgin when he married her, and had asserted as much more than once. (It was a very sore point between them, as Chapuys noted in one dispatch, an issue which continually "raised some scruple in the king's mind" and made him very uneasy.) As to the mass of written opinions he was collecting, the best lawyers in England had declared themselves to be on her side, not his, and if only he would give her permission to seek counsel freely she could find a thousand doctors and lawyers to support her for every one who supported him.

The arguing escalated, yet Katherine refused to back down, and after much dispute Henry left the room abruptly, looking "very disconcerted and downcast." Katherine had succeeded in upsetting him once again. Later that same day, as he sat at supper with Anne, his dark mood persisted. Anne, angry at him for letting Katherine get the better of him, nagged at him.

"Did I not tell you that whenever you disputed with the queen she was sure to have the upper hand? I see that some fine morning you will succumb to her reasoning and that you will cast me off." She was annoyed, for the pattern of mutual recrimination, argument, and moody aftermath kept repeating itself and Anne invariably suffered the consequences. Her annoyance was mingled with fear, for what she said to Henry might very well prove true. He might succumb to Katherine's reasoning, in a fatal moment of weakness.

"I have been waiting long," Anne reminded Henry, "and might in the meanwhile have contracted some advantageous marriage, out of which I might have had issue, which is the greatest consolation in this world; but alas! farewell to my time and youth spent to no purpose at all."[5]

Anne was right, her youth had passed. She was now in her late twenties, no longer a slim girl but an alluring woman, her dark beauty enhanced by the scarlet and crimson gowns the king ordered for her and the diamonds set in hearts he gave her to wear in her thick black hair. The fey enchantment she had radiated as a girl had receded, the quivering hind had been replaced by a lioness, splendid in her fierce courage and daring.

The transformation had been forced upon her, for she stood embattled, surrounded by assailants of many kinds. The pope and the other churchmen denounced her as immoral for her scandalous mode of life and for appearing to be, whether or not she actually was, King Henry's mistress. The courtiers ranged themselves against her in varying attitudes of hostility, from withering superiority to angry contempt. Her relatives, who now found themselves in the uncomfortable position of being at the mercy of her whims, had begun to distance themselves from her without ceasing to advance themselves through her. Henry, who certainly desired her, had begun to consider how he might possess her, and any children she might have by him, without making her queen. The people she hoped to make her subjects wanted to kill her. And Katherine, with her supporters on the continent, was doing her best to call in every weapon of the papacy and the empire to dislodge Anne from her place at King Henry's side.

Probably Anne alone realized how grim her situation was. She seems never to have had an adviser or protector or even a close confidant to lean on. There is no one, apart from Henry, mentioned in the chronicles or other records of the time as giving Anne guidance or particular support. Her father, though forceful and wily, was hardly the sort of man to offer benevolent counsel. Her uncle Norfolk, a hard and callous man who treated his wife with conspicuous brutality, seems not to have had any affection for Anne, and was by this time well on his way to becoming her enemy. About Anne's relations with her mother, sister and brother the records are oddly silent, though here too we may presume that if any of them had been important to her the ambassadors would surely have mentioned the fact—adding recommendations about how to exploit the intimacy.

All but alone then, with her father and uncle ready to condemn her if she made a false step but without the comfort or relief of an older mentor, Anne steeled herself to outbrave the daily hazards of her precarious position.

Of all the vexations she faced the most galling and least tractable was the king's continuing weakness for Katherine and Mary. He saw them less often now than he once had done, but still too often to please Anne. Occasionally Henry, Katherine and Anne all occupied apartments in the same palace, no doubt leading to embroilments among their servants and petty warfare over chambers and provisions and other household trivia. Anne had Henry to herself during the vacation months of summer and early fall, but at the great festivals of Christmas and Easter Katherine still held her place. And, exasperating woman that she was, the worse things were made for Katherine the more gallantly she resisted. Aided by the austerities she had practiced all her adult life—fasting, vigils that interrupted her sleep, predawn prayers —she marshaled her spiritual energies to withstand whatever humiliation and persecution were thrust upon her. In vain Anne placed spies in her household, and made it all but impossible for her to communicate with anyone who might help her, in vain Henry sent deputations of councillors to browbeat her and wear her down; she was outwardly unmoved, though the inner strain on her was very great. "Wherever the king commanded her, were it even to the fire, she would go," she maintained. But she would never voluntarily renounce her rights as queen.

Mary was as bad. Taking her beloved mother as a model she was obedient but stubbornly unyielding when it came to recognizing any irregularity in her parents' marriage. Her mother might be called Mistress Katherine, but she was still Princess

Mary, the king's daughter and princess of Wales. Henry came to see her and "made great cheer with her" occasionally—as much to remind the world that he had a legitimate successor as for his own fatherly pleasure—yet she knew he could hardly wait to marry Anne and father a son who would take precedence over her. And she knew that Anne was jealous of her and wanted her out of the way. Anne was said to hate Mary "as much as the queen, or more so, chiefly because she sees the king has some affection for her." When Henry praised Mary in Anne's presence she became "very angry, and began to vituperate the princess very strangely."[6]

Nothing made Anne more short-tempered and snappish than to be reminded of Katherine and her daughter. Encountering one of Katherine's ladies, Anne told her "that she wished all the Spaniards in the world were in the sea." "For the honor of the queen, she should not say so," the woman answered. Anne burst out "that she did not care anything for the queen, and would rather see her hanged than acknowledge her as her mistress," ending the exchange.[7]

As to the Hapsburg armies, those fearsome hordes which the more cautious of the king's advisers had envisioned overrunning England ever since 1527, let them come. Anne was urging Henry to be fearless where the emperor was concerned, saying that he could do no real harm and that, should he try, her family would put ten thousand fighting men into the field at their own expense for the defense of the realm.[8]

Anne's bravado had a hint of desperation about it. She spurred Henry to extremes not only because it was in her nature—and his, at his best—to take bold risks but because, for her, time was running out. She and Katherine were poised in delicate balance, Anne with the full weight of King Henry's formidable will on her side, Katherine with just enough strength and obstructionism to make up a counterweight. But time was on Katherine's side, especially now that the murderous fury of the Londoners had shown itself. Unless she gained the protection of marriage and the crown soon Anne might lose her chance forever. Unless she pushed Henry to the limit now, some other way would be found to secure the succession, the king would fall back to a compromise which would allow Katherine to retain her titles and dignity.

For the king was tiring. He had been trying to do the work Wolsey had once done for him, yet he lacked Wolsey's genius for administration and his decades of experience. And Wolsey had been a tireless, compulsive worker, whereas Henry worked in brilliant bursts, followed by long hours of vigorous exercise while his mind was at rest. It was no good trying to delegate the work. Norfolk was a continual disappointment, More was opposed to the divorce on grounds of conscience and therefore unsuitable to pursue matters of policy. Boleyn was too ambitious to be trusted, Suffolk trusty but mediocre. The work piled up, the king made heroic efforts to deal with it but fell continually behind, all the while struggling to move ahead with his plan of gathering judgments from scholars all over Europe to lay at the pope's feet.

He struggled manfully, yet month after month his energy flagged and his body began to betray him. He turned forty in 1531, and felt the weight of his years as he never had before. A chronic varicose ulcer on his thigh gave him excruciating pain, and never wholly healed. He could no longer walk or ride tirelessly, his magnificent horses were idle much of the time. His voice gave out from shouting in frustration at his advisers, and then he developed sore throats and head colds. Above all, the increasing strain of his personal life, the agonizing indeterminacy of the divorce hounded his wits and carved deep lines in his boyish features.

He missed Wolsey, he freely admitted it. Without him the burden of government was simply too great to carry. Every time he saw Katherine or Mary he had to harden himself to their entreaties, and to his own residue of feeling for them. Every time he returned to Anne afterward he felt the hot blast of her rage. He no longer had the comfort of a wife, only the silent martyrdom of the woman he had rejected and the vociferous injury of the woman he was risking everything to possess.

It was no wonder his head ached and he had to walk with a golden walking stick. Wearied by his labors, his brain taxed by worry, he tried to sleep but could not. Insomnia made him susceptible to illness. Periodically he succumbed, and was reported to be "ill in bed in consequence of the grief and anger he had lately gone through."

Anne watched it all, goading Henry to increase his labors yet knowing that he could be driven only so far. No one man could cope with both the unending tasks of government and a tense and painful personal life for long. Anne dared not let up her pressure, yet she feared a backlash. Indeed she had already begun to feel its sting.

Henry warned Anne on one occasion "that she was under great obligation to him, since he was offending everyone and making enemies everywhere for her sake." It was a reproach; he was telling her in a roundabout way that the price of making her queen was proving to be too high. It was not just that he was making enemies because of her; he was losing friends and loved ones, while gaining little, so far, in return. Anne and her allies had pressed him to execute Wolsey, now they were pressing him with equal firmness to cut himself off entirely from Katherine and Mary. It was the only way, they told him. Not to appear decisive in his treatment of them was to weaken his endeavors at the papal court.

Much as he desired Anne and feared to think that she might leave him, Henry could not help but compare her to Katherine, whose behavior toward him, even during quarrels, was far different. Katherine was a more worthy opponent, she handled him with much greater finesse. She wore him down, waiting her chance and then turning his own weapons against him. Anne bludgeoned him with threats and accusations, arousing his fears yet never coming close to delivering a mortal wound. Anne troubled him, but she also made him resentful—and his resentment was dangerous.

Gradually Henry was beginning to chafe under Anne's arrogant, unbridled language. He went to Norfolk and complained, not once but several times. The duke told his wife, who told Katherine, who told Chapuys, and soon the whole court knew of it. Anne, the duchess remarked, would soon "be considered the ruin of all her family." Her rash temperament would be her undoing. The king was displeased at Anne's "words and authority." "She was not like Katherine," he had said to the duke, "who had never in her life used ill words to him." In his darkest hours he wondered whether Katherine, standing in the shadows of his mind, was really such a liability after all.

15

"The king of England sent out his letters, to his nobility, prelates, and servants, commanding them to be ready at Canterbury, the xxvi. day of September, to pass the seas with him, for the accomplishing of the interview, between him and his brother the French king."

The cortege that passed along the Dover road glittered in the sunlight. The gleaming copper of the engraved saddles, the metal hasps of the huge traveling chests, the gold buckles and buttons and chains of the riders' clothing shone brightly as the procession advanced at an unhurried pace toward Dover Castle. The king and his lady were journeying to France, with a thousand attendants to accompany them. Everyone felt certain that when they returned, they would be man and wife.

For why cross the Channel, if not to escape the incessant hoots and jeers that greeted Henry and Anne wherever they went? Once they were out of England they would be safe from the kind of incident they had encountered the previous summer, when two or three times crowds of women had gathered to shout and hiss at them as they rode northward from London on a hunting progress. The king had become so disconcerted by the angry crowds that he had finally ordered his entire party to abandon the progress and return home.

If he and Anne were not free even to ride out hunting without harassment, how could they ever hope to carry through a dignified royal wedding? Unless of course they left the country and went to Calais or Boulogne, where King Francis and his guardsmen would be waiting to add their protection to King Henry's own escort. The French king's support would lend political ballast to Anne and Henry's union; it might even tip the scales in favor of approval from Rome, though that possibility had by now become exceedingly remote.

The long train of mounted riders, carriages, and pack animals moved on, deepening the ruts in the narrow dirt track they followed and sending up showers of mud. The courtiers appointed to travel with the king and Anne had assembled at Canterbury the day before, October 9, 1532. They were to embark the following afternoon, weather permitting, for the English-held town of Calais. A few days later, once Henry and his companions were certain that no brigands lurked outside the town walls and that the French were not plotting any treachery, they would venture onto French territory. The two kings would meet near Boulogne, then ride together to the town where after several days of ritual cordiality they would spend an equal amount of time in Calais and then the English would embark for home. It was not to be another Field of Cloth of Gold; the splendors of that fabled meeting between Henry and Francis twelve years earlier could never be equaled. But it would be an opportunity for the kings to talk face to face about their overlapping interests, about the obstinate perseverance of the armies of Charles V (who had just gained a major victory over the Turks) and, most urgently, about King Henry's intended marriage to Anne.

He did intend to marry her, come what may. Not in some distant, shadowy future, but soon. With or without papal approval—almost certainly without it. But that no longer mattered, for Henry's view of the church, and its relation to monarchy, had undergone a gradual change over the last several years. In his thinking, and in that of his new chief servant Thomas Cromwell, the time-honored deference paid by kings to popes was inappropriate. Rightly viewed, England was an autonomous realm, and her king had powers which made him inviolably sovereign within it. His sovereignty extended, in fact, to cover not only his lay subjects but the clergy too, thus he was supreme in matters involving the English church.

These views were to be embodied in a series of parliamentary statutes which Cromwell had already begun to draft in the fall of 1532, as Henry prepared for the meeting with Francis. Whatever happened, he would not be dissuaded from pursuing the course he followed—a course which would inevitably lead him to claim England's autonomy from the church of Rome. But by the time he made that claim, Anne would be his wife.

Six weeks earlier he had made her a peer in her own right, granting her the male title marquess of Pembroke (a rank lower than that of her uncle Norfolk but higher than that of her father). On the day of her creation, at Windsor, she was dressed in a crimson velvet surcoat furred with ermines, her hair flowing loose and unbound, covered with jewels. Her dark eyes bright with triumph, her head held proudly, Anne must have been a handsome figure as she approached the king, escorted by two countesses, the officers of arms at the castle and a party of noblemen. Her cousin Mary, Norfolk's daughter, held her furred mantle and her coronet.

Anne knelt before Henry, and her patent of nobility was read out. Significantly, the patent called for the title to descend to Anne's male heirs—not her male heirs "lawfully begotten." Should she bear the king an illegitimate son he would inherit Anne's rank and the lands and income that went with it. Henry then invested her, draping the long velvet mantle around her shoulders and setting the gold coronet on her head. She thanked him, and distributed gifts among the officers who attended her, before retiring to her apartments—no doubt with increased hauteur.

All the leading courtiers had been forced to watch the ceremony, and to contain the resentment they felt. Yet they knew that Anne's creation as marquess of Pembroke was a preliminary to her ultimate elevation into the ranks of royalty, and as she reached the threshold of queenship their smoldering rancor blazed up. They balked at dancing attendance on Anne on her journey to Calais, and denounced the accoutrements of royalty with which she surrounded herself. She had as many servants as Katherine did, and flaunted them. For a time she ordered the motto *Groigne qui groigne* sewn onto their liveries. ("Complain who will!") Her cupboards and dining table sagged under the weight of her heavy gold and silver platters and bowls and goblets. Her robes shone with jewels, even the bed Henry gave her as a New Year's gift in 1532 reflected the light in its lustrous gold and silver coverings.

But it was all a pretense, an elaborate hoax. Anne was a sham queen, giving herself airs and stepping outside the bounds within which society and morality constrained her. Nothing about her was real: not the queenship she played at, not the marquessate she flourished (no woman had ever held such a title in her own right before—why should Anne?), not the exalted pedigree the king had invented for her. The Boleyns, according to this elaborately painted genealogical tree, were an ancient family descended from a Norman knight. Anne's spiteful aunt, the duchess of Norfolk, knew differently; she snatched up the offensive document and tore it to bits, "blazoning it forth very bitterly."[1]

Most unreal of all was the masquerade Anne was carrying on in traveling to Calais with Henry, posing as his queen. Nearly all the women of the court were outraged, and of the men, Norfolk tried to excuse himself from attending because of illness while the earl of Oxford and others complained that the expedition would tarnish Henry's reputation and result in ruin. Suffolk, who privately warned the king that Anne had been on intimate terms with one of his gentlemen and was therefore unfit to become queen, spoke out so strongly against the interview in meetings of the Privy Council that Henry snapped at him and put him in his place. But Henry could not control his sister, Suffolk's wife. Perhaps recalling another journey to France years earlier, when Anne had been the youngest and most insignificant of her attendants on her way to marry the French king, the duchess "stoutly refused" to serve Anne, and insisted on staying home.

Katherine too did her part to protest the hypocrisy of Anne's queenly pose. When Henry ordered her to surrender her jewels so that Anne could add them to her traveling wardrobe, Katherine refused. How could Henry possibly expect her to meekly hand over the symbols of her position to the sinful hoyden who had usurped her place? It was bad enough that Henry had already adorned her with dozens of his own jewels—including twenty splendid rubies and two diamonds which he ordered his goldsmith Cornelis Hayes to reset for her. It was equally insulting that Anne should preen herself insufferably in preparation for her meeting with King Francis, issuing orders to dressmakers and silkwomen and buying extravagantly costly gowns and kirtles. Did Henry seriously believe that Katherine would give Anne a treasure in royal jewelry as well, especially when there was such good reason to believe that Anne meant to wear the jewels at her wedding?

When Norfolk came to take possession of the jewels Katherine told him "that she could not send jewels or anything else to the king, as he had long ago forbidden her to do so." Besides, she went on, "it was against her conscience to give her jewels to adorn a person who is the scandal of Christendom, and a disgrace to the king, who takes her to such an assembly." Of course, if she received explicit orders for the jewels she would surrender them, she added—knowing that Henry and Anne were to leave in a few days and that it would probably take longer than that for the cumbersome paperwork to be completed, brought to her, and expedited.

Henry was angry, but because the journey was postponed for other reasons he was able to have orders drafted to Katherine, her chamberlain and her chancellor officially requesting what he desired. The documents were delivered by one of the king's chamber gentlemen, who relayed the message that Henry was surprised to find her uncooperative, when so many other women —even the affronted duchess of Norfolk—had complied with similar requests. Katherine apologized and sent all the jewels she had.[2]

The procession of nobles and gentlefolk, servants and baggage, guardsmen and clerics approaching Dover Castle was far shorter than originally planned. From three or four thousand the number of royal attendants had been much reduced, for several reasons. First, apart from Anne and twenty or so of her women only the men of the court were making the crossing with the king. The exclusion of ladies was embarrassing but unavoidable, for none of the respectable women of the French court would associate with Anne, only the courtesans, and to prevent dishonor to Anne all of them had to be excluded from the meeting of the two kings. With the French women excluded, the English women had to be excluded also. Then there was the plague danger, which had been escalating so severely over the past month that the king had come very near to canceling the expedition altogether. As it was, he lowered the number of his attendants still further and had them embark from several ports instead of congregating in a single contagious mass at Dover.

Neither the postponements nor the other disappointments seemed to lower Henry's spirits. He talked of nothing but his journey to Calais, busying himself happily, as Anne did, with the details of protocol, lodgings, provisions and dress. He wrote to King Francis about a number of things: Would he see to it that any imperialists who might be at Boulogne were removed? Would he kindly leave the notorious courtesan Madame de Vendôme, whom he proposed bringing with him as Anne's appropriate counterpart, at home? And would he please extend a personal invitation to Anne to come to the meeting, as it would give her the greatest pleasure imaginable? There were lists of guardsmen to scrutinize and ships to inspect. Calais was to be stocked with four days' provisions for the visiting French and their horses, with quarters assigned to the men of highest rank and space for tents to all the others. And what if it rained? Henry and his purveyors must have asked themselves. The weather could be tempestuous in mid-October, the winds high and the rains torrential. A fine spectacle it would turn out to be if water poured down on the kings and their retinues, spoiling their finery and turning the pageantry into a mud-covered fiasco.

The sea was calm on the following day, the weather fine, and the royal party embarked without incident for Calais. They had a swift, smooth crossing, and all the notables of the town turned out to receive them and to escort Henry and Anne to their lodgings in the Exchequer. For the next few days, as the English waited for word that King Francis and his retinue had arrived at the appointed meeting place near Boulogne, there was little to do, but a great deal to think about. Rumor had it that Henry would marry Anne when he brought Francis back to Calais with him. A French prelate would perform the ceremony. Anne had hinted before her departure that her hopes would at last be fulfilled in Calais, but—possibly to save her pride in case of disappointment—she had also let it be known that she would not agree to a ceremony held anywhere but in England, "where queens are wont to be married and crowned."[3]

While Henry occupied his time inspecting the walls and towers of the town and devising new fortifications for it—one of his particular pleasures—Anne was immobile. Probably she did not leave the Exchequer, for Katherine had her partisans in Calais just as she had in London, and Anne would not have wanted to provoke their antagonism. Had her status been unclouded she would have been entertained by the ladies of the town, and by King Francis's sister Marguerite and her attendants. (King Francis's wife Eleanor could hardly have been expected to be hospitable to Anne, as she was the sister of Charles V and thus Katherine's niece.) As it was, she would have no formal social role to play at all. Even her meeting with Francis, whom she had last seen a decade earlier, when she left his carefree and licentious court, would have to be informal.

But though she was not on view Anne was far from inactive. Having been a prime mover of the royal meeting she did her best to obtain all the advantage she could from it. To return from Calais a bride was no doubt her highest goal, no matter what she said to the contrary. Indeed there is some reason to believe that her original hope had been to arrive in Calais already married. She spoke angrily to Gregory Casale, Henry's friend and representative in Rome, when she encountered him in Calais, accusing him of incompetence for "not managing her affair better, for she had hoped to be married in the middle of September."[4]

Short of a wedding, the best that could be accomplished would be to win the support of the French king and clergy. To this end Henry sent a battery of learned men to France ahead of him to put his case before the French; if they could be favorably persuaded, it was thought, the wedding might at least be hastened.[5] Even to hasten it would mean a good deal, for mounting pressures made a swift settlement desirable. The Scots were threatening war, a large Hapsburg army was said to be massed in Flanders, ready to descend on the English-held enclave in France. The pope, who for several years had been forbidding experts in canon law and other scholars to render independent judgments on the validity of Henry's marriage to Katherine, had recently moved on to censuring Henry for his conduct and pressuring him acutely to expel Anne from his court and restore Katherine. And beyond these specific imperatives was the increasing strain of international notoriety. Henry's quarrel with the Roman church, accompanied by his baldly disgraceful life, troubled all Europe. "There are three grievous evils in the church," one of the emperor's correspondents wrote: the invading Turks, the Lutheran heretics, and the divorce of Henry VIII.

Ten days after his arrival in Calais Henry rode out of the town at the head of a long train of some six hundred noblemen and men at arms. Within a few miles they came in sight of the French, waiting in a valley near the village of Sandingfield. The two kings spurred their magnificent horses toward one another, closing the distance that separated them like two eager jousters. Only instead of clashing like jousters they embraced, five or six times, and then each embraced the principal noblemen in the other's suite. The two kings made a splendid picture, both tall and broad-shouldered, Francis dark and devilish, Henry fair and with a hearty and open countenance that belied his forty-one years. Though they had sworn beforehand to keep expenditures low, each wore a fortune on his back, Francis in crimson velvet and cloth of gold, Henry sparkling in a coat covered with pure gold braid studded with pearls and precious stones.

Riding on hand in hand, they stopped to drink a cup of wine together at "a little thicket over a fountain" that marked the boundary between French territory and the English Pale, then went on to meet a vast company of mounted French nobles and guardsmen who escorted them to Boulogne. There they spent the next four days, with Francis entertaining Henry lavishly and, behind the scenes, conferring with him and with his scholars and legal experts. Francis was said to be "in a great passion" because of reports from Rome to the effect that the pope was publicly blaming him for instigating his allies the Turks to invade the emperor's lands. It was not the best time to convince Francis to sponsor the scandalous union of Henry and Anne; even Henry's magnanimous gift of three hundred thousand crowns—a sum equal to that which Francis still owed Henry for his ransom —failed to assuage his anger.[6]

Still the formalities of courtesy between kings had to be observed, and so Francis paid Henry the compliment of watching him joust and admiring his horsemanship, and Henry in return played tennis with the French princes and gambled in the evening with the lords of Francis's court. The two kings exchanged gifts of horses, and Francis received Norfolk and Suffolk as companions of the Order of Saint-Michel. The same courtesies continued when the entire party moved to Calais, only now all was done at Henry's cost. And there was another difference: Anne.

"Madame Anne lives like a queen at Calais," one observer remarked, "and the king accompanies her to mass and everywhere as if she was such."[7] The balls, masquings and banqueting hosted by the English were enough to convince everyone not directly associated with the royal parties that a wedding was indeed imminent. And Francis sent Anne a gift worthy of a bride, a huge diamond worth fifteen thousand crowns. At one supper the two kings dined in a room whose walls were sheets of cloth of gold, their seams hidden by gems. When they had eaten the last of their many courses a troupe of masquers entered. Anne was among them, "with seven ladies in masking apparel, of strange fashion, made of cloth of gold, compassed with crimson tinsel satin," knit with golden laces. With the eight ladies in gold were four others in crimson satin; all were disguised by their masks. Each of the masquers took one of the French lords as her dancing partner, and when in the course of the dancing Henry unmasked the ladies Francis discovered—hardly to his surprise—that his partner was Anne.[8]

"Madame Anne is not one of the handsomest women in the world," wrote a Venetian who saw her in Calais. "She is of middling stature, swarthy complexion, long neck, wide mouth, bosom not much raised, and in fact has nothing but the English king's great appetite, and her eyes, which are black and beautiful, and take great effect on those who served the queen when she was on the throne."[9] The Venetian was almost certainly a hostile witness. Another contemporary thought Anne was more beautiful than Henry's blond, blue-eyed former mistress Bessie Blount, the mother of Henry Fitzroy and among the most stunningly lovely women at the court.

Probably Francis, who was as fond of women as ever, appraised Anne's looks to his heart's content. Then he took her aside and talked with her—quite possibly telling her that, given the unpleasant realities of his diplomatic and military position, he could not lend his sanction to her wedding. Perhaps she already knew this; perhaps, given the decisive shift in Henry and Anne's relationship, it no longer mattered. Before very long he took leave of her, and Henry escorted him back to his lodging.

In a few days the French left for home, but not before Francis had agreed to intervene in the divorce dispute in a way that might persuade Pope Clement to delay punishing Henry and Anne for a while longer. Two French cardinals were sent as envoys to Clement to ask him for a judgment on the case—to be delivered in France. If he would agree to leave Rome, where he was a constant victim of Hapsburg pressure, to render judgment then Henry would agree to accept that judgment, whatever it might be. It would be months before this proposal was made, considered, and either implemented or denied. And a few months was all Anne needed.

For by this time Anne seems to have decided that there was only one way she would ever become queen. Much as Henry desired to marry her, much as he swore, "in great anger, that he would not allow the pope to treat him as he had done, that the pope had no power over him," that "he was resolved to celebrate this marriage in the most solemn manner possible," still he hesitated. The risks were simply too great, and becoming greater month by month. He dared not take the ultimate step. Nature would have to take it for him.

It is possible that Anne had been Henry's mistress for a long time. Stories of her pregnancy, her miscarriages, her immoral life were almost as old as the love affair itself. But whatever the truth of those stories, in the fall of 1532 the two were certainly sleeping together. Then, if not earlier, Henry knew the sweetness of possessing the woman he had yearned so long to possess. And Anne became alert as never before to changes in her moods, her appetites, the workings of her body, watching for the first faint signs that their union had begun to bear fruit.

16

*"The king after his return, married privily the
lady Anne Boleyn, . . . which marriage was kept
so secret, that very few knew it, till she was great
with child, at Easter after."*

Anne may have begun to suspect that she was pregnant
during the Christmas festivities. Or possibly it was not until after
the first of the new year of 1533, as the courtiers were preoccupied with the lucrative giving and receiving of New Year's gifts,
that the menses ceased and she felt the earliest churnings of her
queasy stomach. Whenever it was, the symptoms were undeniable—and overwhelmingly welcome. She was carrying King
Henry's son.

Yet for several months at least no one knew. No one, that is,
but the few family members and friends who gathered, on January 25, "without any one of them having been summoned for
that purpose," to witness the simple, secret wedding of Henry
and Anne. The wedding took place, according to the Spanish
ambassador's informant, in hiding and in haste, a furtive meeting of the bride and groom, the bride's parents, her brother, and
two of her women.[1] Tudor wedding ceremonies were always
brief, but this one may have been limited to the whispered vows
of the bridal couple, followed by a rapidly pronounced blessing
and prayer, then by the swift scattering of the witnesses to other

parts of the palace. If Henry and Anne exchanged rings they did not dare to wear them, nor did Anne dare to give in to her increasing indisposition. Everything had to be as before, save that now the parents-to-be were husband and wife, and their child would be born legitimate.

What was remarkable about the wedding and its aftermath was that the secret held. No one betrayed the fact of the marriage, there was no gossip among the servants that reached the ears of the ambassadors. It was common knowledge that, as one official put it, "there is nothing done or spoken but it is with speed known in the court." Yet for a time, no word of this most momentous event leaked out and in fact among Katherine's supporters exactly the opposite presumption prevailed. Maybe Henry would never marry Anne at all, they were beginning to say. Maybe she would never rise higher than marquess of Pembroke. Maybe—was it really possible?—the king was finally becoming tired of Anne, his "great folly" abating at last.

And if the likelihood of a marriage between Anne and Henry was lessening, then there was no harm, the pope and his advisers reasoned, in issuing the bulls confirming Thomas Cranmer as the new archbishop of Canterbury, even though Cranmer was a client and adherent of the Boleyns and a known supporter of the divorce. Archbishop Warham, who had stubbornly taken Katherine's side, had died, and with his death the way was cleared for the king to appoint a man who would do his bidding. Cranmer was just the man. A committed advocate of Lutheran views— which meant, in the early 1530s in England, no more than that he advocated clerical reform, an end to corruption and to teachings such as the doctrine of purgatory which exploited popular credulity—and an Oxford scholar, Cranmer was also a married priest. Most important, he "did not hesitate to say openly that he is ready to maintain with his life that the king can take the lady for his wife."[2]

The need to keep the wedding secret was tied in with Cranmer's confirmation, for should word of the furtive ceremony reach Rome the pope would refuse to issue the confirming bulls for the new archbishop, knowing what use he would make of his office. Yet the simplicity of the ceremony was appropriate for other reasons too. At forty-one and thirtyish Henry and Anne were hardly young lovers, they were not the sort of bawdy bridal couple to form the focus of days of drunken conviviality. Weddings were customarily raucous parties beginning with "superfluous eating and drinking" early in the morning and ending with the bride and groom in bed together, inviting their friends into their bedchamber for a postcoital drink. In between were hours of processing and recessing, "with a great noise of basins and drums," feasting, and every sort of "vice, excess and misnurture." The guests sang "vicious and naughty ballads" to the bride and groom, played kissing games and amused themselves "lifting up and discovering damsels' clothes." The solemnity of matrimony was completely lost in diverting obscenity, to the dismay of moralists. The sacred bond between husband and wife, one of them lamented, "is nothing regarded but blemished with all manner of lightness." [3]

Then too, Henry may have been a nervous bridegroom eager to say his vows and get the whole thing over. Glad though he undoubtedly was to be marrying Anne—partly to appease her unceasing demands—and legitimizing her child, he may have flinched slightly at the finality of pledging himself, once and for all, to this sharp-tongued woman who knew so well how to upset him. Anne would not be the sort of devoted wife Katherine had been; though tart and argumentative Katherine had remained fiercely loyal to him, while Anne enjoyed threatening him with her displeasure and the implicit withdrawal of her affection.

It was never wise to marry a woman one was in love with, contemporary writers cautioned. "I would not counsel ye to marry her, with whom thou hast been in amours withal," wrote the Spanish humanist Vives, "whom thou flatterest, whom thou didst serve, whom thou callest thy heart, thy life, thy mistress, thy light, thy eyes, with other such words as foolish love doth persuade." Henry had loved Anne with no ordinary love. Married to her, he could expect to be doubly at her mercy. How could a man command his wife with husbandly authority if he had once laid his heart at her feet as her doting slave?

Apart from this, Anne possessed in excessive measure many of the qualities to be avoided in selecting a wife. Never choose a wife who is proud, handbooks of domestic advice warned, or one who wears ornate garments or who talks too much or too harshly. Quiet speech indicates a good disposition, but "silence becometh a woman," and a man ought to make his choice "by his ears rather than his eyes." Anne's pride and expensively elaborate dress were exceeded only by her vituperative, voluble tongue; clearly she had everything against her.

"Women are of two sorts," one preacher remarked, "some of them are wiser, better learned, discreeter, and more constant than a number of men, but another and a worse sort of them, and the most part, are fond, foolish, wanton flibbergibs, tattlers, triflers, wavering, witless, without council, feeble, careless, rash, proud, dainty, nice, talebearers, eavesdroppers, rumor-raisers, evil-tongued, worse-minded," and more.[4] Katherine, Henry would have had to admit, belonged to the first category. He would have the rest of his life to find out whether or not Anne belonged to the second.

Given the prevailing family tensions Anne's hurried wedding may have been fortuitous. Her brother George, who had just returned from the French court, was in good humor as the king had made him a present of a costly horse litter in token of his favor. Her uncle, however, had no use for her and did not hesitate to tell her so. Nonetheless, he was prepared to play up his role as uncle to the queen, and with Boleyn and three others he ordered special, "perfectly impenetrable" armor from Brescia to wear at her coronation jousts. Sparks flew between Anne and her father, who was now a marblehearted elder statesman of fifty-six. For several years he had been trying to dissuade Henry from marrying his daughter, though whether his objections were grounded solely in Anne's personality or in a sensible concern over the international consequences of the marriage as well is uncertain. Whatever his reasons, Anne was irked by them, and by him, and father and daughter bristled in each other's company.

It was an irony of Anne's unique situation that her wedding day, the day her bond with the king was sealed, was also the day her isolation became complete. As queen consort she had no peers, as hated royal mistress she had lost what few allies she had. Most of her relatives were appalled by her, and both dreaded her and looked down on her as a vulgar parvenu.

Yet Anne's enemies, had they possessed sufficient detachment, would have had to admit that she had achieved a remarkable feat of ambition on that day. How many women, they might have asked themselves, could have done what Anne had done, wooing, teasing, conniving her way toward power, now muscling aside her opponents, now gaining ground against them by more devious means. For nearly seven years, ever since Henry became enamored of her and began to imagine her as the mother of his heir, she had withstood every sort of insult and frustration, while doing her best to hold him to her. She had tugged at him, urging him on, shaming him when he faltered. Not that her ambition had been any stronger than his desire, exactly, but where he had roused himself to activity in fits and starts, Anne had been unrelenting. Stubborn, hardheaded persistence, coupled with wary intelligence and her ever elusive allure, had brought Anne to stand at last beside her massive, broad-shouldered bridegroom and recite her vows.

By late March the bulls confirming Cranmer's appointment had arrived, and he was consecrated archbishop of Canterbury. Immediately the king placed his nullity suit in Cranmer's hands, and on May 10 the archbishop convened his court to decide the issue. It was the third time an ecclesiastical court had been convened in England to settle the question of the king's marriage, but where Wolsey's secret legatine court and Campeggio's public one had left the suit unresolved, Cranmer's court came to a swift decision. As it was contrary to divine law, the court decided, and as Pope Julius had erred in thinking he could overcome that impediment by granting a dispensation, the marriage of Henry VIII and Katherine of Aragon was null and void. Following upon the epoch-making act of Parliament forbidding appeals to Rome, the judgment was final according to English law.

Long before this the king had begun to hint broadly to those around him that he had married Anne, and as her heart-shaped face grew rounder and her bosom and abdomen swelled, gossip about her pregnancy flew through the court. (A rumor reaching Venice claimed that Henry and Anne were not only married, but were the parents of a son several months old.) At a feast held in Anne's apartments and attended by several of the principal courtiers Henry was "much occupied with mirth and talk," and directed several of his joking remarks to the duchess of Norfolk —who must have been uncomfortable enough in Anne's presence even before he spoke. "Has not the marchioness got a grand dote and a rich marriage," he teased, indicating the quantities of gold plate displayed around the room, "as all that we see, and the rest of the plate belongs to the lady?"[5]

A preacher was instructed to advise Henry in a sermon (Anne was listening with him) to look to his sins, for he had been guilty of adultery ever since the beginning of his presumed marriage to Katherine. His subjects and counselors, the man went on, ought to urge him to "take another lady," no matter what the pope, who was "against God and reason," might say. "It would be no wonder if he took a wife of humble condition," the preacher concluded, "in consideration of her personal merits." Saul and David in the Bible had done the same thing. The preacher's vehement message scandalized a good many of his hearers, but the king and Anne were pleased.[6]

It remained to move Katherine away from the vicinity of the court—she had been shuttled from one residence to another, but had never been very far away—so that her presence would not offend Anne's burgeoning regality. Norfolk and Suffolk, along with Henry Courtenay, marquess of Exeter and a supporter of Katherine, were sent to inform her that her cause was lost, and that the king had made a new marriage. There was nothing more she could do, they told her, but to yield gracefully and withdraw her appeal to Rome.

She refused to believe that her "most sage and holy" husband could have made a new marriage, she replied. Much as it pained her to disobey her husband, she had no choice; to do otherwise would imperil her soul and disobey the law of God. Far from yielding, she evidently intended to go on regarding herself as queen.

The three royal envoys did not attempt to argue with Katherine. On the contrary, they were almost apologetic, telling her they acted only out of obedience to the king, and taking leave of her with "many gracious words and excuses."[7] Other messengers were more peremptory, informing Katherine that from now on new rules would govern her style of living, which was to be reduced to that of a modest gentlewoman. She would have a small income, but no money to pay her servants' wages. If she was frugal, she would not starve, but there would not be enough to allow her to maintain even the simplest household of attendants. The royal residences would of course be closed to her, since she had no legitimate claim to occupy them any more.

Typically, Katherine had a brave response. Whatever allowance was given her she would be content with, she said. If her servants and attendants had to go, then so be it; she would make do with only two women, her confessor, physician and apothecary. She would take them to live with her wherever Henry ordered her to go, and if her income ran out, then "she would go and beg for the love of God."[8]

Anne was said to hate Katherine more than she had ever hated Wolsey, and to be bent on her destruction. "She will never cease until she has seen the end of the queen," Chapuys wrote, retaining the title now forbidden to Katherine, "as she has done that of the cardinal." Katherine was said to be more concerned for Mary than for herself. Anne had been boasting that she would make Mary wait on her as her maid, which Chapuys interpreted to carry an implied threat that Anne would poison the princess or marry her off to a serving man. Mary was a rival to Anne's unborn child; since Anne's own status would be linked to that child's preeminence in the succession Mary was in a real sense a rival to Anne. Yet Henry treasured his daughter—when he thought about her—and his affection protected her, at least for the time being. Besides, if Anne's child was a boy he would take precedence over Mary, though Mary would still be the focus of any conspiracy that might arise against Anne and her child. Either way, Mary was a living impediment to Anne's security.

Henry had not found a way to announce, directly, that Anne was now queen. But when on Easter eve she appeared "in royal state, loaded with jewels," a mantle of cloth of gold around her shoulders and a suite of sixty waiting maids to attend her on her way to mass, her circumstances spoke for him. She was escorted to and from church with all the solemnities formerly accorded to Katherine, if not more. She was addressed as "queen," not as "marchioness" any longer. (Although Anne was a marquess, a male rank, courtesy seems to have required that the courtiers use the feminine form of the title.) And the preacher offered prayers for "Queen Anne," as he once had for "Queen Katherine."

It had been coming for a long time, this ultimate symbol of the reversal of roles between Anne and Katherine. Anne had been occupying Katherine's apartments, sitting in her place by Henry's side, substituting herself for Katherine as often as possible for years. Yet now that she swept past in her golden mantle, with trumpets blowing a royal fanfare and the personnel of the court forced to bow to her as she passed, just as they had to her predecessor, they were startled in spite of themselves. "All the world is astonished at it," Chapuys wrote, "for it looks like a dream, and even those who take her part know not whether to laugh or cry." Suddenly the phantom queenship had become real.

Uncharacteristically for him, Henry stood by, watching the ceremony with trepidation, wondering how his courtiers would respond. He knew how much they hated Anne, how bitterly they resented having to defer to her. He searched their faces for signs of hostility, and tried to alleviate the tense atmosphere by entreating the men individually to "make their court to the new queen," realizing that he dared not ask it of the women.[9] If they were reluctant to approach her on this occasion, how much more reluctant—possibly rebellious—would they prove to be at her coronation?

For she was to be crowned, publicly and solemnly, in ceremonies planned "to exceed in sumptuousness all previous ones." The coronation would be held as soon as possible, for before too long Anne would enter the final months of her pregnancy and for the child's sake Henry would not want to risk having her jostled and stressed and fatigued then. Preparations were already under way for the crowning and attendant rituals. Letters were being drawn up in the king's name ordering ea_. of the nobles to participate in the festivities, and to provide horses of specific types and colors. Robes for each of them were being ordered from the king's Great Wardrobe, and brought out of storage. Frayed horse cloths were being retrimmed, torn upholstery in the royal litters repaired. Cromwell drew up a list of things to be provided for the queen: robes of velvet lined with satin, a golden cloth of estate and throne, a golden crown. Arrangements were being made for the tourneying that would be held in celebration of Anne's crowning, and this meant more letters of summons, more elaborate matched liveries, more horses. And more expense. Henry was said to be raising loans every day to cover the bills that arrived from his mercers and goldsmiths and silkwomen. To help offset the huge cost he decreed that every man with an annual income of forty pounds or more had to accept the honor of knighthood, with the high expense accompanying it, or else pay a fee. The fees mounted up, though the complaints mounted with them. Few in the kingdom were pleased to subsidize the coronation of the "naughty whore," Nan Bullen.

A particularly large sum was demanded from the Londoners, who grumbled at it, knowing that most of their contribution would subsidize the purse of gold coins traditionally given to the queen as she passed through the city. The contribution had always been made voluntarily; this time, though, the king had to make it mandatory. Anne's efforts to woo the Londoners failed completely; reports of people "murmuring against this coronation" reached the court in increasing numbers. There was no effective way to stop the slanderous talk, the insults and oaths that roared forth whenever Anne's name was mentioned. Yet the king made an effort, ordering all the members of his City companies to refrain from speaking ill of his new marriage and specifically of his bride, and forbidding anyone to mention Katherine's name. Clergy were instructed to teach their congregations to pray "for the king and queen Anne," but not all of them obeyed. One friar who preached at Westminster not only spoke against the marriage, but told the faithful to pray "for the king and queen Katherine, and for the princess." Despairing of any better enforcement of his orders, Henry issued a proclamation offering payment to anyone who denounced a slanderer.[10]

The slanders continued, and as the day of the coronation

approached they broadened into prophecies of disaster. Anne not only was a whore and a harlot, but would be punished as such. There was an old saying, a Warwickshire man told a friend darkly, "that a many should be burned in Smithfield, and he trusted it would be the end of Queen Anne." Signs of doom were all around, people were saying, and had been ever since the king made Anne marquess of Pembroke. Hadn't there been wonders in the earth and in the heavens, prodigies of nature foretelling disaster? And wasn't Anne the danger they warned of? What of the "dead fish of marvellous size," ninety feet long, found stranded on the northern coast just at the time Henry and Anne made their crossing to Calais? And the two other huge fishes caught in the Thames just at the same time, while the tide was flowing unnaturally and the plague was carrying off scores of victims in the capital?

There were stories of an odd wave of suicides in London, of men and women hanging themselves or drowning themselves in the river in greater numbers than ever before, and of unusual lights in the sky. "Toward sunset there fell from the sky, in the southeast, a ball of fire the size of a human head," reported an Italian in London, "which phenomenon, these English consider a prodigy, and draw conclusions thence."[11] Throughout the country prophesiers spread their tales and offered interpretations of ancient folk legends which pointed to Anne as the cause of England's imminent downfall. People remembered that she was said to have marks on her body—the devil's signs—which seemed to confirm the celestial and terrestrial admonitions.

To many people Anne's coronation was more than a venerable ritual of monarchy, it was a symbol of the triumph of evil over good. Katherine, their virtuous and embattled heroine, had been destroyed by Anne, a vice-ridden wench and England's nemesis. Katherine was a saint, Anne a witch. The witch was to be crowned, setting off psychic crosscurrents fearsome to contemplate. "You cannot imagine the fear into which all these people have fallen, great and small," Chapuys reported as the coronation plans went forward, "imagining they are undone."

17

*"After that the king's highness had addressed his
gracious letters to the Mayor and commonalty of
the city, signifying to them that his pleasure was
to solemnize and celebrate the coronation of his
most dear and wellbeloved wife Queen Anne."*

A series of ear-splitting booms shook London, rattling
the frames of old houses and reverberating back and forth across
the city until it seemed as if the world was coming to an end. It
was the sound of the Tower guns and those of the warships
moored at Greenwich, thundering out a welcome to the new
queen as she stepped off her barge at Tower Wharf.

In this, the first of several appearances she was to make before
her coronation, three days off, Anne had ridden upriver in her
barge from Greenwich, accompanied by hundreds of other
brightly decorated craft. The river was full of boats, some carrying painted replicas of the queen's device, a crowned white falcon surrounded by red and white Tudor roses, others with
groups of musicians playing a lively accompaniment to the royal
progress upriver.

Anne stayed for two days in the Tower, then made her coronation procession along Fenchurch and Gracechurch to Lead-
enhall, and thence to Ludgate, Fleet Street and along the Strand
to Westminster. The procession route was as gaudily trimmed
and festive as it had been nearly twenty-five years earlier when

King Henry had ridden to his own coronation as a boy of eighteen. Pageants were erected, according to the king's instructions, which complimented Anne as worthier than the Three Graces, likening her to the biblical Saint Anne, mother of the Virgin Mary, and saluting her nobility, her beauty and—courteously disregarding her swollen belly—her chastity.[1]

No source records Anne's demeanor as she rode along the procession route in her rich litter, whether she made an attempt to smile or nod to the rude, staring populace—among them hundreds who had joined that murderous mob bent on killing her—or whether, pretending not to hear the curses and bawdy insults they shouted at her, she retreated into unseeing hauteur. There were a few shouts of "God save the queen!" but many more of unrepeatable ill wishes for which, had it not been the eve of coronation day, the speakers might have had their tongues cut out or pierced with nails. Few in the crowd took off their caps to show respect, and Anne's fool, "seeing the little honor they showed to her, cried out 'I think you have all scurvy heads, and dare not uncover.' "

It cannot have been easy for Anne, nearly six months pregnant, borne along in a swaying litter down the reeking narrow pathway between the hostile crowds. Marshals rode ahead to divide the people, in order to make way for her, yet she had no real protection; the stench of their unwashed bodies mingled with the common street odors from cookshops and sewers to nauseate her as she passed. The people, she knew, were curious to see for themselves that she was carrying a child—was it really the king's, or the devil's?—and to look at her neck (hidden under a high collar of gold thread and pearls) for a disfigurement they believed she had. She knew they were laughing at her, mocking her and making a joke of the intertwined initials H and A painted and carved into the decorations. Cries of "Ha ha" were mixed with shouts of "Harlot" and "Witch" and reminders of "Good Katherine!" Though Katherine was nowhere in the vicinity, her unseen presence was felt. The German merchants of the Steelyard included in their pageant the arms of Aragon and Castile and the Hapsburg eagle, and placed them, conspicuously, above Anne's white falcon.

The next day was the longest and most exhausting. The ritual of crowning took many hours to complete, as Anne was anointed and invested with her crown, rod and scepter. The ancient liturgy ran majestically on, its oaths and prayers and garbings linking the ennobled commoner Anne Boleyn to England's immemorial royal line. Stiff and punctilious, Anne's enemies took their parts in the ritual, fulfilling the ceremonial functions their rank demanded. Suffolk bore the crown on its embroidered cushion, the dowager duchess of Norfolk carried Anne's train. Her father, his face impassive, escorted her down the aisle of the abbey when the final blessing had been pronounced.

Etiquette and a strong sense of their own dignity prevented them from overt protest against the ceremonies, as did a healthy fear of the king's retaliation. But in private, or rather in the semi-public privacy of the palace, the barbs flew. When Anne appeared wearing a gown with an extra panel of fabric—customary wear for a pregnant woman—her father "told her she ought to take it away, and thank God to find herself in such condition." The two dukes who were present, and several others, heard her answer "that she was in better condition than he would have desired"—a reference to his efforts to prevent her marriage.[2]

At first, queenship seemed to agree with Anne. It was June, the sun shone down on the tiltyard where the king jousted in honor of Anne and on the palace gardens and parks where the courtiers gathered to hunt or dine out of doors. The pleasures of the summer court drove into the background worrisome repercussions of the marriage and the coronation; while the wine flowed and the music played it was easy to forget that the pope had threatened to declare the marriage annulled and to excommunicate Henry.

Anne's apartments in Greenwich were repaired and upgraded in accordance with her new status as queen. Her presence chamber and large bedchamber were newly furnished and provided with hangings and cushions and tables for dining and gaming. She had her throne and canopy, her chapel things and the row upon row of gold plate that, along with her jewels and the lands Henry had given her when she became marquess of Pembroke, constituted her earthly goods. Her apartments became, for a time, almost a court unto themselves, the scene of frequent merrymaking and flirtation. "As for pastime in the queen's chamber," one of the courtiers wrote, "was never more." The ladies who kept Anne company were so preoccupied with "dancing and pastime," he added, that they forgot their absent sweethearts and thought only of the delights of the moment.

In the interval between her wedding and coronation Anne had acquired a fully constituted household, swelling the rolls of her servants until they reached the customary numbers for a queen to possess. Beyond the "great ladies," mature and married, who waited on her there were a number of gentlewomen and waiting maids, the latter young and unmarried. Probably these were among the sixty young women who had escorted Anne to mass at Easter, and no doubt they were among the lively, flirtatious girls who danced away the afternoons and evenings in Anne's first months as queen. A decade earlier Anne had been such a girl herself, a bright-eyed maid of honor in Queen Katherine's household, attracting the attention of Thomas Wyatt and Henry Percy and, in Percy's case, becoming drawn into an intimate liaison that, from the standpoint of political matchmaking, got out of hand.

So it was with the young girls who served her now, tasting the excitement of a court appointment, whispering to one another about the attractions of this or that gentleman, dreaming of a wealthy marriage. The queen's apartments were notorious as a milieu conducive to secret liaisons and pledges of love, sometimes between romantic young people, sometimes between experienced married men and the girls who for the moment attracted them. It was a dangerous atmosphere, and for the first time Anne occupied an uncomfortably constrained position within it, for her very preeminence prevented her from competing with the younger women and her status as a married woman expecting a child made it inappropriate for her to display her customary flamboyance.

Besides, more responsible matters than carefree pastimes had begun to claim her attention. There was her large household to supervise, with its constantly shifting personnel. Each servant wore her livery of blue and purple, with her motto *La Plus Heureuse*—"The Most Happy"—inscribed on it; the names, wages and supply allotments of each of these servants had to be written down and kept up to date, and though there were clerks to do the writing Anne was expected to look over the records and initial them on every page. Her wardrobe demanded attention. The gowns had to be enlarged temporarily, and there were linens to be made up in preparation for her delivery—full smocks with embroidered collars, bedclothes and caps. One list of fabric for her apparel suggests that Anne wore dramatic white and black gowns trimmed with fur and lined with crimson taffeta, the matching "habillaments for her head" made up in white satin.[3] The stark elegance of these gowns must have set off her jewels—which she wore, one observer noted, in great quantities every day.

How much time Anne spent at Henry's side while he conducted business is impossible to estimate, but she was present from time to time when he spoke with ambassadors and councillors. The Venetian envoy Capello greeted her along with the king late in June, and made a note of her answer. "She knew," she told him, "that God had inspired his majesty to marry her, and that he could have found a greater personage than herself, but not one more anxious and ready to demonstrate her love towards the Signory."[4] It was a polite and becomingly modest little speech, surprisingly different in tone from the acerb remarks recorded by others. But then, the Venetian was neither a rival nor an envious relative; he hardly knew Anne.

The bright atmosphere of Anne's early days as queen owed something to the forced departure of Katherine, who was hurried away from Ampthill in Bedfordshire and sent to faraway Buckden in Huntingdonshire, to a crumbling brick manor house many decades old, more a prison than a royal residence. She was kept under strict guard there, and confined to the company of her Spanish ladies in waiting and a few of her most familiar household members. Cut off from news of her daughter, knowing now that neither the pope nor the emperor could dethrone Anne except possibly by fomenting civil war, which her piety found repellent, Katherine was nonetheless in good spirits. She was reported to be cheerful and very much in a mood to heap coals of fire on her enemies' heads by her displays of wifely fidelity. If Anne's servants wore her personal motto "The Most Happy," Katherine's wore new liveries with the initials H and K, for Henry and Katherine.[5]

Support for Katherine was growing, even though Anne now occupied her place and even though Anne's child would soon eclipse Mary. It was not that people expected events to reverse themselves, they knew that Katherine would never be restored to her rights. It was rather that Katherine was becoming a symbol of all that was slipping away: the old faith, with its unquestioned fidelity to the pope in Rome, and the old kingdom, with its beloved young hero-ruler. The long travail of the divorce years had paralleled severe unrest in the church brought to a head by the teachings of Luther and others. And while these teachings had as yet touched the English only lightly, still an unmistakable shift in popular religious sentiment was under way. Nostalgia for the England of ten or twenty years before crystallized around Katherine and her lost cause—and around Mary.

One of the forces feeding this nostalgia and curdling it into opposition to the monarchy was Elizabeth Barton, the "holy maid of Kent."

A visionary whose spiritual gifts revealed themselves when she was a girl of sixteen or seventeen, the holy maid became a nun at the convent of St. Sepulchre's, Canterbury and for years she served as a kind of local oracle, dispensing advice to everyone who asked it. Her fame grew and soon there was a book recording her revelations and the "divine words" God inspired her to speak. People marveled at her ability to predict the future and to see, while in a trance, images of heaven, hell and purgatory and to name the souls she glimpsed there.

But it was the holy maid's divinely inspired views on King Henry and his notorious sweetheart, in the days before Anne became queen, that created the greatest stir. The king had put his soul in jeopardy when he abandoned Katherine, she said, and once he married Anne Boleyn he would put his life in jeopardy as well. His sins made him abominable in God's sight, he was not fit to lead his kingdom. If he married Anne there would be a plague so deadly few would escape it; he himself would be dead within half a year.

The Nun of Kent, as she came to be called, was so influential, and so credible, that King Henry summoned her to court—where she was already well known to a number of prominent men and women—and spoke to her at length more than once, even offering to make her an abbess. She was far from reticent in his presence. In fact she boasted of superhuman powers enabling her to command the wind and waves and to intervene to free souls from purgatory. Henry was highly suggestible and messages from the psychic realm unnerved him. When Elizabeth Barton claimed to have observed devils conversing with Anne and filling her mind with evil, he blanched, knowing that the holy maid and the friars who had begun to publicize her revelations were spreading this story throughout the court and the capital.

It was one thing to tolerate the Nun's slanders against the king's beloved, but when Anne became queen—and the revelations and prophecies took on the character of shrill political threats—Henry had no choice but to silence Elizabeth Barton and those who by this time had begun to exploit her. When she predicted that Henry would be deposed, exiled and sent to hell he had her arrested, along with her accomplices, in July of 1533. Before long she confessed that others had manipulated her, that not all of her revelations had been genuine. Yet in silencing the Nun of Kent Henry had not put a stop to the ground swell of prophesyings and supernatural messages. Clairvoyants appeared at court bearing dire warnings—some of them directed at Anne, some at Henry—and some of those who had formerly been against Katherine and her cause changed their views as a result of visionary dreams.

A letter reached Anne from one William Glover, who signed himself as "dwelling with Sir Henry Wyatt" (Thomas Wyatt's father) and who may have been a servant or employee in his household. For some time, Glover said, he had been receiving messages for Anne but until now he had not chosen to come directly to her with them. The first of these messages had come to him sometime before she was married to Henry.

"A messenger of Christ came to me," Glover wrote, "and commanded me to take a message to you, but I did not believe him."[6] Three nights later the messenger appeared to him again, then a third time three nights after that, this time "in angel form," and Glover agreed to deliver the message, which was that Anne "should have been queen of England ten years past."

Glover took the message to one of Henry's household servants, John Averey, master of the flagons, and left it with him. Then, when Anne became queen, Averey told another member of the household, one Dr. Bruton, about the incident but apparently no one thought either Glover or his divine message important enough to warrant further inquiry.

After Anne's coronation Glover was again visited by a heavenly messenger, who instructed him to inform her that she was pregnant with a girl child "which should be a princess of the land." This, as Glover knew very well, was dangerous and disturbing news, if true. If Anne's child were to be a girl the consequences for the succession would be grave, the international repercussions serious. Even to predict such an undesirable event was hazardous, perhaps treasonous. Yet to withhold God's word was surely worse. Glover went to Dr. Bruton, and told him what had been revealed to him, along with the further revelation that Anne would be delivered of her child at Greenwich.

Bruton put everything in a letter to Anne's chaplain Gwynne, who promptly came, accompanied by her almoner, to see Glover. But for some reason Glover was reluctant to speak of his experiences to the two clerics. Finally, however, the messenger appeared to him yet again and commanded him to either write to Anne or see her in person, threatening that if he did not Christ would "strike." Hence Glover's letter, whose sequel is, unfortunately, unknown.

Anne may never have learned of William Glover's apparitions. Everything upsetting was being kept from her that summer—or nearly everything. The risk of miscarriage had to be avoided at all costs. When bad news came to court the king made certain Anne did not hear of it, taking the extreme precaution of holding meetings of his Council far from the palace, pretending to be going hunting when in fact he was sitting with his advisers. Above all the news from Rome must be kept from her, for the pope, true to his threat, had excommunicated King Henry and declared his marriage to Anne annulled. Her child would be illegitimate in the eyes of Catholic Europe.

Excommunication was more than a spiritual calamity; it carried temporal dangers as well. For five centuries popes had pronounced sentences of excommunication against kings, sentences that were tantamount to deposition. A king who was cut off from the sacraments of the church was, in feudal law, deprived of his rights of lordship. His people no longer owed him obedience. His kingdom could be seized, with the pope's blessing, by another ruler. Should he be looking for a justification to invade, Charles V would have one available now.

But even without any warnings from the spiritual realm, Anne must have worried about the child she carried, and not only about its sex but its health, its survival. So many infants were stillborn, or died soon after birth. Her own mother had lost babies in infancy; her sister Mary had borne Henry a son who was an idiot, and whom Anne "would not suffer to be in the court."[7] Anne's health seems to have been good, and she was, as one who saw her remarked, "likely enough to bear children." Yet so many pregnancies ended tragically that she would be lucky to give birth to a strong and healthy child.

As she entered her eighth month a beautiful bed was moved into her apartments. It was one of Henry's treasures, rarely if ever used. It seemed appropriate that his heir should be born in such a bed, under a satin canopy and surrounded with rich hangings fringed with gold. Regulations for a royal birth drawn up in the previous reign called for a "bed of state," where the queen would lie during her recuperation, in her chamber of presence and for a smaller bed in her privy chamber, where she and her child would be placed immediately after her delivery. There were to be two cradles for the baby as well, one a "great cradle of estate" upholstered in crimson cloth of gold and with an ermine-lined counterpane, the other a carved wooden cradle painted gold.

A final touch was wanted to assert Anne's prerogative. She asked Henry to request from Katherine a "very rich triumphal cloth" which she had brought from Spain and had used to wrap her children in at their baptisms. The cloth, with its reminder of all the babies she had brought into the world only to see them die, was one of the few possessions Katherine had left. The request outraged her, coupled as it was with Anne's remark that very soon she would "be glad to make use of it" to swaddle her child.[8] "It has not pleased God she should be so ill advised as to grant any favor in a case so horrible and abominable," was Katherine's reply. Anne would have to supply her own baptismal finery.

Her time grew nearer. The birth chamber was ready, furnished with braziers for heat and casting bottles for perfuming the air and the array of basins and knives and cruel-looking instruments the physicians and midwives would need. The prognosis was favorable; even the astrologers concurred. Queen Anne would soon give birth to a fine boy. The king decided to christen him either Edward or Henry.

Anne retired to her chamber, as custom required, a month before the birth was expected. She was confined to a darkened room—the August sun and heat were shut out—whose walls and ceiling were draped in thick tapestries. Women came and went in the cloistered darkness, bringing her food and wine, keeping up a tense vigil as they waited for her labor to begin.

Lying here, her flesh heavy and ungainly, Anne burned with humiliation which before long turned to wrath. There was another woman. At least one, possibly others. How could she know how many, shut away as she was and with the court full of women who despised her? Anne was "very jealous of the king, and not without legitimate cause," Chapuys wrote. Other men might look on their wives' pregnancies as an excuse for flirtation, but surely not Henry. Even if her temperament could have allowed her to overlook it, Anne could not have let the incident, or incidents, go by. She was too precariously situated to look the other way while another woman usurped her place.

She confronted him with what she knew, trying to look as formidable as her grotesquely distended belly would permit. Her accusations were harsh, she "made use of certain words which he very much disliked." Ordinarily he would have been disconcerted, at worst stalking off to complain to Norfolk about his hot-tempered niece. This time, however, his reaction was fierce and ugly.

"She must shut her eyes and endure as those who were better than herself had done," Henry told his angry wife. "She ought to know that he could at any time lower her as much as he had raised her."[9]

The quarrel lasted several days. Anne had always been stubborn, and Henry, who until now had always been the one to conciliate and appease, was equally adamant. The courtiers talked in excited whispers about a reconciliation between Henry and Katherine, forgetting that once Anne gave the king an heir Katherine's restoration would be absolutely impossible.

Only a year earlier Henry had remarked deprecatingly that he was forty-one, "at which age the lust of man is not so quick as in lusty youth." He was too old to suffer from "foolish or wanton appetite," he said. He was past his prime. The words mocked Anne now, helpless as she was to prevent his escapades. Where was his "great folly" now, the tenderness he had shown her for so many years, the desire he had always said was for her alone?

The child twisted and kicked in her belly, painfully, unarguably vital and alive. The child would be her vindication, her protection against whatever harm might come from Henry's passing infidelities. No mere mistress could give her husband the heir he needed. Only Anne, now his legal wife and anointed queen of the realm, could do that. Bulky and wretched, she struggled through the last days of her pregnancy in the dim chamber, steeling herself to face the ordeal of her labor and trying not to think of her husband or his wandering heart.

18

*"The vii. day of September being Sunday, be-
tween three and four of the Clock at afternoon,
the Queen was delivered of a fair Lady."*

The pains came, sharp and stabbing, making Anne gasp and then cry out as the midwives tugged at her. She writhed in her wide bed, on the fine lawn sheets, holding her breath and clutching at the cloth underneath her. Hours passed, the pain worsened. The courtiers assembled in the adjoining chamber to wait for the announcement of the birth, talking nervously and nibbling at the wafers and spiced wine provided for them. Mary was among them, pale and blond and exceptionally grave for a girl of seventeen.

As the hours stretched on the talk ranged from the baby's name to the tournaments planned to celebrate his christening to his astrology—he would be a Virgo, given to stern judgment and conscientious in governing, this third Tudor king. No one mentioned aloud the possibility of a female child, or a stillbirth, or the chance—was it a hope?—that Anne might die in childbed.

Then the moment came. There may have been screams from the birth chamber, or Anne may have borne her last pains silently, determined not to give her enemies the satisfaction of hearing her in her agony. The tiny red infant emerged, breathed, cried a weak, newborn's cry. She was alive. But she was female.

The wave of reaction swept through the birth chamber, causing the midwives to shiver with fear and the physicians, imagining the king's anger, to frown and look displeased that nature had not seen fit to conform to their prognoses. Anne, wan and limp from her exertion, her body in the grip of the afterbirth, was told that she had borne a daughter. Her disappointment must have been intense, yet exhaustion soon overcame her and she slept. Someone—it would have had to be someone courageous—was dispatched to inform the king.

A herald appeared in the room where the courtiers waited, made his announcement, and proclaimed the change of succession. The princess of Wales was princess no longer; the queen's daughter now held that title. Mary had expected the announcement, of course, with its insult to her. Probably her poise did not fail her as she listened to the herald. And in any case, she rejected all that he said. In her own eyes she was still princess of Wales, and most of Christendom agreed with her. The surprise of it was that, instead of yielding precedence to a prince, it was to be a princess. A flicker of surprise must have registered in Mary's mild gray eyes to hear that Anne's child was a girl. Her father would be furious. And her mother, once the news was smuggled to her in Huntingdonshire, would laugh out loud and then, when her laughter subsided, say a prayer of thanksgiving.

The laughter of the court was smothered laughter, sensed rather than heard. Yet the hidden smirks and covered smiles were everywhere, heightening the king's annoyance and making Anne feel, as she recovered, not only that she had failed but that she had somehow been cheated or tricked into failure. It had been unfair to expect her to produce a son the first time. A son would have been infinitely preferable, but at least there was an heir now, or rather an heiress, a child with no Hapsburg blood, a child to supplant Mary.

In order to supplant her completely she should have Mary's name. That was the first thought, to name the baby Mary. But by the day of the christening the king had changed his mind: her name would be Elizabeth. It was as Elizabeth that she was christened by Archbishop Cranmer three days after her birth, immersed in the silver font traditionally used for royal infants and attended by an array of notables to bear her canopy and the long train of her purple velvet christening robe. "God of his infinite goodness, send prosperous life and long, to the high and mighty Princess of England Elizabeth!" cried Garter Herald, and five hundred guardsmen and servants with lighted torches escorted the princess from the church to her mother's apartments.

The tournaments that had been planned to welcome the prince of Wales had to be canceled; mortified, the king gave orders for the preparations to cease. Some of Anne's women were quick to try to counteract the presumption that Henry was angry with his queen. Abandon and desert Anne? they had heard him ask rhetorically. Why, he would rather "be reduced to begging alms from door to door," he loved her so much. He loved her more than ever, in fact. But the words rang hollow. Why mention the possibility of abandoning Anne unless it had crossed his mind? For no doubt it had.

Something had soured between the two, that was clear. But how, and why? Had it begun when Henry discovered how profoundly and permanently Anne had alienated the personnel of the court? How after he had elevated her to the rank of marquess of Pembroke none of the titled French ladies would receive her, and how even when she was his wife, and crowned queen, his own subjects refused to bow to the inevitable and accept her? He had gambled on being able to force her into Katherine's place, yet as time passed the hostility toward her hardened instead of melting away as he had hoped. It was as if, perversely, the courtiers enjoyed watching Anne stand precariously at the pinnacle of rank and power; she could go no higher, she would inevitably fall, and they would take malicious pleasure in watching her plummet from her height.

Wherever she was, Anne created drama, with herself at its passionate center. At first Henry had been mesmerized by it, only too glad to take center stage along with her. He was histrionic himself, a natural star performer in the tiltyard, a splendid focal point of court pageantry. But Anne's style of drama was not pageantry but high tragedy, with grand forces pitted mercilessly against one another in relentless struggle. After so many years Henry was beginning to find it wearying, especially since Anne herself had changed from a brilliantly vivacious, sensuous girl into a demanding, shrewish woman.

Once he had needed her, had suffered to be without her. She called forth all his tenderness; she had been his future. Now he often found himself eager to keep his distance from her. She was like a blast of hot air, she made him wince. She was forever goading him, forever bad tempered; she hounded him with her complaints about the German merchants who had insulted her at her coronation, about her spiteful relatives, most of all about Katherine and Mary. It was no wonder he had begun paying court to other women. Husbands had a right to take their pleasure apart from their wives, everyone knew that. Especially when their wives were pregnant. Of course, the wives nearly always complained, but they put up with it. At heart, though, Henry was sentimental, and he must have grieved for the loss of his "great folly," the ecstatic madness Anne had loosed in him and that he had nourished for so long.

Whatever his feelings about Anne, Henry was for the time being committed to the marriage and to its far-reaching results. For months he pressed for an accommodation with Rome (his excommunication had been temporarily delayed), but by early 1534 every tactic had been exhausted. In the first parliamentary session of the new year a series of acts cut England's ecclesiastical establishment loose from the jurisdiction of the papacy and set the king at its head.

The pope, the parliamentary lawmakers asserted, was merely the bishop of Rome; though medieval popes had claimed primacy over all the churches of Christendom, this claim had been false. In actuality the king of England was head of his church just as absolutely as he was ruler of his kingdom. The clergy were under his jurisdiction, answerable to him for their pronouncements and holding their offices by virtue of his appointment. King Henry, the statutes said, now took upon himself the burdens the popes had long ago usurped. He would reform the church, determine its beliefs, and defend it from bondage to Rome.

Without instituting any change in doctrine, the king through Parliament brought about the decisive alterations that separated England from the Roman faith. The priests went on celebrating mass, their parishioners went on receiving the comfort of the sacraments. All that was changed, outwardly, was that fees were no longer paid to Rome and legal cases no longer referred there. To those among the English who had long since viewed the papacy as venal and corrupt the shift in jurisdiction was less a wrenching break with tradition than a welcome reform. They were not, on the whole, aware that any decisive turning point had been reached. Only a few clerics such as Bishop Fisher and percipient laymen such as Thomas More saw the direction in which King Henry was headed. They and others like them would oppose the king, and his changes in the church, to their peril.

With the authority of the pope demolished, Parliament passed the Act of Succession, which declared Mary to be a bastard and named the heirs of Anne Boleyn as King Henry's successors. It also provided for Anne to become regent for her children should Henry predecease her. All subjects were required to swear an oath of loyalty to the new dynasty—an oath which, because it implicitly acknowledged the changes in the church, actually meant denying the pope and accepting King Henry as Supreme Head. In their thousands the people took the oath, with only a few resisting. It was now treasonous to "impugn the king's marriage with Anne Boleyn," though many impugned it privately. People became accustomed to hearing preachers pray for the king as head of the church of England, and then to pray for Queen Anne and her child.

The rhetoric of the new order was becoming familiar, though covert opposition to it did not ebb as familiarity increased. Reports of "slanderous words" against Henry and Anne grew in number. A parish priest was denounced by two of his parishioners for saying "that it was a pity the king was not buried in his swaddling clothes," and that "he hoped to see lady Anne brought full low, and we should have no merry world till we had a new change."[1] Cromwell's informants recorded many incidents of people denouncing Anne and proclaiming their loyalty to

"Queen Katherine," while an increasing number felt pity for Mary and expressed loyalty to her as her father's rightful heir.

It was this that made it imperative that Anne give Henry a son. The baby Elizabeth (the "Little Whore," the people called her, after her mother the "Great Whore") compelled no loyalty. A prince might. And there was still Henry Fitzroy, a vigorous fifteen-year-old. Within weeks of Elizabeth's birth the king had summoned him home from France, where for the previous year he had been staying at the court. Fitzroy was always the fallback candidate, held in reserve in case the unexpected happened and he was needed. Anne meant to be certain that he remained a shadowy, background figure, commanding no popular fidelity and permanently superfluous.

If nothing else, Fitzroy's existence proved that Henry was capable of fathering sons. And indeed by early 1534 Anne was pregnant again, and Henry was looking for her to present him with a boy this time.[2] By April she was said to have "a goodly belly," and there were hopes for a prince.[3]

Anne was made bolder than ever by her expectant state. Mary was her target; she must be subdued, made utterly subordinate to Elizabeth, and to the new little prince who would soon be born.

But Mary was digging in her heels, refusing to accommodate herself to the altered succession in the slightest. Her defiance had begun soon after Elizabeth's birth, when she had been forced to give up her title, her servants and her separate household and join the household of her infant sister. To underscore her inferior position she was told she would have to serve as maid of honor to Elizabeth, call her "princess," and accept the worst quarters in the house for herself. Mary rebelled. She refused to call anyone "princess" but herself, and memorized a formal statement of protest which she repeated whenever anyone addressed her simply as "Lady Mary." She refused to eat at the same table with her half-sister because Elizabeth was given the place of honor; she refused to walk while the baby rode in a velvet litter.

On one level, Mary was a spoiled, disobedient daughter whose pride and obstinacy were unforgivable, especially in an age when parents held godlike authority over their children. Henry punished her disobedience by ordering Norfolk to confiscate what clothing and jewelry remained to her from her days as princess, until she was "nearly destitute of clothes and other necessaries," and told her governess to see to it that Mary deferred to Elizabeth—if necessary, by force. Anne found these tactics inadequate and told the woman (who was Anne's paternal aunt Lady Shelton) to slap Mary and call her the "cursed bastard" she was, and not to allow her to preserve her self-respect by eating in her own room or in other ways avoiding comparisons with her infant sister.

But Mary's quiet, firm noncompliance went far deeper than adolescent rebelliousness or sibling rivalry: it was a question of honor, even of life and death. Chapuys prepared Mary for the worst, telling her that she might without warning be imprisoned, even tortured, to coerce her into acknowledging her illegitimacy. Threats might be used against her, as they had been against Katherine. Her father's agents might kidnap her and compel her, against her will, to enter a convent or to marry a commoner. At one point Lady Shelton told Mary that her father talked of having her beheaded. Katherine was suffering in her isolation, there were rumors that she was gravely ill. Mary was afraid that she might be constrained, as the price of her mother's life, to abandon her rights and acknowledge Elizabeth as princess of Wales.

As Anne's pregnancy advanced, Mary's recalcitrance seemed to increase. She was turning out to be a more stubborn adversary than Katherine, for she had more at stake. It was not only that she was fighting to preserve her right to the throne, to preserve her future. Her behavior was regally defiant. She was showing, by her unwavering, consistent opposition to her downgrading in rank, that she deserved to rule. To do otherwise would mean losing her faith in what sustained her and gave her strength— her Catholicism, and her belief that God was protecting her so that she might fulfill a particular destiny.

It was this sense of her destiny that made Mary so adamant, and that, paradoxically, brought her close to her mortal enemy Anne. For Anne too was coming to believe that she was drawn on by destiny toward an end whose shape was as yet unclear. "God had inspired his majesty to marry her," Anne had told the Venetian ambassador. And if so, God must have intended her to give birth to a son, yet she had borne a daughter instead. If God had wanted her marriage, why had he allowed it to be postponed for years, and tainted, once it was finally accomplished, by excommunication and threats of international reprisals? And tainted, too, by adultery: the king was unfaithful, and brutal toward her when she objected. If destiny ruled her, it was beginning to seem more dark than light, more doom-laden than victorious.

Prophecies foretold that a queen of England was to be burned, Anne said again and again. She wanted to make certain that queen was Katherine, "to avoid the lot falling upon herself." Anne swore she "would not cease until she has got rid of her," and her threats against Mary were equally murderous.[4]

"I am her death and she is mine," Anne said of Mary. Whether or not Elizabeth, or any other child Anne bore, inherited the throne would depend on how successful Anne was in removing Mary from the scene, either by breaking her will or thrusting her aside by violence. And since Anne's survival could no longer by guaranteed by Henry's love for her, it had to depend on her child's preeminence in the succession. It was in this sense that Anne's simple, fateful statement was true. Anne and Mary faced each other across the battle zone of Henry's capricious will. Theirs would be a struggle to the death.

In February of 1534 Chapuys's informants were certain that Anne intended to poison Mary. An odd incident at court suggested this. Nicholas Hawkins, Henry's ambassador in Spain, died suddenly and Anne, surprisingly, was more affected by the news of his death than Henry was. "The lady Anne showed more grief at the death of the ambassador than the king himself," Chapuys learned, "and wept bitterly, saying that an apothecary must have given him some medicine which caused his death, implying that he had been poisoned."[5] Apothecaries, poison, and death were on Anne's mind; why else would she presume that Hawkins's death was other than natural? The ambassador, according to word reaching the English court, was on a journey when he collapsed in a village and died. Unless, as is possible, Anne knew something more than this, her presumption seems strange.

Only the day before Henry Percy, earl of Northumberland and Anne's former love, had confided to another courtier "that he knew for certain that Anne had been thinking of having the princess poisoned." "And I must observe," Chapuys added, "that the earl must know something about it, owing to his intimacy and credit with the said Anne."[6]

To judge from Chapuys' accounts—which, it must be remembered, were thoroughly hostile to Anne—her behavior toward Mary was devious and treacherous. Finding that Lady Shelton was unable to curb Mary's obstinacy, Anne wanted to bring her to court, to become her train-bearer and submit to various other humiliations. But thinking that Mary's undeniable beauty and goodness might soften Henry's heart toward her, Anne reconsidered, deciding that a better course would be to leave Mary buried in the country with Elizabeth, making certain that Henry saw her as infrequently as possible. On at least one occasion Anne went so far as to exchange messages with Mary herself.

While at Hatfield visiting Elizabeth, Anne sent Mary a message, asking her to pay Anne a visit and to honor her as queen. If she agreed to this one compromise, Anne's message said, she would be "as well received as she could wish," and the gesture would result in her regaining her father's "good pleasure and favor." She could count on being treated "as well or perhaps better than she had ever been," Anne assured Mary. And all Anne asked was a little courteous deference to her position as queen.

Mary's reply was curt and insulting. She "knew not of any other queen in England than madam, her mother," she said. However, should Anne, whom she called "the king's mistress," be willing to intercede with her father on her behalf, she would be most grateful.

Controlling her anger, Anne tried once more. She urged Mary to reconsider, and to come to court. If only she would show Anne a measure of respect she would gain so much, and at so little cost to herself. But Mary was stubborn, and in the end Anne threatened her. When even this failed Anne "returned home highly disappointed and indignant, fully determined to put down that proud Spanish blood, as she called it, and do her worst."[7] Anne's worst was very dangerous indeed, as Chapuys warned Mary, but she would increase her danger tenfold if she followed Anne's suggestion and went to live at court. Once there she might well arouse Anne's suspicion and jealousy, which were very lively just then. Anne might seem friendly, yet disguised as friendship, her enmity might be deadlier than ever. Fearing a reconciliation between father and daughter, she might indeed try to have Mary killed. [8]

Along with Anne's pregnancy, another fortuitous event was in the offing in the spring of 1534. Another meeting between Henry and Francis had been proposed, and Henry was reported to be "very desirous of it, and in wonderful haste to go." He wanted Anne to be present as well, pregnant or not; in fact he was pretending that Anne was the moving spirit behind the meeting. She may have been, but even without her there were pressing reasons for the two kings to confer.

Since their talks in Calais a year and a half earlier a good deal had changed, and the interests of France and England no longer overlapped as well as they once had.

Henry, relying on French aid to back him up in an emergency (Francis had promised to put a fleet of ships and fifteen thousand fighting men at Henry's disposal should the emperor invade England), had acted boldly. He had married Anne, become father to her child, altered the succession and canceled papal authority in his realm. His alienation from the Roman church was complete.

At the same time that Henry had been moving away from the pope, however, Francis had been moving closer toward him, hoping to persuade him to ally with the French and with other Italian powers in a league against Emperor Charles. A conspicuous sign of the Franco-papal amity was the marriage of Francis' second son Henry, duke of Orleans, to the pope's niece Catherine de' Medici. Francis hoped to remain allied with England while advancing his ties to Rome; Henry was making this difficult. And while Francis sent a reassuring message that, however wide the breach between England and Rome, he would still stand by Henry with arms and men in the event of an invasion, nonetheless the assurance seemed disingenuous. And besides, Henry had hoped to persuade Francis to break with the Roman church just as he had, on jurisdictional rather than theological grounds. Henry badly needed allies, and was currently attempting to make new ones among the Lutheran cities of Germany. These efforts, and Francis' long-range plans, needed to be talked out if England and France were not to diverge past the point of reunion.

Anne, her "goodly belly" growing, was clearly in no condition to undertake a Channel crossing. The prince must not be endangered. But Henry could go alone, leaving her as temporary regent in his absence.

"I am informed by a person of good faith," Chapuys wrote in June, "that the king's concubine had said more than once, and with great assurance, that when the king has crossed the sea, and she remains *gouvernante*, as she will be, she will use her authority and put the said princess to death, either by hunger or otherwise."[9]

Anne's brother tried to caution her against bloodshed, telling her how furious Henry would be if any harm came to Mary (and wouldn't she be glad to wound him, as he wounded her by his infidelities?) and warning her against her own rashness. But he only succeeded in arousing her bravado. She didn't care, she told him, not even "if she were burned alive for it after."

19

*"O wavering and newfangled multitude! Is it
not a wonder to consider the inconstant muta-
bility of this uncertain world!"*[1]

Anne's baby would be born before long, most likely late
in the summer. Once again the birth chamber was prepared,
midwives and physicians engaged, linens sewn for mother and
child. The princely cradle was brought out of storage, along with
the christening mantle and the hangings for the great royal bed.
Cromwell busied himself with drawing up lists of procedures and
necessities "for the queen's laying down," and all the implements
and furnishings used when Princess Elizabeth was born were
reassembled in the queen's apartments.

All this went on, yet the surviving records of the court are
oddly silent about it. It was as if, having occasioned high hopes
and, ultimately, deep disappointment once before, Anne could
not be trusted to perform satisfactorily this time. There was an
air of tentativeness about her pregnancy, or at least about the
reporting of it, and an air of indifference in the way she and her
unborn child were treated by the king.[1]

This time Henry seems to have made no attempt to protect
Anne from shocks or disturbing news. Whereas in the previous
summer he had gone out of his way to adjust his itinerary for

her benefit, now he went where he liked, when he liked, occasionally staying where Anne did but more often lodging at a variety of country houses while Anne remained behind. How he occupied himself when he was not hunting she could not know for sure. Possibly he was keeping company with the beautiful young woman who had made her so jealous the year before, or with a new mistress, or even—so the gossip went—with girls he kept in a private brothel.[2]

Stories about the king's lechery were probably as exaggerated as they were widespread, but they cannot have made Anne easy in mind about him. He was amorous, people said. He was inordinately fond of women, always eying them and remarking on their attractions. He liked a salacious tease: he once told his bawdiest courtier, Francis Bryan, to whisper suggestively to Mary while dancing with her, and enjoyed watching Mary blush and stammer out a genteel but embarrassed reply. When Wolsey was alive there had been rumors that the cardinal pimped for the king; now the story went that Henry kept maidens "over his chamber," who satisfied his desires. And when he tired of these maidens, and of the women of the court, he kidnapped nubile strangers.

That was the tale, at least, of a man who had sworn vengeance on the king for abducting his "pretty wench." The man and his girl were out riding in the countryside near Eltham, where Henry often stayed during the summer season. Suddenly they met the king, who rode up to the girl, "plucked down her muffler and kissed her, and liked her so well that he took her from him."[3] There was nothing the angry lover could do but complain, and tell the outrageous story to everyone he met. Yet even so, all Henry had done was to exercise his *droit du seigneur*, a custom which, however it may have clashed with his protestations of virtue and chivalry, was clearly his to claim. And the girl had stayed with the king.

One such story led to another, and merged plausibly with the image many of his subjects had of Henry as a voluptuary who had put away his good wife in order to enjoy his brazen concubine. He did little but "enjoy and use his foul pleasures," many of them believed. "If thou wilt deeply look upon his life," said one clerical critic, "thou shalt find it more foul and more stinking than a sow, wallowing and defiling herself in any filthy place. For how great soever he is, he is fully given to his foul pleasure of the flesh and other voluptuousness."[4] No woman was safe from him, gossip said; the old story of how he had seduced not only Mary and Anne Boleyn but their mother Elizabeth was now revived and retold.

All this was in itself worrisome to Anne, yet she was aware of a larger worry. For the loosing of Henry's concupiscence was a symptom of a broader malaise. "Inwardly," Chapuys wrote about him in April of 1534, "his spirit is not at rest."[5] Once again, as in the mid-1520s, shadows were lengthening over Henry's life, darkness was closing in. There was his unhappy marriage to contend with. Life with Anne was hellish, she gave him no peace, and scolded him mercilessly when he tried to find it with other women. She might or might not give him the son he needed; he no longer counted on it. And whose fault would it be if she did not? Hers, or the fault of a cruel fate that he seemed destined never to escape? Or was it his own fault? In his blackest hours he may have thought so. "Am I not a man as other men are?" he demanded of Chapuys when the latter pressed him about the likelihood of Anne's bearing a son.[6] "Am I not a man as other men are? Am I not a man as other men are?" He hammered the ambassador with the question three times, revealing, by his bullying, the extent of his insecurity.

The shadows were lengthening, he was slipping back into the pathless confusion that had assailed him a decade earlier. He was losing that sense of rightness, of divinely guided congruence, that had once buoyed him out of his depression and that had kept his will firm as he fought to gain his freedom from Katherine and, ultimately, from the pope. That certainty had always been somewhat brittle; the more loudly he asserted his own rightness the less convincing he was. The birth of Anne's daughter had shaken his confidence, and as his marriage deteriorated his self-doubt deepened, revealing that his conviction had shallow roots indeed. He lacked patience; instead of waiting, giving Anne a second chance and enduring the thankless interim he rushed ahead to involve himself with other women, embittering the already cankered marriage past the point of redemption. His recklessness, his heedless self-indulgence told her how little she mattered to him. She no longer had his heart or moved his will.

Having lost these, she had little else left to her, beyond the redheaded infant daughter she saw once in a while and the women and men who, on a daily basis, served her and kept her company. Of these women, few names have come down to us. Beyond Anne's mother and sister (who was at court until the fall of 1534), there were her sister-in-law Jane, George Boleyn's wife; her cousin Mary Howard, Norfolk's daughter, who had married Henry Fitzroy in 1533; Margaret Lee, Thomas Wyatt's sister, who was said to be Anne's closest intimate, and such hostile female relatives as the duchess of Norfolk. There were others, such as Lady Worcester, Lady Wingfield and Nan Cobham, who would figure prominently in Anne's later history.

Lady Wingfield held a grudge, probably because Anne had lashed out at her in some way in the past. She had been allied to Suffolk's faction, and that in itself would have made her Anne's enemy, but very likely there were personal grounds for bad feeling as well. "Madam, though at all times I have not showed the love that I bear you as much as it was indeed," Anne wrote in a conciliatory letter to Lady Wingfield not long before she became queen, "yet now I trust that you shall well prove that I loved you a great deal more than I made feign for; and assuredly, next mine own mother, I know no woman alive that I love better. And at length, with God's grace, you shall prove that it is unfeigned." What occasioned this letter is unknown, but Lady Wingfield was not mollified by it, and wanted her revenge.

In the company of these women Anne carried on her ordinary existence, to some extent a prisoner of her condition as she waited for her child to be born. For amusement she played cards with them, gambling away the gaming money the king allotted to her, or she watched them dance while her musicians played. Anne was a musician herself—one poem saluted her as a second Orpheus, a better harp player than King David, playing so sweetly that she charmed the lions and wolves—but whether she continued to perform as queen we don't know. Most of her women were illiterate, but those who could read read to Anne, probably from the popular romances with their tales of lovers sundered and reunited, heroic knights, giants and fairies and dragons. No doubt there were many idle hours, with little to fill them but gossip and intrigue, the gossipers fortified by trays of marzipan and comfits and goblets of sugared wine.

The women talked of clothes, of the current fashion in kirtles, cut "large and long with double placards," of the scarcity and great expense of cloth of silver "because none but great personages wear it." Anne had her tailor John Skowtte make her fur-edged damask or velvet gowns lined with black satin, in her preferred colors of russet and carnation and deep orange. With them she wore sparkling headdresses, trimmed with matched pearls or with the diamonds the king had given her in years past. Once Henry had paid attention to her dress and adornments, even supervising the choice of embroidery patterns to be used on her gowns and hoods. Now she had only her women and the men who sometimes kept her company to admire her, and she could not trust any of their flattery to be sincere.

Flattery, vanity, the dread of aging and of lost beauty. To what extent Anne fought the signs of age and strain we don't know, but other women underwent hours of prolonged, often torturous treatment to arrest wrinkling and freshen sallow skin. They bleached their complexions with lemon juice and whitened them with sulphur borax or "dead fire," sublimate of mercury. Because of its "malignant and biting nature," dead fire ate away at wrinkles and lines and scars, yet it did its mortifying work without causing the woman unbearable pain. It was widely used, even though the penalties of overuse were grotesque. "Such women as use it about their face," a contemporary wrote, "have always black teeth, standing far out of their gums like a Spanish mule, an offensive breath, with a face half scorched, and an unclean complexion."[7]

To soothe their tormented flesh they then applied oil and fat to the skin, and added buttermilk or wine to their bathwater, cleansing their faces with rosewater or cherrywater or applying a mask made of egg whites to tighten away wrinkles. This done, they painted themselves with cosmetics. First came a layer of white lead, or ceruse, mixed with vinegar and applied to the face, neck and breasts. Then alum was spread over the cheeks, turning them a raging pink, and the lips were reddened with crystalline mercuric sulphide or cochineal, a dye made from alum, gum arabic and crushed insects. The ceruse dried and withered the complexion, and the alum—which, in its pure form, was so corrosive it was used to dissolve metals—"burned, shrivelled and parched" it.

Presumably the overall improvement was thought to be worth the long-term damage. Yet in women past their first youth the deteriorating effect of the chemicals must have made them more macabre than alluring. Their complexions were permanently tinted yellow or green or red, their teeth were rotten, they looked far older than their years, their faces wrinkled "like an ape" and their nerves so affected by the dead fire that they trembled as if palsied. "The tender skin will rivell the more soon," Vives warned, "and all the favor of the face waxeth old and the breath stinketh, and the teeth rusten, and an evil air all the body over, both by reason of the ceruse and quicksilver." Time might consume beauty, but the devouring chemicals consumed it faster, and turned even attractive women into pathetic relics of their youth.

The summer days passed, but without the usual summer diversions. Anne could not hunt this season, her greyhounds were idle and her Irish hobbies grew fat in the stables. She had her little lapdogs, however. One of her gentlewomen wrote that Anne "set much store by a pretty dog," preferring males to bitches and becoming extremely attached to them. Early in 1534 Francis Bryan received a dog as a gift, "which the queen liked so well that she took it from him before it had been an hour in his hands." A favorite was "little Purkoy," which delighted her so that "after he was dead of a fall there durst nobody tell her grace of it, till it pleased the king's highness to tell her grace of it."[8] Purkoy was mourned, but the marmosets and ring-tailed monkeys sent as pets to the women of the court from the New World she found repellent. "The queen loveth no such beasts nor can scant abide the sight of them," wrote John Hussey, a serving man familiar with the life of the queen's apartments. Anne did enjoy "a pleasant singing bird," a linnet, that hung in a cage in her chamber, though, and told Hussey that she "liked it very well."

Anne presided over a large complement of household officers, from her lord chamberlain Lord Borough and vice chamberlain Edward Baynton to her mistress of the maidens Mrs. Marshall to her surveyor John Smith. Yet her circle of familiars seems to have been extremely narrow; her fool, her few women friends, her rakish cousin Francis Bryan, and Francis Weston, the athletic privy chamber gentleman who played cards with her and often came away the winner.

Her brother George, whom the king had often sent as his envoy to the European courts in recent years, was made lord warden of the Cinque Ports in June of 1534. Wyatt wrote of him that his arrogance outshone his cleverness; evidently he was no more loved than his sister Anne. A letter he wrote to a diplomatic colleague in 1530 reveals little about him except that he could not write either Latin or Italian well and that he found his endless journeying somewhat tedious and looked forward to returning home "to pass time as others of my friends doth." He was a member of the king's circle of intimates, but of his closeness to Anne—or to his elder sister Mary—there is scant trace.

Mary Boleyn Carey moved briefly into the limelight once again in the summer of 1534. Her life as a widow had not been easy. After William Carey's death in 1528 she had found herself all but destitute. Deprived of her late husband's income, she had been reduced in her "extreme necessity" to pawning her jewels, and her unloving father was reluctant to provide for her.[9] Anne was mildly dutiful toward Mary, but hardly warm. Then it was discovered that Mary had disgraced herself; she was pregnant. Anne was furious, and Henry no less so. Mary was ordered to leave court at once, and she obeyed.

But once she was safely away, she wrote to Cromwell, explaining her situation and asking him to mediate between her and her royal sister and brother-in-law.[10] The truth was, she wrote, that she had secretly married a soldier serving in Calais, William Stafford, three months earlier. The child she expected was his. The secrecy of their marriage displeased the king and queen even more than her choice of bridegroom, she acknowledged; the indiscretion of her pregnancy was the crowning blow.

"But one thing, good master Secretary, consider," Mary wrote, "that he was young, and love overcame reason. And for my part I saw so much honesty in him, that I loved him as well as he did me; and was in bondage, and glad I was to be at liberty. So that for my part I saw that all the world did set so little by me, and he so much, that I thought I could take no better way but to take him and forsake all other ways, and to live a poor honest life with him."

They and their child could live that poor honest life, Mary felt sure, if only Anne were not so severe in turning her back on them. They had no one to turn to, for Anne and Henry were implacable, Thomas and Elizabeth Boleyn refused to hear them, and Norfolk and George Boleyn were hardhearted ("I dare not write to them," she said, "they are so cruel against us"). Cromwell was her only hope.

"And seeing there is no remedy, for God's sake help us," she pleaded, "for we have been now a quarter of a year married, I thank God, and too late now to call that again." And besides, there was the child to think of. She urged the secretary to appeal to Henry to allow Stafford to come before him, "that he may do his duty as all other gentlemen do," and to convince Henry to melt Anne's resistance. Their case could not be more piteous, she wrote, yet her happiness shone through her words, the happiness of a woman who believes she has found a good man.

"For well I might have had a greater man of birth and a higher, but I ensure you I could never have had one that should have loved me so well nor a more honest man." If she had it to do over again, and had free choice, she would marry him all over again, despite the trouble they found themselves in. "I had rather beg my bread with him," she concluded staunchly, "than to be the greatest queen christened."

Poor as she was, and disowned by her family, Mary's story had come to a happy ending. It was for this, quite possibly, that Anne could not forgive her.

It was time, and more than time, for Anne to "take her chamber," to enter that period of absolute seclusion which had to precede the birth of her child. But August came and went and the formality did not take place. Then it was September, the days were growing shorter and the fields were golden. Her term had run. If she had a miscarriage, it went unreported. With no official explanation, the expectation of a birth dissolved, there simply came a day when Anne's "goodly belly" was no longer in evidence. Henry had experienced such things before; Katherine had had false pregnancies early in their marriage, unexplained swellings and deflatings that left her physicians baffled. Perhaps Anne's symptoms were of a similar kind, or perhaps there was in fact a miscarriage, undergone in the greatest secrecy and kept even from the alert ears of the ambassadors' spies.

Either way she had failed, and to punish her for her failure Henry returned to his sweetheart, the "very beautiful damsel of the court"—possibly one of Anne's own maids of honor—whose name has not come down to us but whose influence with the king increased as Anne's waned. She was more than a passing infatuation; she had been his favorite for some months at least. Who she was, whether she was fair or dark, girlish or mature, dazzling like Anne herself or shyly seductive is impossible to say. (The "very beautiful damsel" may have been Jane Seymour, though there is no particular reason to think so.)

The infatuation was quite public, everyone witnessed it. It was also pointedly political. The young woman was allied with that vast majority of the courtiers who opposed the Boleyns, and who preferred Mary to Elizabeth as heir to the throne. Alignments shifted, the scales of influence tipped further against Anne and her child.

Anne fought back, trying to drive the woman away from court, but the king prevented it, telling Anne "that she had good reason to be content with what he had done for her, which he would not do now if the thing were to begin, and that she should consider from what she had come, and several other things."[11]

It was a great deal to bear: her all-powerful husband's ugly words, the presence of his other love, inescapable and nerve-rending, Anne's depression over her unsuccessful pregnancy, and the physical strain it had caused her, the repeated blows to her pride. She had to bear up under it all—or lose all. She had somehow to find the strength to battle on, to regain whatever margin of her husband's lust was required for her to conceive again. Fertile, she had hope; barren, none was left to her.

It would take all her strength, yet that fall her strength began to seep away. Slowly Anne began to lose the keen edge of her audacity, her aggression blunted. Always in the past she had thrown herself into conflict, now she hesitated. A part of her shrank back. Her dark eyes had always been both wary and intelligent, now they were apprehensive.

The king was firmly in control, Anne had lost her leverage. At times she followed him around, as one of her critics said, "like a dog its master."

20

*"Is it not a world to consider the desire of wilful
princes when they fully be bent and inclined to
fulfill their voluptuous appetites, against the
which no reasonable persuasions will suffice; little or nothing weighing or regarding the dangerous sequels that doth ensue as well to themselves
as to their realm and subjects? And above all
things there is no one thing that causeth them to
be more wilful than carnal desire and voluptuous
affection of foolish love."*

The wind was shifting. The courtiers, ever alert, sensed it
and began to trim their sails. The king was no longer satisfied
with his wife, the ugly quarrels that erupted between them were
not lovers' quarrels but outbursts of pure enmity. They were like
wild animals, caged together by a cruel keeper; they longed to be
free. Anne never could be, there was no way out for her. But
Henry, who had rammed his way clear of a constricting marriage
once before, would extricate himself from this one as well. It
was only a matter of time.

There was a change in the wind, but the new direction was
not yet clear. Would the young woman Henry pursued now be
the permanent focus of his attention—and therefore of influence and patronage? Or would she be merely the first of several?
Opportunity loomed: could the king's amorous fancy be guided,
as it had been guided before, in a particular direction?

For now the courtiers rushed to make themselves useful in
promoting the new love, emboldening the king to deceive and
defy his queen and disassociating themselves as rapidly and completely as practicable from the Boleyns. Overnight the favored

young woman became the eager center of attention, while Anne was all but deserted ("which abated a good deal of her pride and arrogance," it was said). Even Mary took heart when she received a message from the new favorite, "telling her to be of good cheer, and that her troubles would sooner come to an end than she supposed, and that when the opportunity occurred she would show herself her true and devoted servant."[1]

Anne wanted the girl out of court, out of sight, and thought of a way to get rid of her. In this she found an ally in Jane, Lady Rochford, her sister-in-law. But the plan backfired; instead of Henry's sweetheart it was Lady Rochford herself who was banished from the court. The new love continued, and with it Mary's resurgence. The favorite was "quite devoted" to Mary, and was said to be "busying herself in her behalf," so that by late October of 1534 the former princess was receiving visits from nearly all the prominent courtiers, to Anne's "great annoyance." Not long before Mary had been in fear of her life; now, amazingly, she was catered to, even privileged. When Chapuys saw her he was surprised at how her gaunt sickliness had given way to round-faced good spirits. Like her father, Mary defied Anne. When Anne came to visit Elizabeth—whose household Mary still shared—she wanted to see Mary as well, but Mary refused. There was no exchange of threats or guarded courtesies between the two women this time. Mary simply had her way.

It was as the locus of power at court was shifting that word arrived from Rome that Pope Clement was dead. A year or two earlier the announcement might have made Anne gloat with satisfaction. Now, coming as it did as she was struggling to hold her own, her pleasure in hearing it was undercut by the knowledge that Clement, before he died, had no doubt gloated over what his agents told him about her. Cromwell, who made no effort to restrain his delight that, as he put it, "this great devil was dead," could afford to indulge in noisy jubilation. Anne could not.

The vast clandestine realignment was under way, the dissolving and sealing of alliances, the whispered speculations, the bargains made and broken. Anne had watched it happen twice before, on a grand scale: first when a coalition had taken shape around her, to dethrone Katherine, and later when another had dethroned Wolsey from his high place. New webs of alliance were being spun now, secured where possible by personal ties and linked to a slowly emerging political axis. It was chilling, this dispersing and congealing of human greed. And it was made even worse by the entanglements of blood ties, so that to political treachery was added the sharp sting of family treachery, family conspiracy. Norfolk, jugular in his instincts and full of ugly spite toward the Boleyns, stood to benefit from their fall from grace, and gathered new allies around him. The Boleyns were far from being his only in-laws; he had a host of others, among them several girls as attractive as Anne had been a decade earlier. He could use one of them as he had used Anne, now that she was becoming expendable.

Relations with the French in the fall and winter of 1534–35 revealed just how expendable she was. Toward the end of November Francis sent an envoy to England, Philippe Chabot de Brion, admiral of France. He was a familiar figure to Anne, who remembered him from her girlhood at Francis' court and who had renewed her acquaintance with him at Calais two years before. But personal familiarity counted for nothing, she found, where diplomatic interests clashed. Chabot brought a painful message, which was that, although Francis was prepared to stand with Henry in his assertion that his marriage to Katherine had been invalid, he was not prepared to accept the alteration in the succession. In fact, he wanted to revive an old agreement calling for the betrothal of his son the dauphin to Mary.

Mary again! She was eighteen, quite lovely in her fragile blond way, despite her chronic illness. She was unarguably marriageable, while Anne's baby would not be for many years. But Mary remained stubbornly faithful to Rome, refusing to acknowledge the Act of Supremacy which, earlier in the month, had officially made Henry Supreme Head of the church in England. And she was legally barred from the succession, legally declared illegitimate. The fact that, despite all her handicaps and ineligibilities, Francis still found it prudent to choose her over Elizabeth as the more likely to inherit the throne was unnerving; what did he know, or sense, of Anne's future and Elizabeth's?

The French envoy's behavior toward Anne was equally dis-
quieting. He ignored her. He did not bring her a gift, or convey
greetings from Francis, or even greet her himself. The neglect
was highly significant, and Henry, whose own honor it touched,
finally asked Chabot whether he would like to pay his respects to
the queen. "As you please," he answered, and proceeded to
insult her more by his perfunctory courtesies than he had done
by his neglect. Henry had been warned by one of his agents in
France that the French theologians and legists held the view
that Mary was legitimate; beyond this there was the unspoken
but inescapable stigma of notoriety and scandal that clung to
Elizabeth through her mother. To these influences were added
several others impelling Francis to dissociate himself from Elizabeth and Anne. Just at this time he was being wooed by his
inveterate enemy Emperor Charles, who naturally preferred to
see the French prince wed Mary. And the new pope, Clement's
successor Paul III, was doing his best to lure Francis away from
the English and their ecclesiastical rebellion.

All the same, it was aggravating to Anne that Chabot and his
entourage were lavishly entertained by Henry Fitzroy and his
wife—Norfolk's daughter—as well as by Norfolk himself. Always
before, Anne had entertained the Frenchmen, priding herself
on her fluency in their language and her ability to charm and
entertain them in their own style. This time no opportunity was
offered her. And to increase her humiliation, her husband
brought a number of handsome young women to court to orna-
ment the entertainment. His favorite was there, her youth and
beauty a reproach to Anne. He flirted with her one night in full
view of Anne, making the latter react, loudly and conspicuously,
with a prolonged outburst of bitter laughter. She must have
drawn a good deal of attention; Chabot, who was seated beside
her, was embarrassed by it, and by her.

"Do you mock me, madam?" he asked indignantly.

Anne was convulsed with laughter, she could not answer him
at first. When her laughter subsided, she explained. Her explanation was brash. Her husband had gone in search of one of the
Frenchmen, then had encountered his sweetheart, who had
made him forget the Frenchman and everything else! It took

toughness to make the painful truth sound like a wry joke. The envoy was taken aback by Anne's boldness, and reported the incident in full to his master in France.

Although Henry and Anne celebrated Christmas lavishly that year the celebrations were marred by the tensions with the French. Henry continued to talk with confidence of a meeting with Francis in the coming months, announcing it to the court and saying he "considered it certain." But in fact he had little ground for confidence, and Anne even less. For Anne, Christmas brought confrontations with her husband and her vengeful uncle.

She clashed with Henry over his favorite, telling him that the girl "did not do either in word or deed the reverence she expected." She touched a nerve, as usual, and he became very angry. She was always complaining. Nothing ever pleased her, she kept at him day and night. His anger triggered other thoughts about Anne. How could he rid himself of her? And how soon? He had been discussing it with some of his councillors. There was no question that her involvement with Percy—now the earl of Northumberland—would allow him to secure an annulment. He had always known that. The obstacle was Katherine; while Katherine still lived, Henry could not set Anne aside without taking her back. Yet as long as Anne remained queen England's diplomatic situation was bound to worsen, or so it appeared. If France deserted England, as seemed more than likely, Anne would be a very dangerous liability. And in the meantime she brought him no joy as a wife, barren of sons, lacking the quiet decorum suitable to a queen. He countered her complaints about his sweetheart with harsh complaints of his own, turning his massive back on her and shouting about how she never gave him any peace.

Exchanges such as this only made Anne's temper worse, fraying her nerves and leaving her high-strung and bright-eyed with malice. She took her feelings out on Norfolk, heaping such abuse on him "as one would not address to a dog." He stormed out of her presence, hurling obscenities at her as he did so, the least offensive of which was "Great Whore." Before long he had his revenge. He brought his comely niece Margaret Shelton to court, and in a matter of weeks she had not only captivated the king but completely supplanted the previous favorite. She was Lady Shelton's daughter, Anne's cousin; of her appearance and temperament nothing is known. But she was not a partisan of Mary's, and she was, presumably, obedient to her relatives, and grateful for her opportunity.

Now Anne had her attractive cousin to contend with, along with her other worries. She needed a son, but had shown no signs of pregnancy for months. Was it her fault, or Henry's? How often they slept together, and whether—as would be whispered later—Henry was at times troubled with impotence is beyond discovery, but her anxiety was clearly increasing. In a fleeting conversation she had with another French envoy, Palamède Gontier, in February of 1535 she could not prevent herself from revealing the terror she lived with.

She was at first imperious with Gontier, tossing off complaints and accusations. But her façade soon dissolved to reveal the frightened, hounded woman beneath. She urged the Frenchman to convince his superiors, and King Francis, to do what they could for her, "so that she may not be ruined and lost, for she sees herself very near that, and in more grief and trouble than before her marriage."[2] Her words were startling in their candor: grief, loss, ruin. She looked careworn, Gontier thought. Her anguish was eating at her, making her look older than she was. And there was more behind her words, something or things she did not dare reveal for fear her enemies might overhear her. "She could not speak as fully as she wished," she told Gontier, "on account of her fears, and the eyes which were looking at her, her husband's and the lords' present. She said she could not write, nor see him again, nor stay longer."

Anne was trapped. It was plain to Gontier, who reported that "she is not at her ease on account of the doubts and suspicions of the king." The French were still refusing to commit themselves to a betrothal with Elizabeth, questioning her legitimacy to an extent which angered Henry and which was directly related to their rapprochement with the Hapsburgs. The resurgent power of the emperor acted like a magnet, deflecting all lines of force; it was not only the French who felt his pull, now Henry was succumbing. (Or was it merely that Henry no longer had any reason to resist, now that Anne no longer mattered to him?)

In January Henry had offered the emperor a callous bargain. If Charles would agree not to intervene militarily in English affairs for as long as Henry lived, then Henry would promise not to mistreat Katherine. The succession issue would remain undecided for as long as Henry lived; once he was dead the rival claimants would contest for the throne. It was a horrifying prospect, for with Henry dead Anne and Elizabeth would have no chance whatever against Mary and her cousin Charles and all the forces he could bring to bear. For Henry to propose such a bargain was tantamount to abandoning Anne and her child, once and for all.

The stakes had risen. Weary and strained as she was, Anne had only two choices, to give up or to fight back. Once again she summoned her courage.

"The concubine has suborned a person to say that he has had a revelation from God that she cannot conceive while [Katherine and Mary] are alive," Chapuys wrote in a dispatch at the end of March. She was adopting the tactic of the Nun of Kent (who had been executed in the previous year for using it), harnessing the power of the supernatural to promote her political ends. The psychic or mystic Anne found (and she may not have "suborned" him, as Chapuys believed; like William Glover, he may have approached her) took his prognostications to Cromwell, and perhaps to Henry. Certainly Anne told Henry about them, playing on his awe and dread of the unseen and on his growing insecurity.[3] Katherine and Mary were no more than "rebels and traitresses deserving death," Anne insisted. It did no good to keep such persons alive. Now she had reason to believe that it did great harm. Her current barrenness was linked to their survival, her fruitfulness to their extinction.

In the spring of 1535 a bloody terror was settling over England. New treason laws made it worth a man or woman's life to criticize the king or slander the queen or challenge the royal supremacy. Proclamations and pamphlets circulated in every town warning the king's subjects that they had an obligation to take note of any treasonous words they might overhear and report them—or else suffer serious penalties. The reports came in in their hundreds, arrests were made, people disappeared into the royal prisons and a good many did not reemerge. So widespread were the denunciations that it was rumored that Cromwell had organized a vast espionage network. In reality there was none, but fear fed the rumor; like Anne, who complained of the "eyes looking at her," the English saw eyes everywhere and were constantly frightened of secret informers and false accusations and of one another.

Most of all they feared the king, whom they saw as a monstrous, depraved figure, consumed with bloodlust. For King Henry, it seemed, had lost his reason, and was ordering many of the saintliest and most admirable men in England to their deaths.

First to die were four monks, hanged at Tyburn in their religious dress, their religious status mocked by the barbarity of their treatment. They were not merely hanged, but disemboweled, still living, and as a final dishonor their beheaded corpses were paraded through the streets and their severed hands and feet were nailed to the city gates. Norfolk, Boleyn, Fitzroy and other prominent courtiers came to watch the executions, and there was speculation that the king was present in the crowd of onlookers as well, in disguise and wearing a mask.

The shock of this unprecedented event was still fresh when a second set of executions took place. Three monks suffered, holy men whose only crime was that they refused to swear an oath to uphold the succession—refusing not out of disloyalty to the king and queen but because the wording of the oath contained a denial of papal authority.

A few days later came the greatest shock of all. The aged John Fisher, bishop of Rochester and for years the king's firmest and most outspoken clerical opponent, was led to the scaffold on Tower Hill to die. Fisher was a pitiable figure, white-haired and withered, made wretched by long imprisonment. Yet Henry showed him no mercy, nor did he respect Fisher's status—conferred on him by Pope Paul III during Fisher's imprisonment—as cardinal of the Roman church. Fisher's death, coupled with the execution of the revered humanist Thomas More shortly afterward, horrified the devout throughout Europe. Both Fisher and More had international reputations as men of learning and sagacity, admirable men prepared to face death for conscience's sake. That Henry should order them to their deaths went beyond tyranny: it put him beyond the pale of honor, even of sanity. In his inhumanity he had taken leave of his reason.

The heads of the condemned traitors—many called them martyrs—grinned down, black and rotting, from their places on London Bridge. The arrests increased, people watched one another fearfully and, at court, watched the queen and Margaret Shelton to see who would win out.

It was June, but summer refused to arrive. Heavy clouds hung black in the dull sky, rain poured down on the new grass and drowned the crops in the fields. "Ever since these executions began it has rained continually," went one report from London, "and they say it is the vengeance of God."

Anne, conspicuous and forceful once again, presided at her husband's side during that freak season. The strain she lived with gave a harder edge to her passion, sharpened her shrewd wits. Next to her maids of honor, young, pale beauties whose ripe charms were subdued by their soft voices and modest behavior, Anne stood out in stark contrast. Gaunt, thin, her eyes large and haunted, her black hair hidden beneath a jeweled cap which revealed the hollows in her heart-shaped face, Anne was both startling and vulnerable. Her words underscored her sense of doom-laden drama.

She "ventured to tell the king that he was more bound to her than man can be to woman," Chapuys wrote, telling him that "she had extricated him from a state of sin, and moreover, that he came out of it the richest prince that ever was in England, and that without her he would not have reformed the church, to his own great profit and that of all the people."

Her arguments tumbled over one another in a fever of articulacy. She was vainglorious, full of her old hauteur and boastful of her place and importance. She had moved events; by moving the king she had brought about momentous change. One thing remained to be done to round out the bloodletting. Let Katherine and Mary suffer as Fisher and More had suffered, as the traitor monks had felt the pain of royal displeasure. Let them suffer, or as sure as death, Anne would never conceive another child. With all her power Anne urged Henry to complete his sanguinary work, to wipe the slate clean of traitors so that his son—his and Anne's—could be born into a peaceful, loyal realm.

Henry, bemused by the horrors he had unleashed, seemed for a time to listen. He kept Anne with him now, no one mentioned Margaret Shelton. Anne, to soothe his dismay at the abrupt shattering of all his diplomatic efforts, gave grand banquets for him with masquing and plays, making him forget the pain and fear that ate at him as he laughed at the mummeries and drank goblet after goblet of sugared wine. There was to be no bargain with the emperor. The French had proved treacherous, and Francis had taken to slandering Anne, saying "how little virtuously she had always lived and now lives." Pope Paul, in retaliation for the execution of Cardinal Fisher, declared a holy war against England and invited the European sovereigns to fight under his banner. Katherine and Mary were behind it all, Anne told her tormented husband, the cause of every evil plaguing the kingdom. And Henry, his vigilance relaxed, heard her and "doted upon her more than ever."

For once her voice was hushed. There were no stories of the queen's shrill anger that summer, no bitter clashes of will between Henry and his wife. She lashed out at others, vituperating the French, accusing Norfolk of trying to gain power at her expense, telling Cromwell she "would like to see his head cut off." But to Henry she was balm and nurture.

Cut adrift from the community of monarchs, the object of unprecedented censure and contempt, the king was struggling to put together a new coalition of powers, a Protestant alliance centered on the Hanseatic city of Lübeck. It was a futile venture, but for a few months it provided the surgence of a fresh beginning. While Francis was content to mock Anne and laugh at her husband, and while the emperor was concentrating all his strength in a massive campaign against the Turks in North Africa, Henry and England could still gain time.

The rain pelted down on the roofs of the hunting lodges,

shutting the king indoors and forcing him to spend his idle hours with Anne. He had chosen to take her on progress with him this summer, a progress that extended more deeply into the countryside than usual and that lasted well into the fall. Perhaps out of fear of the treason laws, the people did not gather to block the muddy roadways or shout at the royal party as they passed. Far from the court, closed in on one another and yet alone with their separate, troubling thoughts, Anne and Henry reached a fragile equipoise. It was to be their last fleeting season of calm.

21

*"O madness, O foolish desire, O fond hope, O
greedy desire of vain honors, dignities, and
riches, O what inconstant trust and assurance is
in rolling Fortune!"*

Praised be God who has freed us from all suspicion of war!"
cried Henry when he heard that Katherine was dead. He tried to
put out of his mind all thought of how she had died, doubled
over with violent stomach pains, vomiting uncontrollably, unable to eat or drink or sleep. She did not want to die alone, like
a brute beast, she had told Chapuys. Yet when the end came no
one she loved was with her, she had died attended by strangers.
Between spasms of pain she had roused herself for one last effort:
to write to the man she still thought of as her beloved husband,
telling him that she longed above all else to see him once more.
All this Henry tried to suppress as he paraded through the court,
shouting his relief and joy to everyone he encountered.

The event was providential, there was no questioning that.
England had been delivered from a serious threat of invasion by
the forces of Charles V, forces fresh from victory over the Turks
in Tunis. Only a month earlier, in December of 1535, Pope Paul
had issued a bull declaring that Henry no longer had any right
to the throne he occupied, and that whoever took it from him
would be carrying out a papal mandate. The emperor could have

launched his armies, relying on the reports from his informers which assured him that many of the English would desert their sovereign and assist the invaders, so great was their hatred of Anne and of the altered succession. Had the invasion come, Henry would have been all but powerless to resist it. The French would not have come to his aid, nor would the Lübeckers or the Danes or any of the lesser northern powers he had recently been cultivating in vain.

The crisis had made plain how defenseless he was, as long as he remained cumbered by a personal life which constricted his and England's diplomatic and political fortunes. His discarded wife was a rallying point for rebellion and the occasion of invasion; his discarded daughter Mary aroused sympathy and loyalty and made the people hate Elizabeth and Anne; while Katherine lived and Anne remained queen none of the great powers would agree to become his ally, and all were susceptible to being turned against him by the new and stronger pope. Clearly his marriage to Anne and the large-scale religious and political changes that had flowed from it were at the heart of all his difficulties.

But now he had been extricated from those difficulties by Katherine's fortuitous death—a death so fortuitous, in fact, that a great many people believed she had been poisoned. After she drank "a certain Welsh beer," Katherine's physician told Chapuys, her health had begun to deteriorate. Some "slow and cleverly composed drug" must have been put into the beer by unseen hands. If Katherine had been poisoned, Henry did not want to know it, any more than he wanted to know that she had died yearning for the sight of his face. All he wanted to think about was that her nephew, pragmatic and statesmanlike as he was, would no longer threaten invasion—as long as he was convinced that Mary was safe and well treated.

It was too bad Mary was not keeping her mother company, Thomas Boleyn remarked sourly when he heard of Katherine's death. Yet he took his cue from the king and talked expansively of the prospects for rapprochement with the empire, saying nothing of the probability that this turn of events would affect his daughter's future for the worse. George Boleyn too was conspicuous in his public rejoicing, though in private, with his sister, he was not at all sanguine.

Anne was at first joyful when word reached her that her rival was dead. She rewarded the messenger with a substantial gift, and took heart when she saw Henry, dressed from head to foot in cheerful yellow and radiating exhilaration, sweep two-year-old Elizabeth up into his arms and carry her from room to room. Anne put on yellow to match him, but much as she might have liked to emulate his elation she found it impossible. Katherine's death made her own dangerous position all the more precarious. While Katherine lived, she had been safe; Henry had been unable to divorce her. Now that she was dead he could afford to dispense with his second marriage and contemplate a third. Only one thing stood between Anne and disaster: the child she was carrying.

She was pregnant again, her child was expected in July. The prognosticator who had sworn that she could not conceive as long as Katherine and Mary were alive had been wrong. And this pregnancy was certain, her condition was unambiguous. Her dearest wish was to have a son, she wrote to Marguerite of Navarre. As to Henry's dearest wish, it was somewhat harder to determine; though he too wanted a son, he might have preferred the child to have a different mother.

His new sweetheart, Jane Seymour, was pallid, unintelligent, and, according to the imperial ambassador, unchaste. "She is of middle height, and nobody thinks that she has much beauty," he wrote. Her figure was quite ordinary, her manners "rather haughty." The Seymours were undistinguished, save for their fecundity. (Jane had nine siblings; her brother Edward sired twelve children.) Yet Jane had attracted Henry when he visited her father's house of Wolf Hall in Wiltshire while on progress the previous fall, and shortly after the king's stay there Jane became a maid of honor to Queen Anne.

It has often been remarked that what Henry liked about Jane was that she was completely unlike Anne, but this is a distortion. Pale, purse-lipped and prim as she was, Jane resembled the queen in one very important respect. Like Anne she was brave enough to take on the outsize, fearsome king, though he was twenty years her senior and though he had shamefully mistreated two wives. While he was certainly capable of charming gallantry, Henry was not notably kind to his woman. Jane had courage. Encouraged by her two ambitious brothers Edward and Thomas, she accepted the king's flattery but shielded herself from his lechery, all the while putting up with "much scratching and by-blows" from his mistress the queen.

To celebrate England's rescue from peril banquets and jousts were held at court over the next several weeks. The king kept up his elaborate sartorial displays and his exuberant spirits, indulging himself and allowing himself to forget that he was long past the age for vigorous athletics. As a younger man he had been among the finest jousters in Europe; his horsemanship was unsurpassed. Now he tried to recall past glories by entering the lists once again. As luck would have it, he met with a potentially fatal accident. He was unhorsed and fell heavily to the ground, and before he could get up his huge warhorse fell on top of him. He was knocked senseless, and for a full two hours lay unconscious, apparently near death, before he finally roused himself and—to everyone's enormous surprise—resumed normal activity almost at once.

Anne was not watching the tourneying. Possibly she was in bed, keeping her movements to a minimum for her child's sake. Or possibly she had been forbidden to attend the spectacle, so that Jane Seymour could watch it in peace without worrying about her mistress's slaps and blows. In any case Anne was informed of her husband's mishap by her ungentle uncle Norfolk who, even if he conveyed his message curtly and without gratuitous injury to Anne, must have set her pulse racing with suppressed hostility by his very presence in her apartments.

According to one account, the news "was announced to her in a manner not to create alarm," and after hearing it Anne "seemed quite indifferent to it." But she was nervous and anxious, and had been ever since Katherine's death. Her husband's attachment to her maid of honor Jane was very worrisome, as was, given her obstetrical history, her pregnancy. She was said to be extremely harassed and agitated, sometimes anguished to the point of tears. Coming at a time of such nervous strain the shock of Henry's accident must have taken its toll on her health. Six days after hearing of it she suffered a miscarriage.

The dead fetus, the midwives who examined it said, "had the appearance of a male."[1] How and why they determined this, whether at Henry's request or Anne's (both had reportedly been "almost sure" that Anne was carrying a boy), we don't know. But from the moment he heard of it, his "great disappointment and sorrow" manifest, Henry seems to have closed his heart and his life to Anne. "I see that God will not give me male children," he muttered, and did not contradict the generally expressed opinion that Anne had a "defective constitution," and was incapable of bearing a liveborn, healthy son.

Nor did he contradict the gossip about his intending to make a third marriage. He would merely treat Anne as he had treated Katherine, people said, finding grounds for an annulment and then marrying Jane Seymour. Anne would follow in Katherine's footsteps, her daughter Elizabeth in Mary's. Both would be sent away to remote country houses and would remain buried there, all but forgotten, while Jane's children were born and grew to maturity. It would be much easier for Henry to discard Anne than it had been to discard Katherine, for Anne had no powerful relatives who could put armies into the field in her defense. Her Boleyn kin no longer had any influence, while her uncle Norfolk could be counted on to side wholeheartedly with the king against her.

Henry had everything to gain from getting rid of Anne. Save for one useless daughter she was barren, and it was evident he could not afford a barren wife. The son he needed had to be born soon, so that he would be of age and prepared to rule by the time Henry died. The longer the barren marriage lasted, the less likely it would be that Henry's heir—Jane's son—would reach maturity in time. Divorcing Anne would redeem Henry, to an extent, in the eyes of his subjects and of all of Christendom. So the arguments went, arguments made more plausible by Henry's frequent visits to Jane in her brother's apartments—visits that were discreetly chaperoned by her relatives—and by the handsome presents he gave her.

Anne's miscarriage had no impact on the unending festivities that continued to be held in and around London. At the end of February, six weeks and more after Katherine's death and nearly a month after her interment, they still went on. Henry hardly spoke to Anne. He came to her chamber once, while she was still in bed, but was brusque and distant. "When you are up I will come and speak to you," he was overheard to say, "with much ill grace," as he left the room.[2] The state of her health, mental and physical, her possible complications did not concern him. For in fact he already considered their marriage to be at an end.

Applying to his second marriage the same blend of superstition and eccentric logic that had enabled him, in his own mind, to justify walking away from his first, Henry had arrived at the conclusion that he had never really been married to Anne. Just as his union with Katherine had been barren of sons because it had been cursed from its inception, so his union with Anne must be invalid—because Anne was barren of sons. In Anne's case, the marriage had, he now believed, been brought about by witchcraft; having been seduced into it unnaturally, by means of enchantment, he had every right to consider himself free of it now that he perceived the truth.

Enchantment it had been, though not the kind the king meant when he claimed "in great confidence, and as it were in confession," that Anne had long ago put him under a spell. His feeling for Jane Seymour had none of the fire or intoxication of the love that had taken possession of him ten years before, lifting him out of himself and making him see the world through new eyes. The emotion he felt for Jane was controlled and manageable, fondness rather than passion, appropriately pragmatic and sensible for a man of his stage of life selecting a nubile young woman to give him children. But the desire he had felt for Anne was something entirely different, utterly unique and—so it pleased him to think—so alien to normal human experience as to have been triggered by sorcery.

Anne had bewitched him, but at last he was breaking free of her spell and finding her attempts to clutch at him repellent. She tried desperately to exonerate herself from blame for her miscarriage by claiming that it was "the love she bore him" which was responsible for her loss of the child. Her love, she swore, was "greater and more vehement than that of the late queen, so much so that whenever she heard of his loving another woman but her, she was brokenhearted." He had broken her heart by his wooing of Jane; she had miscarried in consequence. This sort of entreaty, combined as it was with backhanded accusation, was as irritating as it was sordid. Anne was crawling to him now, her misery arousing not his compassion but his impatience. He did not want her near him. He ordered her to stay at Greenwich while he amused himself in London, letting his advisers, principally Cromwell, grapple with the question of how best to put her aside.

From this point on Anne's story turned on the contriving and implementing of a plot to destroy her, a plot designed by Cromwell and carried out by a coalition of her enemies. But Anne's fate was, throughout, in Henry's hands. His was the decision to allow the vicious play of faction to work against her, knowing that, even if she had been strong enough to mount a counterfaction of her own, Cromwell was more than equal to the task of crushing it. Henry could at any moment have intervened to protect Anne, but he chose not to. At bottom he feared her power over him, her seemingly unquenchable resilience. She disturbed him deeply, and would go on disturbing him even if she ceased to be queen, even if she ceased to be his wife. While she lived, he would never be completely free of her.

It was this enduring bond between Henry and Anne, no longer a bond of love but no less strong for that, which led Anne's enemies to devise not merely her removal from the throne and banishment from court but her death. Alive, she would always be a danger to them.[3] And once it was decided that Anne must suffer execution, it was but a short step for Cromwell to plan her downfall in such a way that his own political fortunes would prosper.

Among those who blocked his path to supremacy at court were Anne's father, who held the coveted office of lord privy seal, and her brother George, who though he had begun to go into eclipse was nonetheless still one of the two most influential of the privy chamber gentlemen. Others among the privy chamber staff, who formed a powerful clique there, also hindered him, as did Norfolk. If it were to be discovered that Anne was embroiled in treasonable adultery with certain privy chamber gentlemen, including her brother, then Boleyn and Norfolk would be dragged down along with Anne and her alleged paramours. The entire Boleyn-Howard network at court would collapse like a house of cards, leaving Cromwell and his supporters to inherit the lucrative, influential offices they vacated.

It was a bold and risky plan, requiring the aid of a variety of courtiers committed to Anne's overthrow. Cromwell brought them together, the Seymours, the disgruntled officers of Anne's own household, Anne's cousin Nicholas Carew, and a group of Mary's staunchest supporters, conservatives in religion and fired by disinterested loyalty to the Aragonese succession. These, and their adherents, denounced Anne in Henry's presence, telling tales and making insinuations about her behind her back. Lady Worcester, daughter of the Marian supporter Anthony Browne, accused her of immorality. So did one Nan Cobham, and another of Anne's maids.[4]

Then there were the deathbed slanders of Lady Wingfield, widow of Richard Wingfield who was a client of Anne's enemy Suffolk. Lady Wingfield, a woman considerably older than Anne, had become Anne's servant in the 1520s and had been in a position to observe and share in the deepest secrets of Anne's private life. In her last extremity—she died no earlier than January 1533—Lady Wingfield was said to have described Anne's appalling lechery and promiscuity, "so that there was never such a whore in the realm."[5]

All this was grist to the mill, and the king, knowing what the consequences would be, allowed the gossip to swirl around him and allowed his own suspicions to mount. Informally, by innuendo, a case was being built against Anne; at some point soon the accusations would have to be brought out into the open and examined fully. At last on April 24 a special commission was appointed to investigate and punish treason—and specifically the possibility of treason by the queen and others. The commission worked swiftly and perfunctorily. Within six days the first arrest was made, and the others followed quickly.

Cromwell cast his net wide. A number of people were arrested or detained, but in the end only six were indicted: the queen and her brother, two of the leading privy chamber gentlemen, Henry Norris and William Brereton, and two younger men, Francis Weston and Mark Smeaton, who had no political significance but whose youth and good looks lent plausibility to the erotic charges. Weston had been raised at Henry's court, and had been a royal servant and close companion of the king for ten years. Brereton, who was Fitzroy's deputy and so tied in with Fitzroy's father-in-law Norfolk, was a royal agent and confidant who had played a prominent part in the campaign to rally support for Henry's divorce from Katherine in the late 1520s. And Norris, who had served both Henry and his father for twenty years, was chief gentleman of the privy chamber and Henry's trusted right-hand man. No one stood higher among the king's intimates, or had greater responsibility, for Norris controlled the king's coffers, the most vital financial office of the court.

The shape of Anne's alleged treason was mapped out. According to her accusers, her infidelities had begun in 1533 and had continued unabated ever since. She had betrayed the king repeatedly, adding to her sexual trespass the stain of political conspiracy. She had plotted Henry's death, and had sabotaged the succession, she had committed sins too vile to enumerate, bringing dishonor on her husband and the realm as well as on herself and her daughter.

There was not the slightest expectation that any of those accused would be able to defend themselves, or that they might have a chance for acquittal. Even before the arrests were made writs were issued summoning men to a new Parliament which would occupy itself with legislation relating to the queen's treason and to changing the succession. Behind a façade of legality, corrupt witnesses were supplying false evidence to be used to justify judicial murder. Anne's death was a foregone conclusion.

Anne knew that the scope and intensity of the political maneuvering against her had increased, though she may not have realized how grave and how immediate her peril was. She knew that Mary was in the ascendent once again, and that her little Elizabeth, for all the boisterous attention Henry had paid her in January, could be disinherited at any moment. Mary was the rising star, even Cromwell now showed marked deference toward her and had joined her party. Anne attempted a reconciliation with Mary, instructing Lady Shelton to assure her that Anne would be like a second mother to her, if only she would abandon her obstinate insistence on her succession rights. Lady Shelton, "in hot tears," begged Mary to give in, but Mary, who knew of the faction building against Anne and who like everyone else expected that Jane would soon take her place, saw no reason to. Anne was graciously but firmly rebuffed.

At Easter the emperor made overtures to both Henry and Anne—not just to Henry alone—in order to pave the way for closer relations between England and the empire. Yet his cordiality toward Anne was misleading. It was motivated solely by his concern that Henry, once he divorced Anne, might marry a French princess. And anyone was preferable as queen of England to a relative of Francis, even the notorious Anne Boleyn.

Within weeks the emperor learned that his messages of good will had been misdirected. He ought to have approached Jane Seymour, he was told. Before the season was out Jane would be queen. Henry was pursuing Jane with more dedication than ever, charmed by her maidenly propriety and warmed by her generous advocacy of Mary. He continued to give Jane presents and to speak of their future together, yet when he gave her a purse of gold sovereigns she refused it. That sort of gift, and the intimacy it implied, would have to wait until they were married.

Hating Jane, feeling the coils of conspiracy tighten around her, aware that she was so closely watched she could do nothing to save herself, Anne lived out her last months. Perhaps she told herself that in the end Henry would be lenient with her. Perhaps she counted on his affection for the bright, redheaded little daughter she had given him, who though she was not yet three years old was remarkably quick-witted and high-spirited, a very exceptional child for a girl.

Carrying Elizabeth in her arms, she tried to approach Henry

on April 30, six days after the treason commission convened. The court was at Greenwich, and Henry stood looking out a window of the palace into the courtyard below, his face a mask of suppressed anger. He was aware of Anne and Elizabeth, but did not acknowledge them or speak to them. For he was also aware that Mark Smeaton was to be arrested that day and that Cromwell was on his way to conduct Smeaton's interrogation. Smeaton would be made to confess, and his confession would be used to counteract the denials of Norris, Weston, Brereton and George Boleyn. Anne would be taken away and locked in the Tower, and in a little while he would never have to see her again.

22

*"If eyes be not blind men may see, if ears be not
stopped they may hear, and if pity be not exiled
they may lament the sequel of this pernicious
and inordinate carnal love, the plague whereof is
not ceased (although this love lasted but a
while)."*

From Greenwich Anne was taken by barge to the Tower, "in
full daylight" on the second of May. Her scant escort—only
Norfolk, two other court officials and four women—was proof
of her disgrace, and she was not granted the privacy of a night-
time passage. Earlier in the day she had been questioned by the
councillors, who were in possession of a very damning piece of
news. Mark Smeaton had confessed to being her lover.

Afterward Anne was to complain that she had been "cruelly
handled" during the questioning, with Norfolk saying "Tut, tut,
tut" and shaking his head at her, and the others accusing her of
adultery and announcing that she was to be seized and imprisoned in the Tower. One of the men could not keep his
thoughts straight, Anne said scornfully. Another, the controller
William Paulet, treated her with gentlemanly courtesy. But none
of them regarded her dignity, or gave her the reverence she
deserved. For a queen to be so "cruelly handled was never seen,"
she insisted regally, though the composure with which she spoke
soon deserted her.[1]

As soon as Anne was immured within the high, thick walls of

the Tower compound she was put into the custody of her jailer, constable of the Tower William Kingston. Kingston's letters to Cromwell describe Anne's words and behavior during her imprisonment. They reveal her wayward moods: she was by turns the haughty, offended queen, the bewildered, piteous victim, the nervous, overstrained woman on the verge of hysteria.

"Mr. Kingston, shall I go into a dungeon?" she asked him.

"No, madam. You shall go into the lodging you lay in at your coronation."

"It is too good for me," she answered, adding, "Jesu, have mercy on me." As she said this she knelt down and broke into tears, her prolonged weeping ending in wild laughter. It was a pattern that was to recur often. In her sorrow she would "fall into a great laughing," as if she suddenly saw herself at the heart of a vast absurdity.

She asked him some time later that evening to ask the king to allow her to have the sacrament in a little room near her chamber, so that she could pray for mercy. "For I am as clear from the company of man as for sin as I am clear from you," she insisted. "And am the king's true wedded wife."

Later still she asked, "Mr. Kingston, do you know wherefore I am here?" He said, following the king's orders, that he did not know—when in fact, as both he and Anne were perfectly aware, he was familiar with the charges against her. Getting no response, she then asked after the whereabouts of the king, her father and "her sweet brother." He had not seen King Henry since the previous day, Kingston told her, at the May Day jousts in the tiltyard at Greenwich; her father Kingston had seen "before dinner in the court," her brother he had last seen at York Place (though he undoubtedly knew that George Boleyn was in the Tower, having been brought there some hours before his sister).

Another exchange Kingston thought was worthy of record came when Anne touched on the accusations she knew were being made.

"I hear say," she said, "that I should be accused with three men. And I can say no more but nay, without I should open my body." "And therewith," Kingston wrote, she "opened her gown." It was a dramatic gesture, meant to underscore the vehemence of her denial while at the same time demonstrating the impossibility of proving her innocence.

"O Norris, hast thou accused me?" she went on. "Thou art in the Tower with me, and thou and I shall die together. And Mark, thou art here too." The rhetorical questions were melodramatic; one wonders whether Anne was trying to find a way to move the imperturbable Kingston. "O my mother," she went on, "thou wilt die with sorrow." And then, unexpectedly, Anne mentioned one of her accusers, Lady Worcester, saying that she "much lamented" because "her child did not stir in her body." When Kingston's wife, who was present, asked Anne why Lady Worcester's child did not quicken, Anne answered, "for the sorrow she took for me."[2]

Kingston recorded a final poignant exchange he had with Anne on her first night in the Tower. "Mr. Kingston, shall I die without justice?" she asked. "The poorest subject the king hath, hath justice," he told her. "And therewith she laughed."[3]

There were four women attending on Anne: her aunt Lady Boleyn, wife of Thomas Boleyn's brother James (who was a supporter of Mary), Mistress Coffin, whom Kingston relied on to repeat everything Anne said to her, Mistress Stonor, and another woman whose name has been lost. Lady Boleyn and Mistress Coffin slept with Anne on her pallet bed; Kingston and his wife and the other two women slept "at the door without." The women were not of Anne's choosing, quite the opposite. They were "such as she never loved," she said. Yet their unwanted companionship did not make Anne withdraw into silence.

On her second day she spoke to Mistress Coffin about Henry Norris.

Norris had told Anne's almoner the previous Sunday that he would swear that Anne "was a good woman," she said.

"Madam, why should there be any such matters spoken of?" Mistress Coffin asked.

"Marry, I bade him do so, for I asked him why he did not go through with his marriage, and he made answer that he would tarry a time. Then I said, 'You look for dead men's shoes, for if

aught came to the king but good, you would look to have me.'
And he said if he should have any such thought he would his
head were off." And then, Anne recounted, she had threatened
Norris, saying she "could undo him if she would," and a quarrel
ensued.

Later Anne talked about Weston, saying that she had spoken
to him because he was in love with her cousin Margaret Shelton,
and not his own wife, "and he made answer to her that he loved
one in her house better than them both. And the queen said,
who is that? It is yourself," Weston answered. And then, Anne
explained, she "defied him."[4]

To these incidents she added a third, telling how Mark Smeaton was only in her chamber once, at Winchester, when she sent
for him to play for her on the virginals. "I never spake with him
since," she swore, "but upon Saturday before May Day, and
then I found him standing in the round window in my chamber
of presence. And I asked why he was so sad, and he answered
and said it was no matter." "You may not look to have me speak
to you as I should do to a nobleman because you be an inferior
person," Anne had told Smeaton. "No, no, madam," he answered, "a look sufficed me, and thus fare you well."

All three encounters, as Anne described them, illustrated
nothing more sinful than a virtuous queen's haughty refusal of
the erotic worship of her inferiors. If Kingston had hoped she
would break down under the strain of her imprisonment, and
confess to indiscretions of whatever sort, he was disappointed.

In fact, after an initial period of disorientation Anne seems
not only to have recovered her poise but to have recovered her
customary bravado as well. "One hour she is determined to die
and the next hour much contrary to that," Kingston said, but a
good deal of the time she acted as if she were convinced that she
would escape death.

One day she was "very merry, and made a great dinner," and
soon afterward called for her supper, wondering aloud where
her jailer had been all day. After supper she sent for Kingston
and asked him herself, "Where have you been all day?" When
he told her he had been with the prisoners, she began to com-

plain of the way she had been treated when she was first arrested, reiterating how outrageous it had been for a queen to be denied her full dignity.

"But I think the king does it to prove me," she added, laughing and "very merry." Henry was toying with her, testing her loyalty. He never meant for her to be condemned.

"I shall have justice," she said then, more soberly.

"Have no doubt therein," Kingston answered her.

"If any man accuse me I can say but nay, and they can bring no witness." For the moment at least, she was confident that her guilt would be as hard to establish, for her accusers, as her innocence would be hard for her to prove. Had she forgotten the power of perjured testimony, and did she really believe that her enemies would scruple to make use of it? Or had she simply convinced herself that the entire episode was a macabre whim on the part of the king, who would carry it so far and no farther?

Anne's fantasies misled her, fantasies of vindication both divine and human. "I would to God I had my bishops," she told Kingston, "for they would all go to the king for me, for I think the most part of England prays for me, and if I die you shall see the greatest punishment for me within this seven years that ever came to England." "And then," she said, "shall I be in heaven, for I have done many good deeds in my days."

Her mind was wandering. She was not mad, but was clearly lost to sober reason. Her thoughts ran together without order, the grandiose juxtaposed with the trivial. She wanted the women of her privy chamber with her, those she "favored most." She wanted to write to Cromwell. She wanted the royal councillors to come to her, and was greatly surprised that they had not. It would rain every day, she insisted, until she was delivered from her imprisonment. As for her aunt Lady Boleyn and Mistress Coffin, "she defied them all."[5]

The indictments against Anne and the others were handed down on May 10. They stated that the queen, "despising her marriage, and entertaining malice against the king, and following daily her frail and carnal lust, did falsely and traitorously procure by base conversations and kisses, touchings, gifts, and other infamous incitations, divers of the king's daily and familiar servants to be her adulterers and concubines."[6] The "adulterers and concubines" were named, and specific dates for the alleged assignations given. George Boleyn, though he was Anne's natural brother, allowed Anne to seduce him, "alluring him with her tongue in the said George's mouth, and the said George's tongue in hers, and also with kisses, presents, and jewels." Anne and all of her lovers, the indictment stated, were guilty of conspiring the king's death, and Anne had often said she would marry one of her lovers afterward, "affirming that she would never love the king in her heart." The king, becoming aware of these abominations, "took such inward displeasure and heaviness" that "certain harms and perils have befallen his royal body."

The roll call of Anne's "malice and adultery" went on and on. She was guilty of mocking the king and laughing at his clothes and person; she made fun of the ballads he wrote; she told her sister-in-law Lady Rochford that the king "was impotent, having neither vigor nor strength." Nor were these light indiscretions, for they had the cumulative effect of spreading doubt about Elizabeth's paternity. George Boleyn, among others, questioned whether she was the king's daughter—though some people said he himself was her father.

The four commoners were tried on May 12, all but Smeaton professing innocence of the charges. Smeaton confessed to adultery, but not to conspiring the king's death, and his admissions were forced from him by torture or the threat of torture. All four men were condemned to die the death of traitors—that is, to be hanged, then cut down and disemboweled, their bodies hacked into quarters and decapitated.

"Around the throne, thunder rolls," Wyatt wrote in his celebrated poem about the events of May 1536. In the week that opened with the condemnations of Norris, Weston, Brereton and Smeaton the court reverberated with that thunder. Because of his past involvement with Anne, Wyatt himself was in the Tower, uncertain whether he would live or die, but many others who found themselves still at liberty feared for their lives, and wondered whether Cromwell's juggernaut would eventually crush them too. The courtiers lost little time speculating about the guilt or innocence of the accused, rather they devoted every waking hour to sifting rumors and to positioning themselves to profit from the misfortunes of the condemned. The spoils to be shared were sizable. Beyond the estates and offices of the accused men and the rents and incomes derived from them, there were furnishings and tapestries and even clothing. It was important to know exactly who would be punished and how extensively; besides those who would be executed, there would most likely be an outer circle of men tarnished by the scandal who would lose their positions and possibly their lands while salvaging their lives.

But it was very difficult to petition the king or Cromwell for the coveted spoils of tragedy. Cromwell was overwhelmingly preoccupied with the unfolding events at the Tower and at Westminster, while the king shut himself away, seeing no one but Jane and his immediate intimates (or what was left of them), walking in his private garden for exercise and emerging from the palace only at night, to ride on the river in his barge.

Henry's outward behavior as he waited for his wife and his close companions to die was enigmatic. On the one hand he put up a show of horror at the vice and criminality that were being brought to light. When Fitzroy came to him on the evening of Anne's arrest Henry wept, saying that the boy and Mary were both lucky to have "escaped the hands of that accursed whore, who had determined to poison them."[7] Yet at the same time, lest he lose dignity by appearing to have been completely duped by the conspirators, he hinted that he had suspected Anne of infidelity and treason all along. Above all, he said, he had no desire in the world to get married again—unless his subjects begged him to.

No one believed this. Everyone knew that, unless he had a sudden change of heart, he would soon be married to Jane Seymour. The fact that he had moved Jane away from court, installing her in Nicholas Carew's house seven miles away, was no indication to the contrary, nor were the people fooled by his festive nightly excursions to "banquet with ladies." They thought it in poor taste, in fact, for the king to disport himself in lively company, surrounded by music and singing, while his court was in such an uproar and while many of those he had once loved—however misguidedly—were awaiting death. "People speak variously of the king," Chapuys wrote. "It will not pacify the world when it is known what has passed and is passing between him and Mistress Seymour."

On May 15, just two weeks after she had been brought to the Tower, Anne was tried by her peers, her uncle Norfolk at their head. Her father was not among them—though Chapuys noted that he would have been perfectly willing to sit in judgment on Anne and her brother, just as he had done on the other prisoners a few days earlier. The trial was brief. There was relatively little testimony to present in any case, and as Cromwell admitted later, much of what there was was never put to the court at all. No depositions of witnesses or interrogations of prisoners have survived, nor have the statements made by Norris and Smeaton.[8] Had Anne been allowed to prepare a defense, she and her lawyers could have challenged, at least, the dates assigned by her accusers to her meetings with her lovers. On a number of those dates the court was miles away from the site of the supposed adultery, and this would not have been difficult to prove. On procedural grounds too, able lawyers might have been able to argue on Anne's behalf, for even the judges appointed by the king objected to legal irregularities in the conduct of the trials.[9]

But ably defended or not, in the end the outcome would have been the same. Judgment was handed down, that Anne "be taken to prison in the Tower, and then, at the king's command, to the Green within the Tower, and there to be burned or beheaded as shall please the king." George Boleyn, tried separately, defended himself so well and rebutted the charges so skillfully that several people present wagered ten to one that he would be acquitted. But he had no more luck than his sister, and was unanimously condemned.

The men died first, on May 17, speaking a few words each, acknowledging themselves to be sinful—as all Christians are sinful and come short of divine grace—yet not confessing to any of the crimes they were to die for. George Boleyn's speech was longer, an exhortation to the onlookers to follow the teachings of the gospel and to pray for his soul. "He hoped that men would not follow the vanities of the world and the flatteries of the court," an eyewitness noted, "which had brought him to that shameful end."

That same day Cranmer pronounced Anne's marriage to Henry invalid, claiming that because of Henry's relationship with Mary Boleyn, Anne and Henry had been related within the prohibited degrees when they married. Elizabeth was declared to be illegitimate.

Anne was forced to watch her brother die, to hear his last words and then to see him kneel before the headsman to receive the deathstroke. Four times more, as she looked on, a familiar figure mounted the scaffold, composed himself, and knelt to die his bloody death. The condemned men were by a final mercy spared the agonies of hanging and disemboweling, but Smeaton and Brereton's corpses were cut into quarters, and by the time the headsman had finished his work the scaffold must have been slippery with gore.

Knowing she must soon follow the others, knowing all thought of rescue to be futile, still Anne felt hope. At her trial she had said that she was "safe from death"; the following day she had said that "she would go to a nunnery," and was "in hope of life." But the vast absurdity was rapidly closing in around her. If she laughed and showed fleeting glimpses of wry wit, still she spent most of her last hours in prayer, with her almoner, swearing again and again "on the damnation of her soul, that she had never been unfaithful to the king."

On the morning of May 19 she came out into the sunshine and walked up the steps of the newly erected low scaffold on Tower Green. The courtyard was full of people, they crowded into its narrow confines and spilled down the hill and around the walls of the White Tower. They were all English, or nearly all; Cromwell had given orders for foreigners to be removed. Most of them had resented Anne for years, had wished her harm or wished her dead. Yet when she came in sight in her gray gown, looking "very much exhausted and amazed," they did not shout or exclaim—or if they did, those who recorded the scene thought the noise insignificant.

Probably the scaffold awed them, and the Tower precincts themselves, and the guardsmen in the king's livery. In this setting Anne appeared drained of her color and individuality, a temporary participant in a dark ritual whose stages were as well known as those of the mass. She did not stir passion in her audience, but something deeper. Perhaps they sensed that, for a woman, it took particular courage to die. And that Anne's greatheartedness, which had so aroused their hatred while it carried her to power, now helped her to "die boldly," and not to faint or weep.

Only those closest to the low scaffold could see and hear what Anne said, or make out the faces of the four women who attended her. Most could not see her kneel, or remove her headdress, or receive the linen blindfold. All they could see was the executioner as he raised his heavy two-handed sword, then brought it down with a swift stroke. There was a murmuring in the crowd, an indrawing of breath, and then the severed head was held high.

"It is said," Chapuys wrote later that day, "that although the bodies and heads of those executed the day before yesterday have been buried, her head will be put upon the bridge, at least for some time."[10] It was an oddity for a woman's head to be displayed, bloodless and rotting, on London Bridge. To some it may have seemed fitting for the woman who had bewitched the king, whose body, many said, had carried the devil's marks. But within days of Anne's death another legend had begun to grow around her, one that saw in her sorry death a key to her misunderstood life.

This new legend made of Anne a persecuted heroine, bright with promise and goodness as a young woman, beautiful and elegant. True, she was not guiltless, but the suffering the king caused her and the punishment he meted out to her redeemed her in the end and allowed her nobility of spirit to reveal itself. The legend began to take shape in a poem written in London two weeks after the executions by a poet who must have believed that his work would sell to a public still eager to relive the sanguinary events they had witnessed.[11] The poet described how Anne was denounced and taken prisoner, refusing to confess and rising above her certain doom to face her accusers with such calm, quiet dignity that "even her bitterest enemies pitied her."

Composing herself after sentence was pronounced, she was possessed by a transcendent serenity which turned her tragedy into martyrdom.

She took the sacrament repeatedly, the poet wrote, and made ready for death, and when her execution was unexpectedly postponed "she was disappointed—not that she desired death, but thought herself prepared to die and feared that delay would weaken her." She consoled her women several times, telling them that no Christian ought to shun death; she hoped soon to be free of all unhappiness. And as if to prove the strength of her belief she mounted the scaffold "with an untroubled countenance," her face and complexion "never so beautiful."

So heartrending yet so inspiring was the spectacle, the poet wrote, that many wept, overcome by the sound of Anne's voice, at first somewhat low and timid but gathering strength as she spoke. She forgave those who had condemned her, and begged all present to pray for the king, "in whom she had always found great kindness, fear of God, and love of his subjects." Then crying out "O Christ, receive my spirit!" she yielded herself up to die. Faint with weakness, her ladies forced themselves to wrap her head and body in white coverings and to carry them into the chapel for burial.

"The ladies were then as sheep without a shepherd," the poet went on, "but it will not be long before they meet with the former treatment, because already the king has taken a fancy to a choice lady." Anne had played her part in the larger scheme of things, Jane would soon begin to play hers. England's fortunes would take new and unexpected turnings, yet all would be rooted in veiled prophecy, "for nothing notable has happened which has not been foretold." "Other great things yet are predicted of which the people are assured," he concluded. "If I see them take place I will let you know, for never were such news. People say it is the year of marvels."

Notes

*References to L.P., Sp. Cal. and similar collections are
to page numbers, not document numbers.*

Chapter One

1. Controversy over Anne Boleyn's birth date continues, and in the absence of conclusive evidence the biographer is left with educated conjecture.

The Elizabethan historian William Camden wrote that Anne was born in 1507, and the biography of another court lady, Jane Dormer, confirms this. Most writers, for example G. R. Elton, accept 1507 as Anne's birth year although a century ago Paul Friedmann and J. H. Round argued for an earlier date, with Round pushing the year back to 1501. Recently Edward E. Lowinsky, "A Music Book for Anne Boleyn," in *Florilegium historiale: Essays Presented to Wallace K. Ferguson*, ed. J. G. Rowe and W. H. Stockdale (Toronto, 1971), pp. 185-6 and 228, note 71, has revived Friedmann's contention that 1502 or 1503 was the correct year. According to Henry Ansgar Kelly, *The Matrimonial Trials of Henry VIII* (Palo Alto, California, 1975), p. 249 note, Lowinsky is not the only scholar to favor a birth date earlier than 1507, yet 1510 and 1511 have also been suggested.

J. S. Brewer contradicted the view that Anne Boleyn accompanied Mary Tudor to France in 1514, but Lowinsky argues vigorously to the contrary, and given the observation of a French contemporary that Anne appeared entirely French in her bearing and manners it seems likely that she went to the French court as a child and spent her entire adolescence there. But this, like her birth date, is speculation.

Chapter Two

1. Pierre de Bourdeille, seigneur de Brantôme, *Lives of Fair and Gallant Ladies*, trans. A. R. Allinson (New York, 1933).
2. Carolly Erickson, *Great Harry* (New York, 1980), p. 188.

Chapter Three

1. *Letters and Papers, Foreign and Domestic, of the Reign of Henry VIII*, ed. J. S. Brewer, R. H. Brodie and James Gairdner, 21 vols. (London, 1862–1910),III:ii, 856. Hereafter referred to as *L.P.*
2. Edward Hall, *The triumphant reigne of King Henry the VIII*, ed. Charles Whibley, 2 vols. (London, 1904), I, 239; *L.P.* III:ii, 1557–9.
3. According to Paul Friedmann, *Anne Boleyn: A Chapter of English History, 1527–1536*, 2 vols. (London, 1884), II, 324, the marriage took place in 1521, though J. S. Brewer dated it 1520 in *L.P.* III:ii, 1539.
4. On "young master Carey," see *L.P.* VIII, 567 and Friedmann, II, 324. In the 1530s, a boy was shown to visitors and identified as "our sovereign lord the king's son, by our sovereign lady the queen's sister [i.e., Queen Anne's sister Mary], whom the queen's grace might not suffer to be in the court."
5. Carolly Erickson, *Bloody Mary* (Garden City, New York, 1978), p. 56.
6. *L.P.* III:ii, 1415.
7. *Ibid.*, 1213.
8. *L.P.* IV:i, ccxxx.
9. *L.P.* III:i, 76.

Chapter Four

1. G. R. Elton, *Reform and Reformation: England 1509–1558* (Cambridge, Mass., 1977), pp. 206–7; *L.P.* III:i, 369.
2. On who made the proposal, see J. H. Round, *The Early Life of Anne Boleyn: A Critical Essay* (London, 1886), p. 26.
3. *L.P.* III:i, 369, 372. In the index to *L.P.* III the daughter in question is erroneously identified as Mary Boleyn.
4. *L.P.* III:ii, 744.
5. George Cavendish, *The Life and Death of Cardinal Wolsey*, ed. Richard S. Sylvester and Davis P. Harding (New Haven and London, 1962), p. 32.
6. Of course, it must always be borne in mind that Cavendish, a Catholic apologist, wrote his life of Wolsey during the reign of the Catholic Queen Mary, and that he was at pains in his dramatized account to make it plain that Anne and Percy made a binding precontract. What he wrote was meant to coincide with evidence brought against Anne in 1536—true or not—and was, given the status of Anne Boleyn's Protestant daughter Elizabeth during Mary's reign, a matter of extreme delicacy.
7. *L.P.* X, 330; Friedmann, I, 159–61. Percy, while admitting to his wife Mary Talbot in 1532 that he had promised himself to Anne before marrying Mary, always denied having made "any contract or promise of marriage"

with Anne thereafter. Kelly, *op. cit.*, 253–4. Of course, for him to admit otherwise would have been fatal.

Anne, while most likely admitting in 1527 that she had been married to Percy, denied having consummated the marriage until the very end of her life when she may, perhaps, have admitted it to Cranmer. Kelly, *op. cit.*, 16, 50–1, 252,256.

8. Quoted in Lacey Baldwin Smith, *A Tudor Tragedy* (New York, 1961), pp. 58–9.

Chapter Five

1. Round, *op. cit.*, 35, suggests that Thomas Boleyn himself may have been the primary obstacle to the negotiations. Round also questions the presumption often made by Anne's biographers that Piers Butler made exorbitant demands.

2. The imperial ambassador Eustace Chapuys reported that Charles Brandon told King Henry that Anne and one of Brandon's gentlemen had been lovers. Kenneth Muir, *Life and Letters of Sir Thomas Wyatt* (Liverpool, 1963), pp. 21–2. (Muir believes that the gentleman referred to was Thomas Wyatt.) Three corroborating sources—each somewhat dubious in itself, but highly persuasive in the aggregate—describe how Wyatt warned the Council that Anne's unchaste life made her an unfit wife for the king. Muir, *Life and Letters*, pp. 19–23 summarizes the evidence.

3. Muir, *Life and Letters*, p. 15.

4. *Ibid.*, 19–23. Patricia Thomson, *Sir Thomas Wyatt and His Background* (London, 1964), p. 276 surveys scholarly opinion on the degree of intimacy between Wyatt and Anne. Though interpretations have ranged widely recent views favor the presumption of a love affair between the two.

5. Muir, *Life and Letters*, p. 19.

6. Both Jane Popyngcort, who seems to have been a royal mistress, and Bessie Blount were Katherine's attendants. Erickson, *Great Harry*, p. 159.

7. *L.P.* III:ii, 942; IV:i:ii, 525.

8. *L.P.* IV:i:ii, 540.

9. *L.P.* IV:i:ii, 865–6.

10. *L.P.* IV:iii, 3116.

11. *L.P.* IV:i:ii, 871.

12. Wyatt wrote of him after his death, ". . . hadst thou been not so proud,/For thy great wit each man would thee bemoan." Muir, *Life and Letters*, p. 33.

13. *L.P.* IV:i:ii, 639.

Chapter Six

1. Quoted in Muir, *Life and Letters*, p. 19.

2. *Ibid.*, 17–18.

3. Erickson, *Great Harry*, pp. 193–4.

4. *Ibid.*

5. Leviticus 20: 21.
6. Erickson, *Great Harry*, pp. 197, 383.

Chapter Seven

1. Although it is customary to assume that Henry's infatuation with Anne arose in the spring or summer of 1526, that assumption rests on nothing more than the conjectural dating of his love letters to her. In one of these letters, written perhaps in summer 1527, he refers to having been "for more than a year now struck by the dart of love." Henry Savage, ed., *The Love Letters of Henry VIII* (Denver, 1949), p. 33. Hereafter referred to as *Love Letters*.
2. Erickson, *Great Harry*, p. 194; Albert F. Pollard, *Henry VIII*, new ed. (London, 1905, 1951), pp. 147–8.
3. Cavendish, p. 37.
4. Erickson, *Great Harry*, p. 153.
5. *L.P.* IV:iii, 3116. Of course it is possible that another "Master Percy" than the heir to the earl of Northumberland was the object of this errand, or that its purpose had nothing to do with Anne or her past relations with him at all.
6. *L.P.* IV:ii, 1382.
7. *L.P.* IV:ii, 1411.

Chapter Eight

1. *Calendar of Letters, Despatches, and State Papers, relating to the Negotiations between England and Spain, preserved in the Archives at Vienna, Simancas, Besançon and Brussels*, ed. Pascual de Gayangos *et al.*, 13 vols. (London, 1862–1954), III:ii, 110. Hereafter referred to as *Sp. Cal.*
2. Cavendish, pp. 37–8
3. *Sp. Cal.* III:ii, 194.
4. Kelly, *op. cit.*, 26–8.
5. *Sp. Cal.* III:ii, 209.
6. Kelly, *op. cit.*, 29.
7. *Sp. Cal.* III:ii, 276.

Chapter Nine

1. *Love Letters*, p. 28. I follow Savage's translation. Like all Henry's letters to Anne, this one is undated.
2. *Love Letters*, pp. 29–30. Though I have followed Savage's proposed order for the letters, it cannot be overstressed that all attempts to date them or place them in sequence are conjectural.
3. *Love Letters*, pp. 33–4.
4. *Ibid.*, 35–6.

Chapter Ten

1. Hall, II, 97–9.
2. L.P. IV:ii, 1626; *Calendar of State Papers and Manuscripts, Relating to English Affairs, Existing in the Archives and Collections of Venice, and in Other Libraries of Northern Italy*, ed. Rawdon Brown and Allen B. Hinds, 38 vols. (London, 1864–1947), IV, 65. Hereafter referred to as *Ven. Cal.*
3. James Gairdner, "New lights on the divorce of Henry VIII," *English Historical Review*, XI (October 1896), 685.
4. *Ibid.*, 686.
5. *L.P.* IV:ii, 1751,2222.
6. *L.P.* IV:ii, 1779.
7. *L.P.* IV:ii, 1924.
8. *Ibid.*
9. J. S. Brewer, *The Reign of Henry VIII: from his Accession to the Death of Wolsey*, ed. James Gairdner, 2 vols. (London, 1884), II, 273 note.

Chapter Eleven

1. *Love Letters*, pp. 31–2. As this letter was written after Henry's departure from Greenwich on the day Anne's illness began, and before he learned of her condition, it must have reached her—assuming it did reach her—as she sank deeper into the malady that threatened her life.
2. Brewer, *op. cit.*, II, 274.
3. *Ibid.*, 276.
4. *Love Letters*, p. 44.
5. *Sp. Cal.* III:ii, 789.
6. *Love Letters*, p. 47.
7. *Ibid.*, 37
8. *Ibid.*, 50.
9. *Ibid.*, 45.
10. *Ibid.*, 50–1.

Chapter Twelve

1. *L.P.* IV:iii, 2509.
2. *Sp. Cal.* III:ii, 845; *L.P.* IV:ii, 2163.
3. *L.P.* IV:iii, 2509–10.
4. This account of the legatine trial is taken from *Ven. Cal.* IV, 219, Cavendish, 82ff and Hall, II, 150ff.
5. *Sp. Cal.* III:ii, 277.
6. *Sp. Cal.* III:ii, 845.
7. Hall, *op. cit.*, II, 145.
8. *L.P.* IV:iii, 2509.

Chapter Thirteen

1. Cavendish, p. 97.
2. *Ibid.*, 98–100.
3. *L.P.* IV:iii, 2683; *Sp. Cal.* III:ii, 885–6. For a complete inventory of Wolsey's goods see *L.P.* IV:iii, 2763–70.
4. *L.P.* IV:iii, 2679.
5. *Sp. Cal.* IV:i, 366.
6. *Ibid.*
7. *L.P.* IV:iii, 2834.
8. *L.P.* IV:iii, 3035.

Chapter Fourteen

1. *Ven. Cal.* IV, 304.
2. *L.P.* V, 161.
3. *Ven. Cal.* IV, 246.
4. *Ven. Cal.* IV, 245–6, 271.
5. *Sp. Cal.* IV:i, 351–2.
6. *L.P.* V, 101.
7. *L.P.* V, 10–11
8. *Sp. Cal.* IV:i, 634.

Chapter Fifteen

1. Friedmann, *op. cit.*, I, 128 note.
2. *L.P.* V, 591.
3. *L.P.* V, 592.
4. *L.P.* V, 647.
5. *L.P.* V, 605; *Ven. Cal.* IV, 354.
6. *Ven. Cal.* IV, 368.
7. *Ven. Cal.* IV, 365.
8. Hall, *op. cit.*, II, 220.
9. *Ven. Cal.* IV, 365.

Chapter Sixteen

1. *Sp. Cal.* IV:ii, 609, 642, 674. See also Friedmann, *op. cit.*, II, 338–9.
2. *Sp. Cal.* IV:ii:i, 609.
3. C. L. Powell, *English Domestic Relations, 1487–1653: A Study of Matrimony and Family Life in Theory and Practice as revealed in the Literature, Law and History of the Period* (New York, 1917), pp. 24, 27.
4. *Ibid.*, 147.
5. *L.P.* VI, 97. The Venetian rumor is in *Ven. Cal.* IV, 393.
6. *L.P.* VI, 107.
7. *L.P.* VI, 167; *Ven. Cal.* IV, 393.
8. *L.P.* VI, 167.

9. *L.P.* VI, 167–8.
10. *Ven. Cal.* IV, 398; *L.P.* VI, 235.
11. *Ven. Cal.* IV, 357–8, 338, 377.

Chapter Seventeen

1. This account of Anne's coronation is taken from *L.P.* VI, 181–2, 245–51, 263–6, 276–9, 300, 313; *Ven. Cal.* IV, 418–19; Erickson, *Bloody Mary*, pp. 97–100 and sources cited there.
2. *L.P.* VI, 243.
3. *L.P.* VI, 264.
4. *Ven. Cal.* IV, 426.
5. Erickson, *Bloody Mary*, p. 103; *Ven. Cal.* IV, 426.
6. *L.P.* VI, 655.
7. *L.P.* VIII, 214–15.
8. *L.P.* VI, 397.
9. *Sp. Cal.* IV:ii:ii, 788.

Chapter Eighteen

1. *L.P.* VII, 223.
2. *L.P.* VII, 94, 44, 37.
3. *L.P.* VII, 221.
4. *L.P.* VII, 282.
5. *L.P.* VII, 68.
6. *Sp. Cal.* V:i, 33.
7. *Sp. Cal.* V:i, 72.
8. *L.P.* VII, 69.
9. *L.P.* VII, 323.

Chapter Nineteen

1. The story of Anne's pregnancy in 1534 is difficult to untangle. In January she was reported to be pregnant (*L.P.* VII, 37, 44), and in late February Henry told Chapuys that he expected he would have a son before long (*L.P.* VII, 94). (It has been inferred from Henry's statement that Anne was still pregnant in February, but in fact his words are too vague to be taken as absolutely conclusive.) The queen reportedly had "a goodly belly" on April 27 (*L.P.* VII, 221), and earlier that month Henry was said to be eager for the French interview even though Anne was pregnant (*L.P.* VII, 193). In July she was said to be "far gone with child" (*L.P.* VII, 366). By late September she was no longer thought to be pregnant, but whether she had a miscarriage, or whether it turned out that she had been mistaken all along in believing herself pregnant, is left to conjecture. It is also possible that she had more than one pregnancy, and miscarriage, during the first nine months of 1534.
2. *L.P.* VIII, 214–15.

3. *L.P.* XII:ii, 243.
4. *L.P.* VIII, 230–1.
5. *L.P.* VII, 192.
6. *L.P.* VI, 164.
7. Charles Carroll Camden, *The Elizabethan Woman* (Houston, 1952), p. 203.
8. *L.P.* VII, 36.
9. *L.P.* V, 306, 752.
10. *L.P.* VII, 612.
11. *L.P.* VII, 463.

Chapter Twenty

1. *L.P.* VII, 485.
2. *L.P.* VIII, 61.
3. *L.P.* VIII, 169.

Chapter Twenty-one

1. *Sp. Cal.* V:ii, 39–40, 59.
2. *Sp. Cal.* V:ii, 59.
3. The best commentaries on Anne's fall and execution are E. W. Ives, "Faction at the Court of Henry VIII: The Fall of Anne Boleyn," *History*, LVII, No. 190 (June 1972), 169–88 and *Faction in Tudor England* (London, 1979), and G. R. Elton, *op. cit.*, pp. 250–6. Both Ives and Elton believe that Anne was innocent of the charges made against her, that her destruction was the product of factional politics, masterminded by Cromwell, and that the entire episode was particularly sordid and distasteful, even for the often sordid and distasteful Tudor court. Elton blames Cromwell for "willingly becoming the instrument of lying and corrupted proceedings" in order to achieve his own ends at the expense of Anne and those who suffered with her. Ives concludes that "Henry, Cromwell and not a few prominent persons contrived or connived at cold-blooded murder."
4. *L.P.* X, 397, 401.
5. While he doubts that Lady Wingfield's confession "contained real meat," Ives concludes that it was "not necessarily invented," and conjectures that her talebearing concerned Anne's relationship with Wyatt, the tales whispered throughout the clientage of the duke of Suffolk and so reaching Cromwell. Ives, "Faction at the Court of Henry VIII," pp. 172–3 and notes.

Chapter Twenty-two

1. *L.P.* X, 337. This and the other records of Anne's words and behavior in the Tower, written by William Kingston, are printed in *L.P.* X in fragmentary form, taken from damaged manuscripts. The *L.P.* transcription, with its conjectures as to missing words, is followed here. Strype, *Eccle-*

siastical Memorials, had access to the manuscripts in their undamaged form.

2. This may not have been the Lady Worcester who made the accusations against Anne. There were two Lady Worcesters: one was Anthony Browne's daughter Elizabeth, wife of Henry, second earl of Worcester, and the other was Elizabeth, widow of Browne's father the first earl. Among the debts owing to Anne at the time of her death was the sum of £10, owed to her by "the lady of Worcester." *L.P.* X, 382.

3. *L.P.* X, 334.

4. *L.P.* X, 334–5.

5. *L.P.* X, 337–8.

6. *L.P.* X, 361–2.

7. *L.P.* X, 377.

8. Ives, "Faction at the Court of Henry VIII," pp. 170–1.

9. *Ibid.,* 173 note.

10. *L.P.* X, 380.

11. *L.P.* X, 428–31.

Select Bibliography

Original Sources

Amyot, Thomas. "Memorial from George Constantine to Thomas Lord Cromwell." *Archaeologia*, XXIII (1831), 56–78.

Brantôme, Pierre de Bourdeille, seigneur de. *Lives of Fair and Gallant Ladies*. trans. A. R. Allinson. New York: Liveright, 1933.

Calendar of Letters, Despatches, and State Papers, relating to the Negotiations between England and Spain, preserved in the Archives at Vienna, Simancas, Besançon and Brussels, ed. Pascual de Gayangos, G. A. Bergenroth, M. A. S. Hume, Royall Tyler, and Garrett Mattingly. 13 vols. London: His and Her Majesty's Stationery Office, 1862–1954.

Calendar of State Papers and Manuscripts, Relating to English Affairs, Existing in the Archives and Collections of Venice, and in Other Libraries of Northern Italy, ed. Rawdon Brown and Allen B. Hinds. 38 vols. London: Longman and Co., 1864–1947.

Cavendish, George. *The Life and Death of Cardinal Wolsey*, ed. Richard S. Sylvester and Davis P. Harding. New Haven and London: Yale University Press, 1962.

Clifford, Henry. *The Life of Jane Dormer, Duchess of Feria*, transcribed by Canon E. E. Estcourt and ed. Rev. Joseph Stevenson. London: Burns and Oates, 1887.

Hall, Edward. *The triumphant reigne of King Henry the VIII*, ed. Charles Whibley. 2 vols. London: T. C. and E. C. Jack, 1904.

Letters and Papers, Foreign and Domestic, of the Reign of Henry VIII, ed. J. S. Brewer, R. H. Brodie and James Gairdner. 21 vols. London: Her Majesty's Stationery Office, 1862–1910.

Muir, Kenneth. *Life and Letters of Sir Thomas Wyatt*. Liverpool: Liverpool University Press, 1963.

————, and Patricia Thomson, eds. *Collected Papers of Sir Thomas Wyatt*. Liverpool: Liverpool University Press, 1969.

Savage, Henry, ed. *The Love Letters of Henry VIII*. Denver, Colorado: University of Colorado Press, 1949.

Wriothesley, Charles. *A Chronicle of England, during the Reigns of the Tudors, from A.D. 1485 to 1559*, ed. William Douglas Hamilton. 2 vols. Camden Society, New series, XI. London, 1875–77.

Wyatt, Thomas. *Collected Poems*, ed. Kenneth Muir. London: Routledge and Kegan Paul, 1949.

Secondary Authorities

Baldwin, Frances E. *Sumptuary Legislation and Personal Regulation in England*. Baltimore: The Johns Hopkins Press, 1926.

Barker, Sir Ernest. *Traditions of Civility*. Cambridge: Cambridge University Press, 1948.

Beckingsale, B. W. *Thomas Cromwell: Tudor Minister*. London: Macmillan, 1978.

Bellamy, John G. *The Tudor Law of Treason: An Introduction*. London: Routledge and Kegan Paul, 1979.

Bowker, Margaret. *The Henrician Reformation: The Diocese of Lincoln Under John Longland 1521–1547*. Cambridge, England: Cambridge University Press, 1981.

Brewer, J. S. *The Reign of Henry VIII: from his Accession to the Death of Wolsey*, ed. James Gairdner. 2 vols. London: John Murray, 1884.

Bruce, Marie Louise. *Anne Boleyn*. London: Collins, 1972.

Byman, Seymour. "Ritualistic Acts and Compulsive Behavior: The Pattern of Tudor Martyrdom." *American Historical Review*, LXXXIII, No. 3 (June 1978), 625–43.

Camden, Charles Carroll. *The Elizabethan Woman*. Houston, Texas: Elsevier Press, 1952.

Carlton, Charles. "Thomas Cromwell: A Study in Interrogation." *Albion*, V, No. 2 (Summer 1973), 116–27.

Chapman, Hester W. *Anne Boleyn*. London: Jonathan Cape, 1974.

Cunnington, C. W. and Cunnington, Phyllis. *Handbook of English Costume in the Sixteenth Century*. 2nd ed. Boston, Massachusetts: Plays, Inc., 1970.

Davis, Norman. "Two Early Sixteenth-Century Accounts of Royal Occasions." *Notes and Queries*, XX, No. 4 (April 1973), 122–30.

Dodds, Madeline Hope. "Political Prophecies in the Reign of Henry VIII." *Modern Language Review*, XI, No. 3 (July 1916), 276–84.

Donaldson, Peter. "Bishop Gardiner, Machiavellian." *Historical Journal*, XXIII, No. 1 (March 1980), 1–16.

Drummond, Jack C. and Anne Wilbraham. *The Englishman's Food: A History of Five Centuries of English Diet*. London: J. Cape, 1939.

Elton, G. R. "The Political Creed of Thomas Cromwell." *Transactions of the Royal Historical Society*, 5th series, VI (1956), 69–92.

———. *Reform and Reformation: England 1509–1558*. Cambridge, Mass.: Harvard University Press, 1977.

———. *Reform and Renewal: Thomas Cromwell and the Common Weal.* Cambridge, England: Cambridge University Press, 1973.

———. "Sir Thomas More and the Opposition to Henry VIII." *Bulletin of the Institute of Historical Research*, XLI, No. 103 (May 1968), 19–34.

———. "Tudor Government: the Points of Contact; iii: the Court." *Transactions of the Royal Historical Society*, 5th series, XXVI (1976).

———. *The Tudor Revolution in Government: Administrative Changes in the Reign of Henry VIII*. Cambridge, England: Cambridge University Press, 1962.

Emmison, Frederick George. *Tudor Food and Pastimes: Life at Ingatestone Hall*. London: Benn, 1965.

Erickson, Carolly. *Bloody Mary*. Garden City, New York: Doubleday; London: Dent, 1978.

———. *Great Harry*. New York: Summit Books, 1980.

Ferguson, Arthur B. *The Indian Summer of English Chivalry: Studies in the Decline and Transformation of Chivalric Idealism*. Durham, N.C.: Duke University Press, 1960.

Forman, John P. "Cranmer, Tudor Diplomacy and Primitive Discipline." *Sixteenth Century Essays and Studies*, II (1971), 108–18.

Friedmann, Paul. *Anne Boleyn: A Chapter of English History 1527–1536*. 2 vols. London: Macmillan, 1884.

Fussell, George E. and Fussell, K. R. *The English Countryman: His Life and Work from Tudor Times to the Victorian Age*. London: Orbis, 1981.

———. *The English Countrywoman: Her Life in Farmhouse and Field from Tudor Times to the Victorian Age*. London: Orbis, 1981.

Gairdner, James. "The Draft Dispensation for Henry VIII's Marriage with Anne Boleyn." *English Historical Review*, V, No. 21 (July 1890), 544–50.

———. "Mary and Anne Boleyn." *English Historical Review*, VIII, No. 29 (January 1893), 53–60; VIII, No. 30 (April 1893), 299–300.

———. "New lights on the divorce of Henry VIII." *English Historical Review*, XI, No. 44 (October 1896), 673–702; XII, No. 45 (January 1897), 1–16; XII, No. 46 (April 1897), 237–53.

Guy, J. A. *The Public Career of Sir Thomas More*. New Haven: Yale University Press, 1980.

———. "Sir Thomas More and the Heretics." *History Today*, XXX (1980), 11–15.

———. "The Tudor Commonwealth: Revising Thomas Cromwell." *Historical Journal*, XXIII, No. 3 (September 1980), 681–87.

———. "Wolsey, the Council and the Council Courts." *English Historical Review*, XCI, No. 360 (July 1976), 481–505.

Gwyn, Peter. "Wolsey's Foreign Policy: The Conferences at Calais and Bruges." *Historical Journal*, XXIII, No. 4 (December 1980), 755–72.

Hogrefe, Pearl. "Legal Rights of Tudor Women and their Circumvention by Men and Women." *Sixteenth Century Journal*, III, No. 1 (April 1972), 97–105.

Hooper, Wilfred. "The Tudor Sumptuary Laws." *English Historical Review*, XXX, No. 119 (July 1915), 433–49.

Hurstfield, Joel. *Illusion of Power in Tudor Politics*. Creighton Lectures in History 1978 Series. London: Athlone Press, 1979.

Ives, E. W. "Court and County Palatine in the Reign of Henry VIII: the Career of William Brereton of Malpas." *Transactions of the Historic Society of Lancashire and Cheshire*, Vol. CXXIII, 1972.

———. "Faction at the Court of Henry VIII: The Fall of Anne Boleyn." *History*, LVII, No. 190 (June 1972), 169–88.

———. *Faction in Tudor England*. London: Historical Association, 1979.

———. *The Letters and Accounts of William Brereton*. Lancashire and Cheshire Record Society, Vol. CXVI, 1976.

———. "Patronage at the Court of Henry VIII: The Case of Sir Ralph Egerton of Ridley." *Bulletin of the John Rylands Library*, LII, No. 2 (Spring 1970), 346–74.

Kelly, Henry Ansgar. *The Matrimonial Trials of Henry VIII*. Palo Alto, California: Stanford University Press, 1975.

Kelso, Ruth. *The Doctrine of the English Gentleman in the Sixteenth Century*. University of Illinois Studies in Language and Literature, Vol. XIV. Urbana, Illinois: University of Illinois Press, 1929.

———. *Doctrine for the Lady of the Renaissance*. Urbana, Illinois: University of Illinois Press, 1956.

Lehmberg, Stanford E. *The Reformation Parliament 1529–1536*. Cambridge, England: Cambridge University Press, 1970.

———. *Tudor England 1485–1603*. Conference on British Studies Bibliographical Handbooks. Cambridge: Cambridge University Press, 1968.

Levine, Mortimer. *The Early Elizabethan Succession Question, 1558–68*. Palo Alto, California: Stanford University Press, 1966.

———. "Henry VIII's use of his spiritual and temporal jurisdictions in his great causes of matrimony, legitimacy, and succession." *Historical Journal*, X, No. 1 (1967), 3–10.

———. *Tudor Dynastic Problems, 1460–1571*. Historical Problems: Studies and Documents, Vol. XXI. London: Allen and Unwin; New York: Barnes and Noble, 1973.

Lowinsky, Edward. "A Music Book for Anne Boleyn." In *Florilegium historiale: Essays Presented to Wallace K. Ferguson*, ed. J. G. Rowe and W. H. Stockdale. Toronto: University of Toronto Press, 1971.

Mackie, John Duncan. *The Earlier Tudors, 1485–1558*. Oxford: Clarendon Press, 1952.

Maillard, J. F. "Henry VIII et Georges de Venise: Documents sur l'affaire du divorce." *Revue de l'Histoire des Religions*, CLXXXI, No. 2 (April 1972), 157–86.

Mathew, David. *The Courtiers of Henry VIII*. London: Eyre and Spottiswoode, 1970.

Mattingly, Garrett. *Catherine of Aragon*. Boston: Little, Brown, 1941.

Muir, Kenneth, ed. *Life and Letters of Sir Thomas Wyatt*. Liverpool: Liverpool University Press, 1963.

Pardoe, Julia. *The Court and Reign of Francis the First, King of France*. 3 vols. New York: James Pott and Co., 1901.

Parmiter, Geoffrey de C. *The King's Great Matter: A Study of Anglo–Papal Relations 1527–1534*. London: Longmans, Green and Co., 1967.

————. "A Note on Some Aspects of the Royal Supremacy of Henry VIII." *Recusant History*, X, No. 4 (January 1970), 183–92.

Paul, John E. *Catherine of Aragon and Her Friends*. London: Burns and Oates, 1966.

Pollard, Albert F. *Henry VIII*. new ed. London: Longmans, Green and Co., 1905, 1951.

————. *Wolsey: Church and State in Sixteenth-Century England*. new ed. London: Longmans, Green and Co., 1929, 1953.

Powell, C. L. *English Domestic Relations, 1487–1653: A Study of Matrimony and Family Life in Theory and Practice as revealed in the Literature, Law and History of the Period*. New York: Columbia University Press, 1917.

Ridley, Jasper. *Statesman and Saint: Cardinal Wolsey, Sir Thomas More, and the Politics of Henry VIII*. New York: The Viking Press, 1982.

Round, John Horace. *The Early Life of Anne Boleyn: A Critical Essay*. London: Elliot Stock, 1886.

Rust, Frances. *Dance in Society: an Analysis of the Relationship Between the Social Dance and Society in England from the Middle Ages to the Present Day*. London: Routledge and Kegan Paul, 1969.

Scarisbrick, J. J. *Henry VIII*. Berkeley and Los Angeles: University of California Press, 1968.

Sergeant, Philip Walsingham. *The Life of Anne Boleyn*. London: Hutchinson and Co., 1924.

Shore, Miles F. "Henry VIII and the Crisis of Generativity." *The Journal of Interdisciplinary History*, II, No. 4 (Spring 1972), 359–90.

Smith, Herbert Maynard. *Henry VIII and the Reformation*. London: Macmillan, 1948.

Smith, Lacey Baldwin. "English Treason Trials and Confessions in the Sixteenth Century." *Journal of the History of Ideas*, XV, No. 4 (October 1954), 471–98.

————. *Henry VIII: The Mask of Royalty*. Boston: Houghton Mifflin, 1971.

————. "A Matter of Conscience." In *Action and Conviction in Early Modern Europe: Essays in Memory of E. H. Harbison*, ed. Theodore K. Rabb and J. E. Siegel. Princeton: Princeton University Press, 1969.

Stevens, John. *Music and Poetry in the Early Tudor Court*. Lincoln, Nebraska: University of Nebraska Press, 1961.

Stone, Lawrence. "Marriage Among the English Nobility in the 16th and 17th Centuries." *Comparative Studies in Society and History*, III (January 1961), 182–206.

Strong, Roy. *Holbein and Henry VIII*. London: Routledge and Kegan Paul, 1967.

Thomas, Keith. *Religion and the Decline of Magic.* New York: Charles Scribner's Sons, 1971.

Thomson, Patricia. *Sir Thomas Wyatt and His Background.* London: Routledge and Kegan Paul, 1964.

————, ed. *Wyatt: the Critical Heritage.* London and Boston: Routledge and Kegan Paul, 1974.

Vives and the Renascence Education of Women, ed. Foster Watson. New York: Longmans, Green and Co.; London: Edward Arnold, 1912.

Wernham, Richard Bruce. *Before the Armada: The Growth of English Foreign Policy, 1485–1588.* London: Jonathan Cape, 1966.

Wiley, W. L. *The Gentleman of Renaissance France.* Cambridge, Mass.: Harvard University Press, 1954.

Williams, Neville. *The Cardinal and the Secretary: Thomas Wolsey and Thomas Cromwell.* London: Weidenfeld and Nicolson; New York: Macmillan, 1975.

————. *Henry VIII and His Court.* London: Weidenfeld and Nicolson, 1971.

Williams, Penry. "A Revolution in Tudor History?" *Past and Present,* No. 25 (July 1963), 3–56.

Zimmerman, T. C. Price. "A note on Clement VII and the divorce of Henry VIII." *English Historical Review,* LXXXII, No. 324 (July 1967), 548–52.

Index

and daughter Mary's affair with
  Henry, 41, 80
daughter Mary's relationship with,
  41, 80, 224, 225
as diplomat, 13, 23, 30, 38–39, 112
duplicity of, 40
elevated to earl, 157–58
elevated to viscount, 63, 64–65
evening entertainments of, 68–69
in everyday ruling process, 62
Francis's relationship with, 23, 112
and Henry's attraction to Anne, 76,
  80, 82, 83, 103–4, 106
Henry's marriage to Anne opposed
  by, 189
in Howards' patronage network, 39,
  62
imperial pension for, 71
income of, 61–63
Katherine's death and, 240
marriage of, 13–14
Ormond earldom dispute and, 44–
  45, 116
Percy affair and, 51, 83
and plot against Anne, 245, 257
rise to prominence of, 13–14, 38–
  41, 61–65, 103–4, 115–16
tax revolts and, 71
treasurer or controller appointment
  sought by, 40–41
as Wolsey's enemy, 40, 41, 62, 112,
  153
Boleyn family, coat of arms of, 40
Bologna, University of, 161
Borough, Lord, 224
Bosworth Field, Battle at (1485), 14
Bourges, University of, 161
Brandon, Charles, Duke of Suffolk,
  55, 172, 221
  in alliance with Norfolk and
    Thomas Boleyn, 65, 103, 124
  Anne's assumption of queen role
    and, 178
  in Anne's coronation, 198
  evening entertainments of, 68–69
  as evil influence on Henry, 74
  Henry's trip to France and, 178,
    183
  Katherine informed of Henry's
    remarriage by, 191–92
  Mary Tudor's marriage to, 10, 22–
    23, 89–90
  in royal Council, 116, 157
  tax revolts and, 71
  as Thomas Boleyn's rival, 62
  in Wolsey's ouster, 65, 103, 124,
    153
Brandon, Henry, 23

Brantôme, Pierre de Bourdeille,
  Seigneur de:
  on arts of allurement, 20
  on battle metaphors in amorous
    language, 27
  on court intrigues, 28–29
  on Francis, 25, 28
  on goblet engraved with copulating
    animals, 25–26
  on men's power over women, 27–
    29
  on sexual profligacy in French
    court, 25–31
  on women's revenge, 29
Brereton, William:
  execution of, 257, 258
  treasonable adultery charged
    against, 247, 249, 255
Brooke, Elizabeth, 55
Brooke, Thomas, Lord Cobham,
  55
Browne, Anthony, 246
Bruton, Dr., 203
Bryan, Francis (cousin):
  Anne's gift to, 223
  court role of, 55, 224
  Princess Mary teased by, 219
Buckingham, Edward Stafford, Duke
  of, 39
Butler, James, 44
  proposed marriage of, to Anne, 43,
    45–46, 50, 51, 55
Butler, Sir Piers, "the Red," 44–45,
  116
Butts, Dr., 127–28

Cambrai, Treaty of (1529), 154
Campeggio, Lorenzo, Cardinal:
  beard of, 137
  Clement's appointment of, to
    legatine court, 118
  delay in judgment by, 141, 142
  journey to England of, 119, 129,
    132
  popular outrage at divorce and, 139
  presiding over legatine court, 126,
    134, 135, 136, 137, 141, 142, 154
Capello (Venetian envoy), 200
Carew, Nicholas (cousin), 246, 256
Carey, Eleanor (sister-in-law), 130–31
Carey, Mary Boleyn (sister), 12–13,
  35–36, 83, 87
  father's relationship with, 41, 80,
    224, 225
  in French court, 19, 21, 23, 30
  as Henry's mistress, 36, 41, 61, 65,
    75, 76, 80, 159, 204, 220, 258

279

in Henry's break from papacy, 176,
177
Mary Boleyn's secret marriage and,
224–25
royal birth and, 218
in terror of 1535, 235
Wolsey's pleas to Anne and, 157

disease:
divine significance of, 120, 128
plague, 180, 195, 202
sweating sickness, 119–28
divorce of Henry and Katherine, 88–
101, 158–74, 247
Anne's elevation to queenly
prominence and, 143, 158–59
Anne's fears of failure in, 160–63,
168–72
Anne's gratitude to Wolsey and,
130–32
break with church of Rome and,
143, 176–77
Clement's actions in, 117–18, 141–
142, 182, 184
Clement's captivity and, 97, 111,
117
clerics' support for, 159
Cranmer's actions on, 187, 190
delays in, Katherine's position
strengthened by, 171–72
divine curse on marriage and, 73–
74, 90
European politics and, 71–73, 79,
93–94, 95–97, 111, 118, 141–43
Francis's intervention in, 184
French diplomats' awareness of, 92
French support for, 181–83
Henry goaded by Anne in, 162, 168–
169, 173–74
Henry's confrontation with
Katherine over, 98–99
Henry's desire to marry Anne and,
128–30, 159–61
Henry's personal initiatives in, 113,
117
Henry's treatise on, 126–27, 135
international notoriety of, 182
Katherine and Henry's relationship
during 166–69, 170
Katherine ordered out of palace in,
98, 143
Katherine's demeanor during, 166,
170
Katherine's fears of, 90–94
lack of legitimate male successor
and, 71–72, 160–61
legatine court in, 89–90, 94–95, 118–
119, 134–43, 153

popular outcry against, 100–101,
139–40, 159, 164–66, 171
power alignments in Tudor court
and, 79–81
problems in Wolsey's case for, 95
sacking of Rome and, 95–97
treason ascribed to Katherine in,
73, 136
university faculties' opinions on,
161–62
Wolsey's loss of prestige and, 97,
153
Wolsey's scheme for, 88–90

Eleanor, Queen of France, 181
Elizabeth I, Queen of England and
Ireland, 215, 229, 241, 255
birth of, 207–8, 218
christening of, 208–9
declared illegitimate, 258
French views on, 230, 231, 233
in line of succession, 208, 214, 226,
234
mother's downfall and, 243, 248,
249
Princess Mary's recalcitrance
toward, 212–13
England:
in break with papacy, 143, 176–77,
210–11, 216
court life in, see Tudor court
culture and society of, see Tudor
era
French relations with, see Franco-
English relations
holy war declared against, 237
imperial relations with, 33, 34, 37,
71–72, 233–34, 248
royal navy of, 65
succession to throne in, see
succession issue
entertainments, see revels
excommunication:
of Henry, 198, 204, 210
of kings, as tantamount to
deposition, 204
Exeter, Henry Courtenay, Marquess
of, 191

Ferdinand II, King of Aragon, 10, 11,
37, 138
Field of Cloth of Gold (1520), 33, 36,
39, 85
Fisher, John, Cardinal (formerly
Bishop of Rochester):
break with papacy and, 211
in divorce controversy, 95, 136
execution of, 235–36, 237

Henry II, King of France (formerly Duke of Orleans), 216
Henry V, King of England, 70
Henry VII, King of England, 38, 94, 138
Henry VIII, King of England:
as amateur apothecary, 126
anachronistic miltiary vision of, 70
Anne as intended bride of, 102, 105–106, 112, 113, 128–30, 158–61, 176
Anne courted by, 65, 66–68, 74–78, 80–83, 92–93, 102–9
Anne given queenly prominence by, 143, 158–59, 178–79, 192–94
Anne's coronation and, 193–94
Anne's pregnancies and, 203–4, 218–219
Anne's sexual relations with, 108, 184–85
Anne's wedding to, 132–33, 181, 184, 186–88
annulment of Anne's marriage to, 198, 204, 258
Barton's prophecies on, 201–2
Blount as mistress of, 36, 64, 102, 184
in break with papacy, 143, 176–77, 210–11, 216
Butler affair and, 45, 49
Church of England headed by, 210–211, 230
clothing of, 10, 69
courtiers' duties to, 57–58
court of, see Tudor court
daughter Elizabeth's birth and, 208, 209
daughter Mary's relationship with, 86–87, 171, 172, 192, 213, 215, 219
decline in health of, 172–73
demeanor of, during divorce crisis, 116, 166–67
despondency of, 74–75, 172–73, 220
diplomatic alignments under, 10, 11, 32–34, 37, 70–72, 79, 83–85, 96–97, 216–17, 233–34, 237, 239–240
disarray in reign of, 69–71, 74
dissatisfied with marriage to Katherine, 71–74
divine curse feared by, 73–74
divorce documents drafted by, 113, 117
Elizabeth Boleyn as rumored mistress of, 41, 61, 80, 220
evening entertainments for, 68–69

excommunication of, 198, 204, 210
extrication from Anne sought by, 228, 232, 243–45
flotilla of, 65
France invaded by, 10, 70
Francis's meeting with (1534), 216–217
French bride proposed for, 87, 92, 101
gifts exchanged by Anne and, 103, 108, 109
Great Enterprise of, 70–71
as "Great Harry," 70, 75
in Green Castle pageant, 34–35
heir lacked by, see succession issue
illegitimate offspring of, 36, 204; see also Fitzroy, Henry, Duke of Richmond
infidelities of, Anne and, 205–6, 210, 219–21, 226, 228–29, 231–233, 242
Irish manor of, 44–45
in journey to France (1532), 175–84
jousting accident of, 242–43
Katherine confronted by, 98–99
Katherine's battle of nerves with, 167–69
Katherine's death and, 239–40, 241
Katherine's relationship with, 37, 166–69, 170, 172, 173, 174
Katherine's royal jewels requested by, 178–79
lecheries ascribed to, 219–20
in legatine court, 90, 94, 134, 137–138
love letters between Anne and, 102–103, 104–5, 106–9, 124–25, 129, 264
marriage to Katherine ended by, see divorce of Henry and Katherine
Mary Boleyn as mistress of, 36, 41, 61, 65, 75, 76, 80, 159, 204, 220, 258
Mary Boleyn's secret marriage and, 224–25
Mary Tudor's marriages and, 10, 11, 16, 21–23
mental agility of, 68
papal deposition of, 239–40
Percy affair and, 48, 49, 52
physical appearance of, 10
physicality and athletic prowess of, 33, 68, 69, 74, 97–98
popularity of, 9–10
Protestant alliance sought by, 237
ruling process under, 62, 172
sexual appetite of, 76, 81